IF WALLS COULD TALK

GREAT IRISH CASTLES
TELL THEIR STORIES

Robert E. Connolly

MENTOR
BOOKS

First Published in 2004 by

MENTOR BOOKS
43 Furze Road,
Sandyford Industrial Estate,
Dublin 18,
Republic of Ireland.

Tel: + 353 1 295 2112 / 3   Fax: + 353 1 295 2114
e-mail: admin@mentorbooks.ie
www.mentorbooks.ie

ISBN 1-84210-287-7

A catalogue record for this book
is available from the British Library

Cover design and imagery by: Anú Design
Photograph of Blarney Castle incorporated in cover image: Bord Fáilte

Edited by: Claire Rourke / Una Whelan
Design and layout by: Nicola Sedgwick
Illustrations: Nicola Sedgwick
Photographs: Robert E. Connolly

Printed in Ireland by ColourBooks Ltd.

3 5 7 9 10 8 6 4 2

To my wife, Pamela,
with all my love

ACKNOWLEDGEMENTS

Thank you to my brothers, sisters, nieces and nephews for all their encouragement and support. Thank you to my mother-in-law, Pauline Burke, for championing my cause. Thank you to Nicola, Una, Danny and everyone at Mentor Books for taking a chance on such a wild notion as walls talking. Thank you to Claire Rourke for her editing so that people could better understand what I have written. And thank you to the castles for 'talking to me' and providing the inspiration for this book.

BIOGRAPHY

Robert Connolly is a graduate of the University of Notre Dame in South Bend, Indiana, USA holding both a Bachelor's degree in Government and a Doctorate in Law. For many years he practised law in Indiana.

His previous American publications include *Armalite and Ballot Box*, *The Connolly Report*, and *A Time to Mend*, all of which examine the situation in Northern Ireland from an American point of view. In 2000 he published *Farewell to the Fort*, which is a perspective on a decaying Midwestern American City.

In 2003 he published *39 Dawson Street: The Autobiography of a Building*.

An enthusiastic historian, Robert is married and lives in Dublin.

CONTENTS

INTRODUCTION

If only these walls could talk . . . How many times have we used this expression in our conversation? How many times have we thought of its possibility whilst looking at some particularly ancient or historic building?

Of course, walls can talk in ways that we all understand and appreciate. The bullet-ridden walls of the General Post Office tell a story of rebellion and the ultimate independence of Ireland. The richly detailed walls and ceilings of Georgian houses on Merrion Square speak of eighteenth-century wealth and elegance. The musty church walls of St Patrick's Cathedral tell of heroic death and the wasted lives of young men cut down on battlefields in the far corners of the world. If one sits quietly on a rock in the glens of Mayo, it is possible to hear the crumbling walls of a famine cottage telling a story of a different death, no less heroic and no less wasted. Walls do talk but people do not always listen, perhaps because the listening must be done with the eyes, the mind and the heart rather than the ears.

If one accepts the proposition that walls reflect their history, it isn't too great a leap of the imagination to actually consider great buildings as personalities who have seen hundreds of years of human history and would like nothing better than to tell us their real story. After all, historians must rely on hearsay compiled by other reporters and historians who are long dead. Archaeologists must rely on conclusions based on the study of the bits and pieces that remain from these past generations. Buildings, however, have been with us for centuries and they were actually present, direct witnesses to the great events of history. If they could actually speak out loud, what amazing stories would they tell?

Even if you can't accept the proposition that walls talk, I hope you will enjoy this book as a bit of history combined with a bit of craic. After all, I never claimed normality. As my future sister-in-law said to my fiancée, 'You're actually marrying someone who talks to walls!'

MALAHIDE CASTLE

~

I Settling into the Pale (1190–1500)

My dear friends, I should begin by saying that I am delighted to be given this opportunity to describe for you the history of my walls and the stories of my residents and guests. I know that with any castle of my age, or shall we say experience, legends and rumours abound and I am happy to set the record straight, at least to the extent of my first-hand information. I think you will be surprised by much of what I have to say because I suspect that I shall change many notions you might have acquired regarding castles and their purposes.

You see I am not really the type of castle who prides herself on an ability to withstand sieges, catapults and armed ruffians running all over the place. I find such matters highly distasteful and not at all becoming to a castle of my grandeur. I leave those special skills to brother castles like Bunratty or Carrickfergus, whose macho displays have resulted in them being battered and bruised on many occasions. Gentle and refined castles such as myself do not countenance such carry-on. Yet, despite my abhorrence for violent behaviour, you will find that I have been among the most influential and powerful castles in all of Ireland. And while other castles have been reduced to battered shells, I have been little changed through the past centuries. In fact, for eight hundred years, I was the home for only one family – the Talbots of Malahide. I am still, however, one of Ireland's strongholds, not by virtue of cunning deceit or a particularly thick shell, but rather by stateswomanship, honour, loyalty and decency.

First, let me tell you about my beginnings. I owe my existence to a Norman family called the Talbots. A member of this family fought with William the Conqueror at a place called Hastings in England in 1066. After victory at Hastings, the Normans were successful in subjugating the whole of England and the Talbots were well rewarded for their efforts. When the Normans turned their sights to Ireland, the Talbots made their way here as well and, for centuries, I have provided for their comfort and safety.

When the Talbots first arrived in the 1170s, they established a residence very near to where I stand today. That structure was still used when I was built and so I am able to tell you a little about it. The original structure was what is called a motte and bailey castle. The Talbots lived in a wooden building perched high on a man-made hill, called a motte. The residence was surrounded by wood and stone walls for protection. An entrance led from those walls down the hill to another enclosed area called the bailey. The bailey was larger and included many buildings for the soldiers, servants and craftsmen needed to serve the Talbots. Both the motte and bailey were surrounded by yet another wall and, beyond that wall, was a ditch (or moat) providing additional security. This first castle was quickly and easily constructed and served until a proper one could be built.

The Talbots, having become accustomed to the comfort of their ancestral home in a place called Shrewsbury in England, were not interested in a long-term residence at a motte and bailey castle so, in the last decade of the twelfth century, I came into being. My original configuration was rectangular and I was only two storeys in height, though I was made of stone, of course. Beginning with improvements to my basic structure fifty years later, and over the centuries that followed, I was to acquire many additions all of which remain intact to this day. My foundations, however, at the heart of my walls are well over eight hundred years old.

How is it, you might ask, that while most castles the length and breadth of Ireland are little more that crumbling piles of rock, I retain all of my beauty, grandeur and matchless comfort? Of course, a lady never tells *all* of her secrets, but I am delighted to share a few of them with you.

The first Talbot to enter my walls was Chevalier Richard, who came to Ireland with King Henry II. I confess that my memories of this man are rather hazy but certainly not because of my age. Rather, I was in my infancy, not even an enclosed structure, when Richard passed from this world. In addition, I was to house *nine* different Richard Talbots over the centuries. I am sure you appreciate identical names and similar faces cause confusion even among younger ladies and gentlemen.

When subsequent generations were told of the family history, I discovered that King Henry II of England had commissioned one Richard De Clare, who was also known as Strongbow, to subdue Ireland. Strongbow was a Norman knight, the earl of a place called Pembroke, in Wales. As he was the half-brother to King Henry's mother, he was well connected in the English court, which was the reason for the assignment. Anyway, Strongbow was so successful that Henry decided he had better appear on the scene before Strongbow gained too much power and created an independent kingdom. Strongbow willingly submitted to the authority of the king claiming that everything he had done was in the king's name. In return, Henry restored Strongbow's authority over most of Leinster but he carved out Malahide for his loyal subject, Chevalier Richard Talbot.

Chevalier Richard was not only the first Talbot to reside within my walls, but he was very nearly the last. The estate was saved for future generations by the tenacity of his widow, whom everyone called Dolly, the first of several remarkable women to live within my walls. Richard and Dolly had two sons, called Reggie and Adam. Reggie was only a boy when his father died so, by rights, the estate should have passed back to the crown for administration on the child's behalf. Unfortunately, the crown had a tendency to administer such estates in its own interest because a child had no influence. Often by the time the child reached majority (which in those days was twenty-one years) he would find no estate left. Dolly was determined to fight for the rights of her family, as any good woman would, and that discussion was among the first within my walls that I specifically remember.

'I will not have my son cheated out of his rightful inheritance,' Dolly declared, her eyes blazing.

The crown's representative, a snivelling little man called Howard, replied, 'But surely the king will protect the rights of your family. The administration will only last as until your son reaches majority.'

'I may be a woman, but I am no fool,' Dolly fumed. 'Henry, say something.'

Now Henry De Fondres was the Archbishop of Dublin and a good friend of the family because the king had also designated the departed Richard Talbot as advowson, or protector of the church at Malahide. Henry stroked his beard for a time and then replied, 'Why Dolly, how would you feel if I appointed a clerk to serve on behalf of the king?'

'You, Henry, I trust,' Dolly said.

Howard began to splutter, 'You, you, you can't do that. It is the king's right.'

Henry replied, 'Now calm yourself, Howard. I am justiciar to the crown and under an ancient inquisition, of which I am familiar, I am certainly entitled to appoint a clerk to serve in the name of the king. Are you saying that you don't trust me, the king's appointee and the Church's representative, sir?'

There was little that Howard could say. However it soon transpired that Dolly's trust in the archbishop was not entirely justified as sections of the original demesne found their way into the Church's ownership. Dolly objected and the crown eventually took proceedings to protect the estate for her son. In gratitude Dolly pledged that, as long as the Talbots held Malahide, they would support the crown. Being a devout Catholic, she also made a pragmatic decision to support the Church in such a way that they would require her patronage. In subsequent generations, many Talbots were sent off to the priesthood and the family soon included powerful bishops and archbishops. In fairness to Dolly, subsequent generations of the family provided substantial funds to support the Church, beginning with the founding of a monastery at Templeogue in 1259.

I suppose it really didn't matter too much who administered the estate while the heirs were still minors because, although rents were collected and lands maintained, the guardians were not particularly interested in growth and development. As a result, I remained little more that a stone house for several years.

When Reggie finally did reach his majority, he was very sickly and, again, I remained unchanged for several more years. My growth and development truly began after Reggie died. As he hadn't produced a child, his brother, Adam, took over as Lord Talbot. Adam began construction of a three-storey rectangular tower with protective parapets on the roof. A person entered through a gateway into a circular tower, which also contained an enclosed staircase connecting the floors. Adam's son, Richard Fitz Adam Talbot, finished this work and my march to grandeur had begun.

My original keep was built on a limestone rock, which provided a solid foundation that was destined to last through the centuries. My ground floor contained servants' quarters and kitchens while the first floor housed a great hall for the important gatherings of the day. That hall, transformed some centuries later with the addition of dark-oak panelling, seems small to me now but, at the time, I basked in its splendour. The Talbots lived on my upper floors from which they could see the beautiful grounds that stretched as far as the human eye could see, nearly to Dublin Bay.

The early Talbots lived peacefully within my walls, generation succeeding generation, with no physical threat to themselves and certainly not to my wellbeing. Leinster Province generally, and Dublin specifically, were at peace in those Norman times of the thirteenth and fourteenth centuries. My own residents, being of noble birth, were particularly prosperous because they were well connected to both the Church and the crown. The Talbot name soon found itself among the bishops and indeed archbishops of Dublin, members of parliament and even sheriffs of Dublin.

Of course, I was familiar with ruffians occupying other provinces because the crown's justiciar, who was responsible for enforcing the law in the king's absence, would frequently meet within my walls to discuss campaigns against those uncivilised Irish tribes that occupied the far reaches of the country. However, as the fifteenth century dawned, it became clear that those self-same campaigns were beginning to encroach on areas occupied by good Norman stock like my residents. In response, Thomas Talbot, my lord resident at the time, surrounded my walls with a new fortified wall preceded by a ditch with massive gates at the front and back. When Thomas died a short time later leaving his mother, his young wife and his infant son and heir, called Christopher, in residence, those new fortifications did not seem particularly secure. I did not want to imagine what might happen if wild native Irish were to overrun them and take up residence.

I needn't have worried because, in November of 1415, Sir John Talbot, who was also called Lord Furnival, returned from service in France to serve as Lord Lieutenant of Ireland. Sir John was Thomas' uncle and young Christopher's great uncle. Although he was not in the direct line of succession to my estate, he had been reared within my domain and I remembered him as a child. I certainly recall the day he returned to my walls.

Sir John, a powerfully built man with a booming voice, rode through the gates and into the courtyard accompanied by a dozen horsemen in full battle regalia. 'Cecelia,' he roared to young Christopher's grandmother, 'open the door and welcome me home.'

The doors were soon opened and a grand feast was prepared. Cecelia acted as the hostess because the heir, Christopher, was far to young and the boy's mother was not experienced in such matters. I was amazed at the quantity of food and drink Sir John consumed. The meat dishes alone included venison, beef, pork and mutton. Chicken, mullet, trout and mackerel were also served accompanied by eggs, milk cheeses and vegetables. All this was washed down with large quantities of cider and mead. Sir John filled his plate on several occasions before announcing that he was satisfied.

With the feast completed, Cecelia asked Sir John about his plans. 'It is so good to have you back, Johnny, but I thought you were going to be in France for some years to come.'

'As did I,' Sir John replied. 'However our good King Henry feels my fighting skills would be better used in defending Dublin against the likes of the O'Mores, O'Reillys and O'Farrells.'

'That is certainly good news,' Cecelia said. 'Hardly a day goes by that we don't hear of some great house being ransacked and hostages taken. When your brother, my dear Richard, was alive, I never concerned myself with the safety of the family as he was the Sheriff of Dublin of course,'

'You are safe now, dear woman,' Sir John assured her. 'I will post men in your keep and they will protect you until the natives are sorted out.'

'Soldiers! But how will we feed and support them?' Cecelia asked.

'Now don't worry about that because the king has promised compensation for quartering troops,' her guest replied.

Sir John Talbot served five terms as Lieutenant General and protected the English Pale against native chieftains for several years. However, compensation to prominent families who fed and housed his soldiers was another matter altogether and my residents were among those who paid heavily for this defence. Speaking as the unblemished walls of a new castle, I thought the money was particularly well spent.

Of course Sir John, and indeed his family, were often welcomed to my walls whenever the opportunity presented itself and I thought you might be interested in bit of a love story involving Peter, one of his sons. You see while Sir John was fighting the native Irish, some of the Norman landlords were jealous of his success. A bit of a feud developed with one particularly powerful man, James Butler, the Earl of Ormond, from my sister castle in Kilkenny. I won't pretend to understand the nature of the dispute but Sir John bellowed in the most profane language whenever Ormond was discussed. I have little doubt Sir John would have killed the man had he been given the opportunity.

During the time the two men were in a rage at each other, young Peter attended a ball at Dublin Castle and who do you think he not only meets but falls in love with? Only Elizabeth Butler, Ormond's daughter. I thought Sir John's rantings were profane before, but I have never heard the like of those that followed his discovering this romance. Fortunately, there were women in both families who would not allow petty feuds to interfere with young love and, after much cajoling, the match was approved and Peter went off to Kilkenny to marry the young Butler girl. Even more amazingly Sir John and the Earl of Ormond both attended the wedding, resolved their differences and became friends.

Sir John Talbot returned to London in 1418 but continued to be the source of much conversation within my walls because his older brother Sir Thomas took over the defence of the Pale and his younger brother

Richard became the Archbishop of Dublin and Justiciar of Ireland. Both of these men were frequent guests to my walls because they were young Christopher's great uncles. During one such visit, I learned that Sir John, in charge of the entire English army fighting in France, had suffered a very rare defeat at the Battle of Patay. At the time the French were under the command of a girl called Joan of Arc, if you can believe such a thing as a woman commanding an army in battle.

With two Talbots so highly placed in government and Church affairs, I prospered during the 1420s and took great delight in witnessing young Christopher's growth and development. He was a happy boy who seemed to get on with everyone from his great uncles (who were always bringing him little presents) to the stable boys (with whom he practised military skills). Unfortunately in 1430 a dark cloud suddenly overshadowed the sunshine of his youthful spirit and Christopher took ill and died just before he reached majority.

When Christopher died, the line of direct descent was broken and my walls were passed back up the line to Sir Thomas Talbot, Sir John Talbot's older brother and the poor boy's great uncle. The following years were particularly quiet as the household mourned our loss. Also, Sir Thomas was called to parliament by Edward III, designated as Lord Thomas Talbot, and spent a great deal of time in London. Sir John was also the cause of some concern when word came that the French had imprisoned him, so he obviously did not call. The third brother – Richard, the archbishop – was far too busy to spend much time in my walls.

As I look over the years of my existence, I realise there were always periods of quiet calm and periods of intense activity, revolving in cycles, almost like the seasons. When Lord Thomas died, his son – another Richard Talbot – succeeded him, assumed his title as Lord Richard and the quiet calm came to an abrupt end. In some respects, nothing was ever the same again.

The storm began when Lord Richard married a woman called Mary Plunkett, whom everyone called Maud. Now Maud was anything but a typical quiet and reserved mistress, like my previous mistresses, and it took me some time to adjust to her character. While Maud was certainly attractive, she was a large woman who got bigger both physically and in her personality as the years passed. From the moment she entered my walls, her forceful character sent many a man – including, on occasion, her husband – scurrying for the peace and quiet of the gardens outside.

Maud Plunkett was remarkable in another respect. Her first marriage a short time earlier had ended quite suddenly. On the day of her marriage to Walter Hussey, the Baron of Galtrim, her husband had ventured out to investigate a reported problem among his tenants and was killed in a skirmish rendering her a widow on her wedding day. My new mistress was subsequently immortalised by Gerald Griffin, a balladeer who wrote 'The Bride of Malahide', a ballad I heard sung for centuries after. The final verse summarises the tragedy:

> But oh for the maiden who mourns for that chief,
> With heart overladen and rending with grief!
> She sinks on the meadow – in one morning tide,
> A wife and a widow, A maid and a bride!

As long as Maud Plunkett lived in my walls, there was very little peace and no quiet. And perhaps if he had lived, Baron Hussey himself might have yearned for the fate he actually suffered!

Shortly after the nuptials, between Lord Richard and Lady Maud, I began to experience a new phenomenon that has since become a staple within my walls. I had always assumed that when a human being died, their earthly existence was ended and, in keeping with the beliefs expressed by the survivors, the deceased's spirit passed into some other existence. I soon learned that this was not always the case. Apparently the late Baron Hussey, perhaps exasperated both by his failure to consummate his marriage to Maud and her subsequent, quite prompt, marriage to Lord Richard, a serious rival, did not go quietly to his eternal reward. Rather, on the occasion of the anniversary of his death and intermittently during particularly dark and gloomy nights, his spirit appears roaming my halls, staggering under his wounds. The spirit moans about his fate and vows retribution on his former bride and her new husband.

Remarkably, Maud was not the least bit taken aback by these

apparitions. Rather, she would shout at her husband's ghost that he was only being mean in denying her happiness and that he should crawl back into his grave and leave everyone in peace. Once she even took a swipe at him with a broom, which passed through the ghost completely and broke a water pitcher on a stand behind him.

While the first few apparitions took me by surprise, after a time they became a normal occurrence and I thought little more about them. Subsequent residents and guests, however, had an entirely different attitude, as one might imagine.

Lord Richard and Lady Maud had only ten years together but they did produce an heir whom they called Thomas, after his grandfather. Perhaps a decade with Maud Plunkett was enough for any man, but Lord Richard died quietly one night leaving Maud a widow once again. Maude was still a young woman and married a third time to yet another powerful politician, John Cornwalsh, the Lord Chief Justice of Ireland. When she moved to Dardistown Castle in County Meath, I assumed I had seen the last of this woman, an assumption that proved to be completely inaccurate.

In fairly short order, the Lord Chief Justice passed on to his undoubtedly much deserved eternal rest and Lady Maud was once again a widow. Since her child, Thomas, by the late Lord Richard Talbot, was the Lord of the Manor, she chose to live out her third widowhood within my walls. Thomas had married a lovely woman named Jane Sommerton, who could not have been more different to her mother-in-law and Lady Maud was soon in complete control. Jane did not seem to mind deferring her authority and, in one respect, I was the direct beneficiary. A family conference took place in the great room.

'Thomas,' Maud stated, 'Jane and I have decided that this place is entirely too small and not at all fitting for a man of your importance. Particularly as King Edward has designated you Admiral of Malahide and the adjoining seas.'

Thomas, his fingers folded in a steeple under his chin, looked first at his wife who cast her eyes down and blushed. 'Indeed, Mother,' he replied, 'and what do my wife and your good self suggest.'

Lady Maud quickly answered, 'A number of things come to mind but first and foremost is a proper great hall for receptions and dining.

In addition the kitchens and service quarters are woefully inadequate. What I . . . er, we suggest, my dear boy, is that you commission an addition to this place to make it worthy of your title.'

'Our home is two hundred and fifty years old, love,' Jane added quietly.

The ladies' efforts were successful and I enjoyed my first major enhancement with the building of the east wing, with its massive banqueting hall over an extension of services areas on the ground floor. While I was to be extended several times over the centuries, this first addition, I suppose not unlike a woman's first child, is very special to me. I understand that to this day the great hall remains one of the finest medieval rooms in all of Ireland.

Lady Jane never did see the finished product because she became ill and died shortly before its completion. Lady Maud on the other hand did enjoy the fruits of her labour and among the first functions the great hall housed was the marriage of her son, Thomas, to his second wife, Elizabeth Buckley. A few years later, Lady Maud finally joined her husbands in death and was interred with her second husband, Lord Richard Talbot, at Malahide Abbey, which adjoins my walls.

Although she was particularly pesky in her old age and became more and more demanding, I knew that I would miss Lady Maud Talbot. As it happened, I needn't have been concerned because, even to this very day, she has never really left. Within a matter of weeks after her death, the ghost of Lady Maud began to appear – often in conjunction with her first husband. She usually appears armed with her trusty broom and continues to try to take a swipe at the Baron of Galtrim. Surprisingly enough, her last late husband, the Lord Chief Justice, also appears from time to time but his role is far more conciliatory as he attempts to convince Lady Maud that she should come to bed. The three made their first appearance in this form in the last years of the fifteenth century and now, over five hundred years later, they remain with me.

II A Lady in Distress (1500–1690)

Three hundred years passed quickly within my walls as the Talbot lineage continued to produced bishops and archbishops, governors and justices and all measure of nobility who ruled from Malahide Castle. My residents were unwavering supporters of English kings and queens and their loyalty was rewarded with positions of wealth and power. You see I am located within the English Pale – which is an area that includes all, or most of, the present counties of Dublin, Meath, Louth and Kildare. The English took particular care to secure this region and, as a result, neither my walls nor my residents were at risk from the turmoil that found my brother and sister castles from Antrim to Clare to Cork, attacked and brutalised with such regularity. This loyalty and location led me to believe that little would change for many more generations of Talbots.

The prosperity of my residents was reflected in further additions to myself. In the mid-sixteenth century an entire west wing was added. This extension included two new drawing rooms – with a smaller one for intimate groups, family chats and quiet times and the grand drawing room for formal receptions and greeting important visitors. Additional bedrooms and service areas were also added and a few years later a substantial library was annexed to my great hall. Even my greeting hall in the original part of my walls was refinished in intricately carved white-oak panelling. Although yet another Sir Richard Talbot, who was my master at the time, decided white was entirely too bright and had the entire room painted black. Ever since, the old greeting hall became known as the 'Oak Room'.

At the risk of sounding vain, I was at once comfortable and elegant, the perfect combination for any castle, at least in the Pale where stout walls were not particularly important.

As befits a castle of my standing, I hosted many feasts and celebrations that were attended by the elite of Dublin society. It was the result of one such feast that I acquired yet another nocturnal visitor from the spirit world, one I value above all the others. The poor dear's name is Puck. He was a very small man who had been hired as a jester and would entertain at functions held within my walls. When those services were not required, Puck made himself useful by meticulously cleaning anything that became the slightest bit dusty or tarnished. This work, performed in the wee hours of the morning, resulted in an immaculately clean great hall, great drawing room and small drawing room. As it happened, poor Puck fell madly in love with a lady-in-waiting to Lady Eleanor Fitz Gerald, a guest within my walls in the mid-sixteenth century. It seems this lady-in-waiting graced Puck with a smile during one of his performances and the poor man read more into it than she intended. When Puck finally got the courage to press his suit, the girl expressed horror that he should consider approaching her, which broke the poor dear's heart.

The next night, after completing his cleaning duties, Puck hung himself from the minstrels' gallery overlooking the great hall. He was greatly mourned by the entire family and those who were familiar with his antics but few people – perhaps only the lady-in-waiting and myself – knew why he had ended his own life. To my joy, however, Puck returned to my walls and to this day remains secreted in a hidden crevice, which I will not reveal. He now roams the rooms he used to clean, ready to warn of danger to the walls that he loved. In his honour, a tiny door was constructed in the great hall over which an inscription reads 'Puck's Room'. However, I assure you that I know where the spirit of Puck resides, and it is *not* behind that door. A lady castle must be true to her friends so his spirit's home must remain a secret.

When further construction was completed in the early years of the seventeenth century, I began to approach the proportions that remain with me into the twenty-first century. As it happened, however, changes within my walls were not restricted to physical alterations.

How many times have I heard the women within my walls instruct their children with the simple warning that 'pride goeth before the fall'? While the expression had little meaning for me when I first heard it, I now appreciate that the condition of a building and its residents is not static, and pride over one's residents means little with the passage of time. Any hopes that I may have cherished for an unchanged existence were soon shattered, as Malahide and the House of Talbot faced their darkest hours.

The first difficulty my residents encountered was the result of a rebellion led by Rory O'More and Phelim O'Neill in 1641. While in earlier times such revolts in the outlying reaches of the country would have little effect in the Pale, this rising spread and soon engulfed all of north Dublin including several Norman families. My master at the time, Lord John Talbot, had only just inherited his title and lands and he certainly did not want to jeopardise his legacy. I well remember a meeting of the clan, held within my walls, because of the division of opinion expressed.

'I will not declare for or support the rebels,' Lord John proclaimed. 'For centuries this family has had no blemish of rebellion against the crown and now is not the time to change our course.'

Richard Talbot (I do hope you are beginning to appreciate all the Richard Talbots that I have attempted to keep straight over the centuries), Lord John's younger brother, rose in anger, 'You won't tell me what to do. The lords justice are nothing but a pack of useless, old men who line their pockets at our expense, which you should know better than anyone.'

'They are the king's representatives and we support the crown,' was the terse reply.

'Now, John,' a cousin from Belgard also called John Talbot replied, 'it isn't just natives who are rising. Many of our own people, the Old English gentry like Fingal, Slane, King and Netterville are also rising.'

'That is their decision,' Lord John concluded. 'Malahide will not rebel against the legitimate rights of the crown.'

Although, my resident's decision was vindicated when the rising was crushed by James Butler, Lord Ormond from Kilkenny Castle, suspicion fell on Lord John primarily because so many of his relatives, including his brother Richard and the Talbots of Belgard, Robertstown and Carton, were clearly involved. As a result, in 1642, Lord John was outlawed and my walls were forfeited to the Dublin government, although the enforcement order was suspended because, in truth, there was no evidence against Lord John himself. He disappeared for a time to Lambay Island hoping that the whole thing would blow over but in his absence two hundred of Ormond's men occupied my grounds. This crowd's manners were quite offensive and when, to my relief, John returned, I witnessed the inevitable confrontation with Lord Ormond.

'You know me, James,' Lord John began, 'and you know my lineage,

I would never rise against the crown, never. With God as my witness I made that perfectly clear to my various and sundry relatives who felt otherwise. I invite you to interview them all, together or separately.'

'It's not that I don't believe you,' Ormond responded, 'it's just that these are troubled times and the lords justice want me to destroy the castles of rebel lords and burn their fields. I can't be seen to be lenient to suspected rebels even if their guilt is only by association.'

Lord John, clearly troubled, replied, 'And this is my family's reward for six hundred years of loyalty. Guilt by association?'

Ormond seemed moved by Lord John's passion and offered a compromise, 'I'll tell you what, John, and this is just between you and me, we will announce you are under house arrest and you can keep your castle and continue to manage your lands but, in return, you must garrison my soldiers, at least in the short term and ensure that they are provisioned. I will report back that this was necessary to maintain my forces in north Dublin and, when things settle down, the eviction order will be vacated and everything will return to normal.'

Lord John Talbot has little choice but to accept the offer and, throughout the decade of the 1640s, he supplied Ormond with victuals. In return there was peace within my walls and, while soldiers occupied grounds around my walls, they did not invade my rooms. Lord John was a model citizen and Ormond, as Lord Lieutenant of Ireland – and his successor, Clanrickard – provided my residents and myself with insurance against the turmoil of the time. I was to hear a great deal about these problems because they included both a general rebellion by English Catholics, called the Confederation of Kilkenny, and the overthrow of the English monarchy by its parliament under the leadership of Oliver Cromwell.

For all his allegations of treason against the king, Ormond himself had little difficulty transferring his loyalty to the parliamentary forces (or 'roundheads' as they were known) and he quickly surrendered Dublin in 1647. When Cromwell arrived in Ireland in August 1649, Dublin was already in the control of his forces. Luckily for me, because of his agreement to support Ormond my resident, Lord John had effectively been supporting that regime for two years.

Cromwell himself stayed within my walls for a few days and I remember him as a young-looking man with a long face, long nose and thinning hair. He was neither physically imposing nor did he appear to command attention and yet his name was only ever whispered as he was among the most feared men in Ireland. Although his stay was short, word got back to me that when asked, Cromwell declared that if he were forced to stay in our accursed country, the only place he would want to live was within my walls. When I think of the other stories I have heard about him, including his butchery of thousands of innocent women and children, I shudder to think of him as a permanent guest.

Despite his support of the roundheads, which was far preferable to the confiscation of his land and risk to his life, Lord John Talbot remained, at heart, a loyal subject of the British crown. When Charles I lost his head in January 1649, that crown passed to Charles II then living in Scotland. Two years later Charles II fled to France having been defeated by Cromwell. As one would expect, Charles II wanted to regain power, so he sent a messenger by the name of Dean John King to the Marquis of Clanrickard to report back on conditions in Ireland.

King's mission was betrayed and he was forced into hiding, desperately seeking some way to escape. I suppose he was told about Lord John's loyalty to Charles because, late one evening, he turned up at my door. He was shown into the Oak Room where he met Lord John. 'I trust you will forgive my impertinence,' he began, 'but I have been sent by Clanrickard who has assured me you will be able to assist me.'

Lord John replied, 'I see. And in what way might I be of assistance?'

'I require safe and secret transport to the Isle of Man and I understand that your fishing fleet can aid me as I carry important dispatches for Charles II.'

'I'd rather not become involved in such matters one way or the other,' Lord John stated.

Dean King was silent for a moment and then said, 'The Marquess of Clanrickard has suggested that you are in his debt and quite apart from your traditional loyalty to the monarchy, he mentioned that I should call upon your honour in this regard.'

Lord John turned rather red in the face and muttered something about impertinence but he did agree to assist. He sent King and a servant down to the docks from where a boat sailed to the Isle of Man. Some months later, Clanrickard surrendered to Cromwell's forces and my resident's complicity in the King affair was obviously discovered because shortly afterwards one Miles Corbett visited my walls and became the bane of my existence for several years.

Miles Corbett was indeed a Roundhead physically as well as politically. He was a short, little fellow with the oddest eyes – one seemed to wander off while the other was affixed to the object of his attention. His voice was a nasal whine as he sneered at Lord John, 'I'm afraid we can't have disloyal citizens, and papists at that, so near to Dublin.'

'I have no idea what you are talking about,' Lord John replied.

'A little birdie told me that you assisted in a mission to spy for our French friend Charles,' Corbett said.

'I suppose you think you can prove such outrageous allegations,' was the indignant response.

Corbett snickered, 'I don't have to prove anything. Consider yourself under arrest.'

With that, the residency of the Talbots, having lasted since I was erected, was supplanted by Miles Corbett and the Talbots were taken away. They were taken, as I understood the situation, to a place called Connacht. Miles immediately helped himself to a drink from the alcohol stores and made himself at home. Apparently the Talbots were not without influence and, although I was not privy to any discussion on the matter, several months later they returned and it was Corbett who was sent packing. That conversation was quite terse with Lord John informing Corbett that he had been released because of a lack of proof and Corbett responding that Malahide had not seen the last of Miles Corbett.

Some months later, in late 1653, that statement proved prophetic as Miles returned with his family and a troop of Roundheads. He announced that he was fleeing from the plague in Dublin, and that Lord John and his family were being transported to Connacht. Of course Talbot challenged his authority but Miles, acting as Chief Baron of the Irish Exchequer, produced the order of forfeiture, which was then over ten years old and which had been suspended when Lord John reached his agreement with Ormond those many years earlier. 'No one gets the better of Miles Corbett,' he announced as the Talbot family departed into their exile although I was to later discover that they only went as far as Athlone in County Roscommon. After four hundred years of Talbot royalty, I had now passed into the hands of a commoner but, of course, there was little I could do about it.

For seven years I provided shelter and comfort for this rather despicable little man because that, after all, is my responsibility. He was delighted with the accommodation and never tired of quoting his mentor, Oliver Cromwell, who so highly praised the sanctuary of my walls. In fairness, Miles did not allow me to deteriorate and retained a full staff to ensure that I always looked my very best. Though I suspect he did this for the sole purpose of impressing his associates, I certainly appreciated the effort.

There is, however, a detail relating to his occupancy that has been a matter of some conjecture and is discussed within my walls to this day. Unquestionably, Miles Corbett was a radical anti-papist in the tradition of Cromwell. The Talbots, on the other hand were Catholics and some fifty years earlier had acquired a Flemish carving of the Coronation of the Virgin. The relief hung in a place of honour over the fireplace in the Oak Room. The story that I have heard repeated is that the Virgin disappeared from this relief during the time when Corbett occupied my walls only to reappear when his occupancy ended. You should know that this story is a slight exaggeration as the only time the Virgin disappeared was when Miles himself entered the room. It transpired that Miles Corbett was soon the one to disappear, in a manner of speaking.

In September 1658 Cromwell died and, in 1660, Charles II returned from France and was restored to the throne of England. Since Miles had prominently signed the death warrant of Charles I, he must have assumed that he would not be popular with the new king and so he departed Malahide and Ireland in some haste. Two years later, Miles was betrayed in Holland and was eventually taken back to London where he was hung, drawn and quartered at a place called Tyburn.

It was certainly a happy day when Lord John Talbot, his wife Katherine and the children, including his heir – yet another Richard –

returned to my walls. The family promptly settled in and, in a short time, it was difficult to believe they had ever left. Of course further proceedings ensured that those who had been loyal to Charles during his exile were restored to their lands. My resident's own exile, and the assistance provided to Dean John King, which Lord John no longer denied, ensured that the Talbots were fully restored to property and titles.

Of equal importance to my resident, a devout Catholic with a particular devotion to the Blessed Virgin, was that while other restored landholders renounced their faith to ensure the return of their property, my Talbots faced no such requirement. The principal reason was that Lord John's cousin, Sir Richard Talbot (who would eventually become Earl of Tyrconnell and represent Catholic interests in London) was a great friend of the king and had served him well while Charles II was exiled in France. In addition, Sir Richard's brother, Peter, was the Archbishop of Dublin and his support was important to the king's return to power in Ireland.

Lord John and his lovely wife did make an immediate alteration to the landscape surrounding my walls when they removed all external fortifications and filled in the moat beyond those walls. Effectively, I was defenceless against any attack but that was the purpose for the change. Lady Katherine wanted to ensure I would never again serve as a stronghold for a usurper. Since I could not withstand an attack, there would be no reason for the destruction of my walls. My residents also realised from their experience in exile, that no castle was capable of withstanding an attack by the modern cannons that had been introduced by Cromwell.

To prove this point to those in the vicinity who questioned the logic of his decision, Lord John commissioned a cannon to take a couple of shots at the fortification wall. The result was a gaping hole, proving conclusively that stone walls could not withstand a cannon's blast. In the course of that experiment, one shot went wild and actually hit my own walls embedding itself in my side where it remained for a hundred years. I was not amused and the effect is not something I will ever forget. I have occasionally heard rumours that that shot was taken by some relative of Miles Corbett who wanted to reclaim the castle but I can assure you that that was not the case.

On the other hand, rumours to the effect that the ghost of Miles Corbett haunts my walls are accurate as, after his death, he came to join Puck, Maud Plunkett and her two husbands. Miles appears only occasionally wandering about in full armour. If he encounters a human, however, he immediately falls into four pieces and disappears. I suppose it is a credit to my apparent allure that this man, who was so enamoured of my walls in life, could not resist returning in death.

Sadly, Lord John Talbot died shortly after he was restored to me. His son, Lord Richard Talbot, who soon assumed an important post as the Auditor General of Ireland, succeeded him. Lord Richard married his distant cousin, Frances Talbot, who was the niece of the Earl of Tyrconnell, also called Richard Talbot. Earl Richard became the most powerful man in Ireland when Charles II died and was succeeded by James II. He was a fine-looking man, tall and slender, with a broad forehead and piercing black eyes. As Lord Richard had married one of the earl's favourite nieces, the earl attended within my walls on many occasions. He was clean-shaven and wore a long wig as was the style of the day. I remember a particular conversation in my small drawing room that, to my horror, led to the decimation of many in the Talbot line.

The earl leaned back, his legs crossed and one arm stretched over the back of his chair, 'It appears, Richard, that our James has lost his throne in England, and has taken up residence in Paris.'

'Here we go again,' Lord Richard said shaking his head. 'What happened?'

'Well now, James converted to Catholicism in deference to his long-suffering mother, which caused all measure of backlash and that Dutch fellow William seized the opportunity to move in.'

'William?' Frances interjected, 'He is King James's son-in-law. Think of his poor wife. Her husband going to war with her father . . . It would be like Richard fighting you Uncle Dickie.'

'Indeed,' the earl replied, 'but there you have it. The timing could not have been worse because we were very close to a Catholic parliament for Ireland.'

'What now?' Lord Richard enquired.

The earl considered the contents of his glass for a moment before replying, 'I really don't see that we have much choice. You know Billy will be over here as soon as he has things settled in England. If he succeeds here, you can be sure that everything we have done to protect Catholic interests will be lost.'

'Oh, Uncle Dickie, not war again,' Frances groaned.

'And what are the chances of success?' Lord Richard asked.

The earl replied, 'Quite good I should think. Our cause is right because we will be holding Ireland for the legitimate king. I have had control of the army here for some time and most of my top officers are Catholic and support James.'

'And what of the clans?' Lord Richard enquired.

'I should think that between ourselves and William, the native Irish would support our cause,' the earl said. 'When I was in France with Charles during the Cromwellian times, I became well acquainted with The McCarthy, a chap called Donogh from a place called Blarney down in Cork. Charles was quite taken with him . . . named him Earl of Clancarthy as I recall. We got on quite well and Donogh would have some influence in the south. I can't imagine problems there, although one can never tell about Ulster.'

'And when does this war begin? When do I have to start planning funerals for my brothers?' Frances asked angrily.

The earl, his complexion darkening slightly, replied with forced restraint, 'No one likes war, Frances, love. But sometimes it is necessary to fight for the freedom to live as we choose. You know I would not risk my sons unless there was no other way.'

Frances sobbed, 'I know Uncle Dickie, but war . . . I hate war.'

III War and Recovery (1690–1835)

Lord Richard's uncle, the Earl of Tyrconnell was, without doubt, the most powerful man in Ireland and, as I consider my long history, certainly among the strongest leaders this country has ever known. As Lord Lieutenant of Ireland he had full command of the English army in Ireland. Ultimately he was a duke and Viceroy of Ireland. Although King James was deposed in England, the strength of the earl's power ensured that he remained the King of Ireland. My residents and the many important persons who met within my walls knew without question that King William could hardly tolerate this division and that, sooner rather than later, he would turn his attention to Ireland.

Meanwhile, the earl had taken his army into the field driving out Williamite supporters who then fled to places like Derry and Enniskillen. Many of these Protestant landowners had armed garrisons and would rally to William when the time was right. Tyrconnell's strategy was to pre-empt future action and defeat them before they consolidated into a strong army.

I was kept well informed on the campaign's progress, as my great hall was the venue for many meetings, particularly among the various branches of the Talbot family. Many of those people traced their roots to earlier generations at Malahide so they rallied to the support of one of their own. Despite this, opinion was certainly divided. The young men, with little apparent appreciation for their own mortality, trained for battle and were confident of victory, while the women supporting their sons, husbands and brothers, spoke only of death and destruction when they met each other.

The earl himself was a frequent guest within my walls when he was not on one of his many trips travelling the length and breadth of the country in support of King James. I remember him reporting on one such meeting, which had been convened in Blarney Castle down in Cork.

'We have the full support of the McCarthys and their related clans,' the earl announced at one meeting.

'Can we be sure of the McCarthys?' one his nephews enquired. 'You know they have a reputation for, shall we say, expedience.'

The earl responded, 'Indeed. That is why I met with them. Donogh

McCarthy is the head of the Muskerry McCarthys. He is named after his grandfather who I knew well in France. The young man may have been a little reluctant at first, but he understands the situation and his duties. He is also well advised by his uncles and minds what they have to say. I see no problem with the McCarthys.'

'And what of the west?' my own Lord Richard enquired.

'Solid, I should think,' was the reply, 'O'Neill from Bunratty has pledged Thomond and we can expect them to contribute substantial forces.'

'Which leaves the north,' another cousin said.

The earl sighed, 'Yes the north. We had a spot of bother in Derry but I abandoned the siege there because the garrison wasn't a threat and I couldn't be wasting any more time on it. We have no real problem in the northwest but I don't expect much in the way of support either. The northeast is the real problem. I suspect that Orange Billy will use Belfast, or more likely Carrickfergus, to launch his invasion. We have to defeat him before he has a chance to spread into the rest of the country.'

'And what of King James?' was yet another query.

Tyrconnell responded with confidence, 'He will sail soon and I will be there to greet him when he arrives. Our glorious king, my friends, is a fighter.'

Not long after, in 1689, James II did land at Kinsale down in Cork. If the discussions within my walls were to be believed, he brought with him a massive army of French soldiers making victory inevitable. James proceeded up to Dublin stopping along the way in Blarney, Kilkenny and other castles to rally support among the clans that had pledged to Tyrconnell. Eventually he called at my walls in the company of Earl Richard Talbot. As one might imagine, there was great excitement and anticipation as we awaited the king's arrival. While I was always well prepared to provide most gracious hospitality, receiving this guest was a proud moment.

In preparation for the planned feast, my great hall was repainted, woodwork was polished and wall hangings were removed and freshened. When the day finally arrived, I had never looked more beautiful, if I dare say so myself. The king arrived dressed in a long, dark-blue coat, white, knee-length pants with red stockings and a pair of what could best be described as bright-red slippers. His shirt was white and he wore a long silk cravat. King James also wore a long, white wig with curls running well past his shoulders. He was not particularly tall but his face was quite long with a prominent chin and nose to match.

At risk of sounding disloyal, something my residents would never countenance, I was far more impressed with the physical appearance of one of his commanders, Patrick Sarsfield, the Earl of Lucan. Sarsfield was regal in appearance and bearing, tall with powerful shoulders and legs and a jet-black wig similar in style to that worn by the king. Other guests included James Fitzjames, the Duke of Berwick, Richard Talbot, the Earl of Tyrconnell, my own Lord Richard Talbot and a number of clan chieftains who had accompanied James from the south.

As the evening wore on, it seemed to me that the feast was more a celebration of victory than it was an anticipation of battle. Only my resident, Lord Richard, displayed any concern about the outcome.

'You need have no concerns, my good man,' the king said raising his goblet toward his host. 'We shall make short work of William. Is that not right Tyrconnell?'

Earl Richard responded raising his own cup, 'The army is ready, Your Majesty.'

'And the cavalry, Sarsfield?' the king continued.

Repeating the gesture, Patrick also added his affirmation and a number of other chieftains raised their goblets with cries of support.

My resident, Lord Richard replied, 'You give me great confidence, My Lord. I was concerned about rumours that the Pope in Rome had sent hundreds of thousands of pounds to finance William, who is not only very well manned, including mercenaries from Holland, but equipped with the latest in weaponry.'

The king gave a dismissive shrug, 'William has the Pope and we have King Louis. William has the Dutch; we have the French. We, however, also have the Irish,' he concluded toasting the remainder of the gathering.

Again he was greeted with roars of support.

For some time after, the king's forces under Tyrconnell gathered and

Here I am in the early nineteenth century. You can see how the construction of castellated drum towers added elegant height to my vista.

prepared for the battle that was inevitable. I saw little of the preparations as they took place far from my walls. Lord Richard Talbot, perhaps remembering his father's time with Cromwell, remained concerned about the outcome, although in the company of guests he expressed confidence. The women within my walls, however, spoke more about their fears for their sons, husbands, brothers and cousins than they did about any great victory.

Toward the end of June 1690, it appeared that the battle would soon be fought because the reports reached my walls William of Orange had landed at Carrickfergus joining his army of nearly thirty-five thousand soldiers and they were on the march. The Jacobite army with King James at the fore was gathering near the banks of the Boyne river a few miles north of my walls.

At first light on the first of July, Lord Richard gathered in my great hall with eighteen members of the extended Talbot family, including cousins and nephews, for a breakfast that would see the Talbots through a day of fighting. The talk at the table was of the glory that would be earned on the battlefield fighting under the banner of King James. When the meal had ended, the men and young men rode away from my walls shouting the motto of the Talbots: *forte et fidelis* ('strong and faithful'). The women gaily waved their kerchiefs but there was no hiding their sobbing and tears.

All morning and afternoon my residents and I waited for word of the battle and it was late afternoon when a cloud of dust in the distance announced the approach of horsemen. Remarkably, at the head of the troop was none other than King James himself and after giving his horse over to the stable boys he entered and was greeted by Lady Frances.

'What news, Your Majesty?' she enquired after rising from a deep curtsy.

The king, obviously winded after a long ride responded, 'I'm afraid all is lost.'

'Lost?' Frances stammered. 'What happened?'

The king was flustered for a moment, 'What happened, you say? Why the rascally Irish have run away from me. Please have a bath drawn for me.'

Lady Frances had recovered from the initial shock of the disclosure and her face showed an anger I had never seen before. She look straight at the king and said, 'Ran away, you say? It would appear that Your Majesty has won the race.' With that she turned and marched away leaving the shocked king to the servants who attended to his needs.

Over the next several hours, late into the night, men wandered from the battlefields onto the grounds outside my walls. Anxious women and children asked for news of their husbands and brothers but the only real news of the battle was that the Jacobite forces had mistaken a feint for the real attack. They committed their troops to the wrong spot and had been overwhelmed by Dutch mercenaries who were far better equipped and had a great advantage in numbers. The message from the battle was clear – King William had won and he would soon arrive in Dublin.

For several days my walls were in a continuous state of mourning as the bodies of fallen Talbots were borne back to Malahide. I also mourned for the mothers, wives and sisters who had lost their loved ones and I have never known a sadder time. When the final body was buried, fourteen of those who sat down to breakfast just a few short days earlier returned on their shields, never again to bring laughter and joy to my walls.

I joined with my residents in assuming that sooner or later, when William of Orange had established himself in Dublin, the Talbots would be driven from my walls to be replaced by some Williamite who had been loyal to the victorious king. Remarkably, unlike the days of Cromwell when I was cursed with Miles Corbet, that did not happen. Lord Richard continued to manage the estates as if nothing had happened, making all the necessary payments to the new government. I recall him discussing the matter with Frances.

'Have you any news?' she enquired one morning as he returned from a journey into the city. 'Have any orders been given about our beautiful home?'

Lord Richard replied, 'Relax, love. Our new government has better things to do with its time than worry about who supported whom. It isn't like Cromwell's time, at least in Dublin. Most of the administration is the same and they still need grain, corn, meat and produce.'

'But they don't need us for that,' Frances countered.

'Perhaps not,' Lord Richard said, 'but any change now would mean some disruption that they also don't want. I think if we pay our rents, supply our food and completely avoid controversy, we will be left in peace. If Dublin has other plans, there really isn't anything we can do about it anyway.'

Tyrconnell continued to call on my walls occasionally, keeping my residents current on the remainder of the Williamite campaign. Perhaps that too, was a reason my resident's support of King James was not punished with forfeiture. During one visit by Tyrconnell, I heard that William had not been so successful in his efforts to take Limerick, which had resisted his siege. William had departed Ireland, leaving the final battles to his generals. He then announced that continuing problems in Scotland and England required his attention so, unlike the Cromwellian days, King William was not around to seek vengeance against the Jacobites. My family merely adjusted their allegiance to the new strain of English kings and provided loyal service to King William and his successors. With each passing year, the likelihood of their eviction decreased.

My chief resident, Richard Talbot, continued as Lord of the Manor for many years and was one hundred years old when he finally died in 1768. At a time when sixty years was a long life for human beings, his years were even more remarkable than his protecting my walls from Williamite plunder. I would certainly attribute both to Lord Richard's remarkably calm demeanour, particularly in his later years. To this day, I can hear the echo of his voice saying, 'What will be, will be.' On the other hand, I can still see the smiles of understanding from his nieces and nephews to the third and fourth generation as his attitude, speech and even style of dress did not change at all for the last sixty years of his life. Until the day he died, Richard's greatest concern was that my walls would be taken from him in retribution for his family support of King James.

In the ninety-second year of Lord Richard's life, I was to suffer the agony of destruction for the first and only time in my glorious history. I well remember the night as it was particularly dark and chilly so the fires in the small drawing room were burning brightly. At a time when no one was in the room, a burning ingot spat from the fire and lodged between the wooden floorboards. After everyone had retired for the evening, the ingot smouldered and eventually caught fire, and destroyed the entire west wing of the house, including the small drawing room and the great drawing room.

Although there were tears in the old man's eyes as he viewed my destruction, his response was typical of his philosophy. 'Well, we shall have to rebuild this bit, better than before, I should think.' And that is what happened, my great and small drawing rooms were rebuilt with turreted towers at the corners, in the configuration that exists to this day. They were finished in Georgian splendour making them far more elegant than my earlier rooms. An additional staircase hall was also added to ensure that, should I ever be cursed with another fire, my residents would be safe.

I have heard that many castles, having once suffered the ravages of fire, were abandoned. So I was delighted that my ancient resident was so pleased with my past services that he ensured I would rise from the ashes.

Although Lord Richard was happily married to Frances for many of those years, they were not blessed with children and his nephew, Richard (a name which must come as a surprise to you), became the designated heir. Young Richard could not have been more unlike his uncle but, after years of sombre peace and quiet, Richard brought new life and vitality to my walls ending, perhaps forever, the sadness occasioned by that bloody day at the Boyne.

First, Richard married one Margaret O'Reilly much to the chagrin of both families.

'But Dickie,' the ninety-seven-year-old patriarch counselled. 'She is Irish and you are not. It just isn't done.'

'But Uncle Richard, I love her,' the young man pleaded in time-honoured fashion. 'And besides, our family has been in Ireland for six hundred years so if we are not Irish, what are we?'

The old man seemed a little confused at the comment but replied stoutly, 'English of course! You know that the king might not be pleased that you are consorting with an enemy.'

Young Richard smiled at his uncle, 'With due regard, Unc, I don't think the king realises we are here at all, and I do love her, I really do.'

Lord Richard thought about that for a while and appeared to almost fall asleep but then he raised his head and put out his hand taking that of his nephew. 'Well Dickie, my time is almost gone and I suppose whatever will be will be. I can't say I'm happy about the whole thing, but you are a man now and I can only trust that you will do what is best for my beloved home.'

Young Richard did marry Margaret but not within my walls. Margaret was cheerful and pleasant and always had a good word for everyone in Malahide. She was particularly thoughtful to the ancient Lord Richard helping him in his last days and more than nearly anyone she brought joy to my walls. She also delivered children, many children. Eight boys and eight girls attested to the great love she had for the new Lord Richard and he for her, and I was delighted to again hear the laughter and shouts of such happy voices within my walls.

Sadly, Margaret's eldest son, Richard Wogan Talbot, was only twenty-one when his father died but Margaret carried on assuming her husband's role and responsibility without any particular concern for the niceties of heirship or passage of title. Margaret had no interest in withdrawing to widow's weeds when there was a family to rear and an estate to administer. Although Richard Wogan had reached his majority, it was Margaret who made all the important decisions affecting the affairs of the family.

Perhaps Lady Margaret's most remarkable decision was to abandon the Catholic faith that had been such an integral part of the generations of Talbots who lived within my walls. I well remember the discussion in the oak room that seemed to shock even her children.

'But why, Mother, why now when Daneil O'Connell is starting to make Catholicism acceptable again?' Richard Wogan Talbot enquired.

'That is the very reason,' Lady Margaret replied calmly tapping her fingers on the desk at which she sat.

Richard Wogan was certainly puzzled, 'Whatever do you mean? We have been Catholic for all these years when the risk to our land and estate was immeasurable, but now, when a ray of tolerance appears, you want us to change.'

'Yes,' Lady Margaret replied. 'When the Catholic faith was

effectively proscribed, and Catholics had no power, being a Catholic presented no risk to the crown. Because of this, our religion was not a sign of disloyalty. Now, however, the Catholics have voted and put O'Connell into parliament. Surely you understand that the crown sees O'Connell as a threat? Some people are even calling him the uncrowned king of Ireland.'

Richard Wogan nodded apparently following his mother's reasoning, 'But being Catholic does not mean we are disloyal any more now than it did fifty or one hundred years ago. Why should we convert now?'

'Perception, Richard, perception,' Lady Margaret replied patiently. 'We have always been loyal to the crown. Converting from Catholicism, which the crown perceives as a threat to its rule, is a forthright demonstration of our continuing loyalty. I have given this matter considerable thought and I have concluded that our family will not only be protected for generations to come, but will be well rewarded for this gesture of loyalty.'

'But, Mother,' Richard protested. 'What of loyalty to the true Church? Seven hundred years of history . . .'

Lady Margaret moved forward in her chair placing both hands on the desk. 'History, Richard, creates fickle memories. When the Talbots declared their loyalty to the Church and the crown, the two were one and the same. To be loyal to the one was to be loyal to the other. That all ended at the Battle of the Boyne. To support the Catholic king, we disowned the true Catholic Church in Rome, which as you know backed the Protestant King William. Yet that Protestant king allowed your great uncle to keep these walls when he could have easily sent us off to France to join our Catholic king.'

'I see,' Richard replied, 'So loyalty to the crown is more important that loyalty to the Church.'

'Perhaps,' Lady Margaret replied. 'I'm not sure any more of what loyalty to a religion means when we sent fourteen Talbots to their deaths at the Boyne in support of a Catholic against a Protestant who was supported by the Roman Catholic Church. I do know what loyalty to the king means and as the future of this family depends on a choice, I choose loyalty to something I can understand, something to which we have always been loyal, and that is the crown.'

And so it was, that the Talbots converted, nearly en masse, to the

Episcopal Church. The only one who did not convert was Frances Gabriella, who had been named after her great aunt. Frances left my walls and moved to Austria where she married into royalty and never returned.

Margaret was certainly accurate in her assessment of the effect the conversion would have on the fortunes of the Talbot family. Shortly before her death in 1833, she was designated Baroness Talbot when the family was raised to peerage. One of Margaret's sons, John, rose to the rank of admiral in the English navy and another, Thomas, emigrated to a place called Ontario in Canada where he established another branch of the Talbot family. Richard Wogan Talbot succeeded his mother as second Baron Talbot and subsequent heirs inherited that auspicious title.

As you might expect, my own position as an estate owned by a family of peers to the British Empire was also further enhanced from time to time. In 1812 a new fireplace was installed in my Oak Room to commemorate Nelson's victory at the Nile in 1798. A new entrance supported by circular towers with castellated battlements was constructed at the front of my walls. I understand that battlements of that type had been used in early Norman times when archers would shoot down at attackers from between the castellations and the very thought of such a carry-on sent shivers through my walls. Of course in reality this addition served no defensive purpose, as that had long since ceased being a matter of concern, but I suppose it created the appearance of a proper castle as opposed to a great house.

In addition, a wing was added to the rear of my walls to house servants' quarters, stables and, later still, offices for the administration of the estate. By the time the baroness died, having lived for nearly ninety years, my walls appeared very much as you see them today. I had fully recovered from the grief of war and the pain of fire and, at the age of over six hundred years, I could not have been more fit. I credit much of my good fortune to two of my residents, Lord Richard and Lady Margaret, who, between them, guided my fortunes and the destiny of my resident family for over one hundred and fifty years.

IV Eight Hundred Years and Counting (1835–Present)

Having survived the Norman settlement, medieval times, Cromwellian vengeance and Jacobite wars, my recent history has been remarkably easy. After all, a grand lady of my stature and importance deserves to spend her middle years in quiet and unthreatened relaxation. Naturally I have not retired, unlike many other castles who dot the Irish countryside in far more ruinous condition. On the contrary, I have continued to provide unparalleled comfort and welcome not only to my residents but also to the many guests who have called to my walls.

The elevation of the Talbots to the peerage in 1831 was most assuredly a reward for many centuries of loyalty to the English crown. It also brought with it recognition of the family's importance well beyond the shores of Ireland. And, in credit to my residents, the Talbots accepted the responsibility to maintain a certain decorum in family matters and to provide service to the community. When peace returned to the English Pale, I accepted new responsibilities in assisting the Talbots to maintain their place in Dublin and London society.

For example, one resident, Lord James Talbot (the grandson of Margaret O'Reilly Talbot, the first Baroness Talbot) was the fourth Baron Talbot, the second and third being his uncle and father respectively. In addition to his duties to Malahide, Lord James was a Lord-in-Waiting to Her Majesty, Queen Victoria as well as the president of the Royal Irish Academy. Lord James was a fine-looking man with a large and well-shaped head, which was fortunate because he was not blessed with hair on top.

One dark and cold January afternoon in 1854, a messenger arrived at my walls exclaiming that a ship called the *John Tayleur* had wrecked off Lambay Island. Hundreds had been lost and the survivors had been washed up on the shore not far from where I stood.

Lord James gathered the staff and announced, 'We shall open the castle and welcome the survivors.'

'But, sir,' one footman replied, 'we simply do not have the room or facilities to accommodate two hundred people.'

To my delight, his response was prompt and forthright, 'Nevertheless, we have a beautiful, warm house and those people have lost everything. We will provide welcome.'

For the first, but certainly not the last, time, I was transformed into a hospital as well over two hundred wet, tired and injured souls were welcomed into the warmth of my walls. Pallets were set up in nearly every corner of every room and doctors and nurses were called in from all of north Dublin to assist in the effort. I enjoyed the experience and would rate it just below the shouts and laughter of children as my happiest time.

Lord James did more than just order that my walls be made available because he also met with each survivor to ensure that they were comfortable and to enquire if they had any particular need. When the crisis ended, he also set up a substantial fund to assist his guests in beginning their lives anew. I must say that his generosity, as well as the hospitality of my walls, was remarked upon for many years to come.

The fifth Baron, Lord Richard Wogan Talbot, succeeded Lord James and with his accession I was to greet the twentieth century with another most remarkable woman resident. In 1901 Richard Wogan was a widower (his wife, Emily, had died) and the father of a son called James. While away on business in London he met Isabel Blake Humphrey, a widow with seven children of her own and, in December of that year, they were married in London and shortly thereafter came home to my walls.

Despite the demands of her large family, Isabel was as energetic a person as I have ever encountered and, in a very short time, she set about making my walls the social centre of the Anglo-Irish community in Dublin. I was to discover that, in her prior marriage to a well-respected banker in London, she had frequently entertained royalty so she was well experienced in organising and presenting great feasts and balls. On one occasion, however, an unforeseen circumstance caused some embarrassment.

The cook, a jovial woman who was normally quite dependable, had been jilted by one of the grooms for whom she had a particular affection. Her response was to consume the alcoholic spirits that were intended for a pudding – as a consequence she became quite inebriated. The job of finishing the meal's preparation fell to one of the serving maids and the result was, well, a bit unusual to say the least. Lady Isabel, ever the gracious host, responded by increasing the presentation of drink to her guests who, in time, did not seem to notice a problem with the quality of the food.

The following morning the matter was further investigated. Isabel enquired of the butler, 'George, whatever happened to the dinner last night? The soup had little taste at all and the joint of beef was burnt on one side and raw on the other. As for the pudding, it had absolutely no sparkle.'

George replied, 'With respect, Madam, we had a spot of trouble with the cook.'

'Well that much is certainly clear,' Lady Isabel replied. 'What was the nature of the trouble?'

'I understood it to be a matter of the heart,' George replied and then he elaborated on the cook's disappointment.

At this point Lord Richard Wogan interjected, 'And that is the reason she forgot how to cook? Most remarkable it seems to me.'

The butler then explained about the consumption of the sherry concluding, 'She was as drunk as a lord . . . er . . . M'lord.'

After an uneasy moment, Lady Isabel broke into laughter, though her husband, who did not apparently understand the humour of the moment, only managed a chuckle. The normally taciturn George smiled for perhaps the first and only time in my memory. Lady Isabel had a sympathetic talk with the cook who was not sacked for her indiscretion, a fate that would almost certainly have awaited her under some of my earlier mistresses. The incident reflected the goodness of Lady Isabel and further endeared my resident mistress to the entire staff.

While some might view Lady Isabel's penchant for entertaining as a frivolous pursuit for a wealthy socialite, many of the functions were meant to raise support for various charitable causes. I was to hear a great deal about organisations like the Dublin Red Cross, Irish Distressed Ladies, the Mothers Union and the Public Library Guild and I was proud to welcome both committee members and the subjects of these organisations to my walls.

First and foremost, however, Lady Isabel Blake Talbot was a mother. I have the fondest memories of all her children and step-children perhaps because they were the last large family to reside within my walls. The children were happy and vibrant and Lady Isabel always found time to comfort a child when he or she was ill or to 'kiss better' a small scratch.

As I consider all the centuries of my existence, and indeed all the generations of Talbots who have resided within my walls, I believe that those years at the dawning of the twentieth century were my happiest. First, there was no longer any shadow of war or death. I was very well maintained and small restoration projects left me completely revitalised. I was the home to a large family who delighted in laughing and playing in every part of me. I was never without music; Lady Isabel frequently led singsongs while she played the piano. My hours were filled with community meetings and social entertaining and it seemed that the only time silence descended was when the lord and lady were travelling to some exotic place like Egypt or China. Of course when they returned the story of their travels became a reason for even more entertaining. They also never failed to bring back some exotic statue or ornament to adorn my walls and furnishings, which is always appreciated by a lady like myself.

Even into the twentieth century, my residents retained their loyalty to the crown and, when called upon at the time of World War I, we were happy to serve. The grounds outside my walls became a dirigible base from which these giant craft, nearly one hundred and fifty feet long, patrolled the Atlantic in search of German U-boats. The sight of these monsters flying above my parapets was most remarkable, and more than a little frightening as it took fifty men to tether the beasts. I hate to think what might have happened if one got loose and struck me. The pilots and crew were often welcomed into my walls because Lady Isabel believe strongly that it was our duty to provide a home for these brave boys who were protecting our shores.

I remember one occasion when literally providing a home was exactly what she did.

A Lieutenant Smythe-Rogers approached Lady Isabel as she was tending her garden just outside of my walls. 'If you will pardon my intrusion, I should like a word,' he began.

'But of course,' Lady Isabel replied. 'How may I be of service?'

The officer stammered for a moment before responding, 'It seems

Here I am today, 800 years young and clothed with nature's finery.

that one of my men, Miller, has become smitten with one of your housemaids called Sarah, as it were.'

Lady Isabel smiled, 'Well, isn't that wonderful.'

'Quite,' the officer continued. 'But it would appear that they have taken their, er, romance a bit beyond what one would expect from an unmarried couple . . . with . . . er, predictable consequences.'

'Oh dear, and how are they currently disposed toward one another?' she asked.

The officer said, 'Well that is the purpose for my visit. My man appears to be delighted with the whole thing and wishes to ask for her hand in matrimony. As I understand it, she is similarly disposed, as it were.'

'Well then,' Lady Isabel announced clapping her hands. 'We shall have to convene a wedding. What a wonderful thing to celebrate.'

The couple were married in the chapel on my grounds and a grand reception was held on the lawns beyond my walls. When the young man left the military he was promptly hired as a groom and his particular responsibility was tending Lady Isabel's Siddeley Wolseley. I don't believe they make that particular brand of automobile any more but, at the time, it was as fancy a contraption as you would find in Ireland.

Lest you think that my descriptions of this remarkable woman are exaggerated, I was not the only one to appreciate her virtues. In recognition of her many contributions to the people of Dublin and her service to the crown, Lady Isabel was named a Dame of the Order of the British Empire at the beginning of 1920.

Lord Richard Wogan Talbot died in 1921 and was succeeded by his son, James Boswell Talbot. Regrettably, a short time after that Lady Isabel moved back to England and rarely returned to my walls. Her departure left me with an emptiness that, in some respects, has never been filled. When Lady Isabel died a decade later, all of my residents as well as the community around Malahide publicly mourned her passing.

While human life is mortal, the existence of a castle moves forward without pause and in some ways my next mistress was not unlike Lady Isabel. Lady Joyce Kerr was a famous actress in London when Lord James Boswell began courting her. I would certainly commend his good taste because she was quite beautiful with an open and friendly manner. When James returned to my walls with his bride, she captivated everyone she met and a massive festival on my grounds was organised in welcome.

Among those who also welcomed, in a manner of speaking, the new mistress, was her predecessor from a previous century, Lady Maude Plunkett Talbot. Although she had been dead for nearly five hundred years, she, along with my other lingering spirits, would turn up nearly any time change was in the air. These apparitions were well known to Lord James Boswell Talbot so he advised his wife on the proper way to treat these spirits and, being an actress, Lady Joyce performed admirably.

On the night in question Lady Joyce was coming down the back stairwell with a candle to light the way when she encountered first Sir Walter Hussey brandishing his spear and then Lady Maude chasing him with her broom.

Lady Joyce was taken aback but only for a moment and then she commanded, 'You there, Lord Galtrim and Lady Maude, stop this instant.'

I was not surprised to see the two stop dead in their tracks because a similar scene had played itself out with earlier mistresses. Lady Joyce's tone softened slightly as she continued, 'The two of you will stop this carry-on immediately. This castle is in good hands.'

After a slight hesitation, the two disappeared in a puff of cold air. Lady Joyce did not encounter my other spirits, the Lord Chief Justice, who very seldom appeared, Miles Corbett or Puck the Jester but that was merely happenstance in a castle as large as myself. Puck was particularly in evidence when the resident master changed, if only to ensure his legitimacy and security. The only reason my new mistress did not encounter him was that Lady Joyce was not one to wander around in the dead of night when the spirits moved about.

Like her predecessor, Lady Joyce was involved in community affairs and, in 1941 during the Emergency, she had parts of me outfitted as a hospital with beds and all the necessities. Although I never actually welcomed a patient, I was fully prepared to do my part and I am happy to report that Lady Joyce ensured that the Malahide Castle hospital was second to none. My resident mistress was also a strong supporter of the Red Cross and at times it seemed like my walls were more like a warehouse than a castle. In addition to bandages, Lady Joyce bought and stored sugar, wheat flour and other staples against any emergency.

Lady Joyce was the last of a line of remarkable women who lived within my walls. When Lord James died in 1948 Lady Joyce remarried and moved to England where she died in 1980 at the age of eighty-three.

I know that many of my male residents were not only important but became famous in the story of Ireland and England and, perhaps, these women did not receive the same public recognition and respect. You see I was their home during all the centuries and I sheltered them while their husbands or sons were off on some important business for the crown or government – or some useless business like fighting and dying. As a result, I know more than most how truly special and important they were and I do thank you for the opportunity you have given me to honour their memories.

Unfortunately, my latest residents were also not blessed with children. Apart from an occasional visit by distant relatives of Lord James Boswell, or the children of servants or friends, I was deprived of the wonder of little people. After a few decades of years filled with the laughter and play of children, I felt an emptiness that, in some ways, has never gone away.

After Lord James Boswell Talbot died, his cousin, Lord Milo John Reginald Talbot, assumed the title of seventh Baron Talbot De Malahide. Lord Milo was to represent the end of a line of Talbots who had occupied my walls for eight hundred years but, for twenty-five years, I provided him with safety and comfort, just as I had for all his ancestors. Lord Milo had served the crown as a career diplomat in far-flung places like Laos and Vietnam so he was happy to enjoy the peace and serenity of my walls. He never married and spent his hours in the gardens around my walls filling the landscape with rare and exotic trees and flowers. When Lord Milo died suddenly in 1973, his sister Rose Talbot, who was well into her fifties, inherited my walls but circumstances prevented her from every taking up permanent residence and my days as a home came to an end.

Not long after Rose Talbot returned for Lord Milo's burial, she met with solicitors in my small drawing room who explained the problem. Under Irish law a tax is imposed on the transfer of property when someone dies and, with a property as valuable as myself, that tax was quite significant. The contents of my walls, collected over hundreds of years, meant that Lord Milo's estate was so large that his sister did not have the money to pay the tax required by the government of Ireland. Since the government insisted on monetary payment, it appeared for a time that the contents of my walls, including the furniture and artwork that had been collected by my residents over the centuries would have to be sold, leaving me an empty shell.

As a castle I would know very little about the politics of such things but, after eight hundred years of observing residents who were involved at the highest levels of government, I couldn't help but speculate on the process. To the end of the Talbot line, my residents retained their allegiance to the English crown. Lord Milo held a British title, served as a British ambassador and, despite my location in Ireland, never stopped being a citizen of Great Britain. His late cousin, Lord James Boswell, and his uncle, Lord Richard Wogan, who both owned my walls after the formation of the Irish State, were no different. They saw themselves as subjects of the English crown who happened to be resident in Ireland.

I suppose that, because of the nature of my residents, in one respect I never stopped being a part of England, despite the fact that I am located in a totally independent country. In another respect, it is a credit to Ireland that despite over eight hundred years of English occupation, my walls and my residents were allowed to live in peace after the nation became independent. In return, my residents contributed greatly to the community in which they lived. When the Talbot line of descent came to an end, it seemed only right that I should take my place in the country of my creation and indeed existence. I had hoped, however, that there would be a more appropriate method for this transfer, than the decimation of my contents.

However, in 1976 an auction was arranged and potential buyers from all over the world arrived to inspect my contents with a view to stripping me of my grandeur. You see, although my walls might remain as strong and beautiful as ever, ladies of my years grow accustomed to a certain level of luxury and comfort represented by the furnishings that adorn my interior. Each chair, each rug and each table has a special meaning to me because I remember the circumstances, perhaps hundreds of years ago, surrounding its arrival. The portraits and pictures that adorned my walls were like my own album of photographs, to use the modern parlance, and their value to me was incalculable. Only my resident spirit Puck seemed to agree with me and appeared almost nightly howling his protest and perhaps he drove off one or two of those scavengers.

The auction went ahead and the value of my contents ensured that Lord Milo's death taxes would be paid in full. To my delight, Ireland's tourist board, Bord Fáilte, was able to purchase much of the furniture as well as the carpets and draperies so they never left my walls. In addition Ireland's National Gallery purchased many of the family portraits that meant so much to me. While they left my walls for a short time for cleaning and restoration, they were soon returned, albeit on loan. In the end, my splendour remained for future generations to relive history through my walls and their contents.

With the taxes paid, Lady Rose Talbot moved back to her family home in Tasmania, which was also called Malahide. As she was older and had no children, the Talbot line ended and she was the last of her lineage to reside within my walls. Since the costs of maintaining my walls and contents were significant, the Dublin County Council acquired me and I have become a living museum to be enjoyed by visitors from Ireland and around the world.

Although I miss the daily excitement of family life, and particularly the children who once laughed and played within my walls, I have embraced my new existence. In some respects I am even more elegant than at any time in my history because many kind people have contributed beautiful and valuable pictures and furnishings on display within my walls. One picture on loan from the National Gallery that has particularly poignant memories for me is located in my great hall. The painting by Jan Wyck depicts the Battle of the Boyne and is a sad reminder of the fourteen Talbots who ate breakfast together on that fateful day in July of 1690 and never again returned.

Today, well over eight hundred years since I first saw service to humankind, the purpose for my existence has changed completely, as indeed has my loyalty. I am proud to be a living Irish museum enabling people to imagine life within my walls hundreds of years ago. My only remaining residents are spirits of those who have long passed from this world and even they seldom appear so my nights are filled with quiet solitude. Although I do miss the Talbots, I do not bemoan my fate because, in many respects, my service to the people of Ireland, and particularly the schoolchildren of Ireland, makes me particularly happy.

I conclude my story as I began, by saying that I am delighted to have had the opportunity to tell you about my existence. Although of Norman origin, like many of the other great castles of Ireland (including Bunratty, Carrickfergus and Kilkenny) I think you will agree that my history is unlike any other. I have provided a comfortable home to my residents and circumstances have allowed me to avoid the personal agonies of war and destruction, enabling me to be a mother's arms into which my residents always returned.

I am reminded of a phrase from a book called *Golden Opportunities* written by my resident, Lady Isabel Blake Humphrey Talbot. That special lady wrote that the principal gifts a mother should provide to her children are love, patience and hope. I should like to think that, as a castle, that is what I have done.

CARRICKFERGUS CASTLE

~

I How I Became a Stronghold (1177–1280)

I am called Carrickfergus Castle. I have been the rock-solid defender of Belfast Lough and the Antrim coast for over eight hundred years. I have never surrendered and I remain virtually unchanged since my Norman birth in the twelfth century. To be frank, I am not a willing participant in this storytelling of my history. I am not a bard or a poet or any measure of storyteller, rather I am a castle who has always accomplished the task for which I was constructed. This makes my story quite simple – I have held strong against the enemies who would threaten the safety and security of my residents. I have done my job.

Despite my misgivings, I will elaborate on the story of my existence because if I don't, you may get the impression that the proper role for a castle is to provide gala parties like my sister castle in Malahide, or to allow itself to be battered in submission like Brother Bunratty or Sister Kilkenny or to talk its way out of all harm like that snivelling wretch Blarney. From De Courcy to Churchill, I have served and I have protected because that is what a castle does, plain and simple. A castle provides a safe haven for those who seek refuge within their walls regardless of the character, principles or religion of these people. Comfort and convenience are attributes prized by human beings, but a comfortable ruin can hardly call itself a castle. It is better that a castle stands strong and offers little comfort than be a pleasure palace who collapses at the first stiff wind. And so, I will tell you my story.

My original builder was a knight called John De Courcy who had joined Strongbow in the invasion of Ireland. De Courcy tired of the soft life in Dublin preferring further adventure and conquest. The English king, called Henry II, granted his consent for De Courcy to rule Ulster, provided he could conquer it. De Courcy set out with around four hundred knights and, because they were well trained, well equipped and well protected, he won several battles against much larger forces. De Courcy marched further north until he arrived at a rocky outcrop extending into Belfast Lough and known locally as the Rock of Fergus.

I was to discover that Fergus, a Scottish king, was shipwrecked and drowned off the rock and that is how it got the name. (My own name, Carrickfergus, is simply the Irish word for rock combined with that of the departed king.)

This rock, protected on three sides by the sea, was the foundation upon which I rose and upon which I have prevailed, as solid as my foundations, for over eight hundred and twenty-five years. My walls as you see them today were constructed in three stages over the first seventy-five years of my existence so that I now occupy the entire rock. Each of these constructions, including my first walls on the end of the rock, remains much the same as when it was first built.

My existence began in 1177, which makes me one of the first true castles in all of Ireland. I take particular pride in the fact that centuries of battering by time, weather and human beings have not brought me down. And, I can say with the confidence of my years, that I will never be reduced to the piles of rubble, generically referred to as castles, that are strewn across many an Irish field.

The first of my walls to rise upon the Rock of Fergus was my donjon which people today would call a keep. Although it took several years for De Courcy to finish this section, I am grateful to him for his insistence that there be no shortcuts in my construction. When my keep was completed, I rose ninety feet into the Ulster sky. This section is a five-storey square tower with each side exceeding fifty feet. My base on the north side, which faces away from the sea, is nine feet thick while my base on the other sides are over eight feet thick. Given this foundation, built upon solid rock, there was no chance that an attacker could batter my foundation or tunnel under a corner in an attempt to cause me to collapse upon myself.

I will be the first to admit that I have never been a particularly comfortable residence for those who sought my protection, however, I never saw that as a part of my responsibility. The lower floors where the soldiers and public met, though well secured by the width of my walls, were dark and damp with no fireplace for warmth. The middle floors, containing the kitchens and resident halls, had little ventilation and could become thick with the smells of cooking and living. The upper floors served as my principal rooms of residence and offices and could only be accessed by climbing a long and narrow circular staircase. Although De Courcy himself, and later lords of the manor, occupied this floor, it was usually cold and draughty because my walls were defended from these upper floors and the windows were arrow ports from which weapons could be fired down upon an attacker. This floor also had access to the battlements above my roof, which were manned at all times by lookouts.

In those early days, each lower floor contained one large room in which business was conducted during the day and where, at night, soldiers and staff slept wherever they could fine room. The important business was conducted on the top floor and among my first memories of human occupation was a conference held there shortly after my keep had been constructed. De Courcy planned to enclose the yard between the sea and the keep with another brick wall creating an inner ward but his soldiers, who had joined him in search of conquest and adventure, had tired of the life of stonemasons.

One man in particular, called Miles De Chancier, voiced the grievances. 'With all due respect,' he began, 'we have been at this project for three years. I have made countless trips up and down the coast transporting this limestone from the quarries. I don't fight anymore. I plead and beg with the native workers to earn their pay. I spend more time with a trowel in my hands than I do a sword. I am a soldier not a mason or a builder.'

De Courcy, who was a very tall man with long, blond hair, broad shoulders and powerful hands, rose from his chair and glared down at De Chancier. 'Are you not paid well for your service?'

De Chancier cowered noticeably but replied, 'I am, sir, but I joined for adventure and riches it might bring and not merely to find employment. I could have laid stone in Dublin.'

Perhaps the response reminded De Courcy of his own history as his stance softened and he returned to his chair. After a moment he said, 'Yes, Miles, I understand. But don't you see, I would rather have a castle full of live builders than an army of dead soldiers. This . . .this fortress must be impregnable if we are to hold Ulster. Sooner or later the natives will revise their method of fighting and if we don't have a solid base from which to operate, their sheer numbers will overrun us. This castle must be our rock and, until the fortifications are complete, everything we have done will mean nothing.'

De Chancier apparently understood but he protested meekly, 'But the men . . .'

'You tell the men,' De Courcy concluded, 'that there will be plenty of adventure once Carrickfergus is secure. I will guarantee their share of the prizes that await us, including a tenancy on rich land for those who stand by me. They must understand though that, without this rock, we will not hold Ulster and they well have nothing.'

Apparently the men accepted the word of their leader because my inner ward walls continued to rise until an area approximately one hundred and fifty feet by one hundred feet, including the keep, was behind fortified walls. Because my south and west walls abutted the coast, I had begun to approach the invincibility that was to mark my history. De Courcy, in turn, used my walls as the base from which to rule the area covering the modern counties of Down and Antrim as if he were the king.

In fairness, he also kept his word to De Chancier and the other knights as, in what was the typically Norman way, he created baronies and issued charters repaying his soldiers for the loyalty and hard work with grants of land. My resident regularly convened a court within my walls to address the grievances and disputes among his subjects. From the nature of those proceedings, I could only conclude that De Courcy was a fair and reasonable ruler and that peace and prosperity were the order of the day. De Courcy even commissioned the minting of silver coins called 'Patrick farthings' to facilitate commerce.

During those early days of my existence, I also experienced family life for the first time when John De Courcy brought his wife, Lady Affreca, to live within my walls. De Courcy was devoted to Affreca who, like her husband, was tall and slender. Affreca was a Viking princess, the daughter of Godred who ruled the Isle of Man, and she was accustomed to the finer things including the luxury of a far more comfortable accommodation than I could provide.

Affreca was a quiet and gentle person, well beloved by all those with whom she came into contact but she was never particularly happy with her life within my walls. Although she was stoic in accepting her fate and never really complained about anything, her character changed completely when family members from Man visited and it was clear that she missed them far more than she would ever say. I quite liked Affreca and so, for perhaps the only time in my long history, I nearly regretted that I was not better equipped to provide comfort as well as security. I should like to have been able to provide such a noble woman with an accommodation that would make her happy.

I suppose John De Courcy knew better than most that a rock-solid castle is not compatible with style and comfort, even for the benefit of his wife. As a result, little was done to accommodate those who were not so robust and my destiny was not altered.

It could be said that, using my walls as his centre of power, John De Courcy did indeed conquer Ulster. In doing this, he earned the right to rule it promised to him by King Henry II when he set out from Dublin some twenty-five years earlier. Unfortunately for my resident, the nature of the times was not to allow continuing prosperity because others were not so diligent in honouring their commitments. I recall a conversation held in the upper chambers between De Courcy and Eldric, Lady Affreca's brother, who had recently arrived from London.

'I have news,' Eldric began, 'which will not be pleasing to your ears.'

'And what news is that?' De Courcy queried.

'You know, of course, that my father, Godred, and King John are on close terms now that my father has established himself on Man, and that I have been to London on my father's behalf.' Eldric said.

De Courcy replied, 'And what has that to do with me?'

Eldric looked down at the dagger with which he was cleaning his nails and answered, 'It seems the king is concerned about you.'

'Concerned about me?' De Courcy responded obviously puzzled. 'King Henry issued me a charter because I was able to conquer these lands. He specifically reserved rights of homage and fealty and I can only assume that I have contributed more to the royal treasury than nearly anyone in Ireland. Why would John be concerned about me?'

'I am only the messenger,' Eldric continued, 'and although he may have no reason for concern, it seems that John is not like his father, or his brother "The Lionheart" for that matter, and past commitments don't seem to matter to him. He is concerned about the extent of your power, particularly as you are out here in the wilds of Ulster sitting in an impregnable fortress well removed from his authority. Perhaps you should go to him and return your lands to him as a sign of good faith. Strongbow did that and the king immediately returned his estates to him.'

Making the mistake which would cost him a kingdom, De Courcy scoffed, 'I'll do nothing of the kind. The king has nothing to fear from me. I have always acted in good faith and, whatever I have done, it has been in the name of the king. The charter came from his father and I have strictly abided by its terms. I cannot accept that the king thinks poorly of me.'

Eldric sighed, 'For my sister's sake, I hope that you are right and my information is simply rumour. I only hope you know what you are doing.'

Regretfully, my resident was wrong in his opinion of the integrity of King John, as I was to discover. The king's viceroy in Dublin, Hugh De Lacy, summoned De Courcy to a court hearing over a land matter and when my resident refused to appear, De Lacy, with the approval of the king, captured De Courcy's castle at Downpatrick and took control of his territory throughout Antrim and Down as well. This caused De Courcy to march out from the safety of my walls, with flags flying, to revenge the wrong. Unfortunately, that was the last I was to see of John De Courcy as he was defeated at Dundrum and captured by De Lacy.

Eventually, in 1204, Hugh De Lacy took possession of my walls as

The Rock of Fergus in the early thirteenth century. Note my original fortified keep surrounded by curtain walls commissioned by King John himself. I am unchanged today.

the king designated him the Earl of Ulster. De Lacy was most accommodating to Lady Affreca, presumably because the king did not want to offend her father. While De Courcy's properties were forfeit to the crown, the king ordered that Lady Affreca's dower rights be taken from the forfeited property and returned to her. Lady Affreca also departed from my walls to take up residence in an abbey she had founded and that was the last I heard of her.

While De Courcy was well respected by his subjects in and around my walls, the same could not be said for De Lacy. Settlers who had taken property after serving De Courcy were considered enemies and De Lacy sent his armies to take possession of their lands. He also levied heavy taxes on the native Irish, which caused them to rebel and, before long, the peace and contentment of the De Courcy years were well and truly gone. The talk within my walls at the time was that De Lacy had let the power go to his head. In the space of eight years, King John apparently decided that he had chosen the wrong man for Ulster because the word came that the king himself was leading an expedition to rid himself of De Lacy.

Hugh De Lacy did not make the same mistake as De Courcy as he knew better than to confront the superior forces of the king, so he retreated to my walls, destroying and burning the castles he had previously held. Ultimately, King John reached my walls having faced little opposition along the way and it was then that I faced my first siege.

In the days and months that followed, I felt the stings and blows of the arrows and rocks of the mightiest army in Ireland but, to me, they were little more than an annoyance. Although I might have had little respect for my resident, my job was to stand strong and I will tell you with no false modesty, I did exactly that. The King of England may have assaulted my walls for decades, but I would not have surrendered. De Lacy, however, was not so resolute and he, together with his family and close friends, slipped out of my walls and escaped by sea to France. The remaining occupants opened my gates and I had a new resident, King John of England, and I have been legally a property of the crown since that day.

After hosting John De Courcy, a tall and powerfully built man with a reputation as a daring knight who could not be defeated, I was disappointed with King John's lack of regal bearing. He was a smallish, dark man with black hair and a black beard, both well trimmed, and his face seemed etched with a permanent expression of grave concern. While King John only ruled his empire from my walls for a period of ten days in July of 1210, I remember well his conduct of court matters from the great hall on my third floor.

The court was convened with much ceremony and everyone rose and bowed as the king entered the room. After surveying the crowd to be sure that everyone was properly submissive, King John slumped into a massive chair that had been placed at one end of the hall. A desk table was then set in front of him. Most of the business of the day had very little to do with my walls but were matters of state that a clerk brought to his attention and, for the better part of the day, he simply signed documents that were placed in front of him. The time came, however, when the knights who had helped him in taking my walls were presented, including Adam le Butiller, Godfrey De Rupe Forth and Robert Salvagius. Each knight stepped forward and knelt on one knee as the clerk read a proclamation attesting to their noble deeds. The king touched each knight's shoulder with a small baton he held at which time the knight rose, accepted his payment and backed away. The king also signed a decree that four hundred foot soldiers should be paid for their service and other payments were ordered for mariners and carpenters, though none of these people appeared within my walls.

Although his time in my walls was short, King John's impact on my development was to last to this day. I have no doubts but that king recognised the strength and character of my walls, which he had been unable to breach, but he quickly decided to expand them to fortify the entire outer half of the Rock of Fergus. He therefore ordered the constables he left in charge to make further additions to my fortifications.

King John ordered that a second wall be constructed, which meant that all three water-facing sides of the peninsula on which I am located would have walls up to the water line. A further wall on the fourth, north-facing side completed the fortifications and a moat was dug beyond the north wall adding further protection. When the job was completed it was reported that King John declared that I was the most secure castle in his kingdom.

As it happened, I was not yet completely rid of Hugh De Lacy who returned intent on recapturing my walls and so, thirteen years after De Lacy stood on my ramparts, besieged by the king, the king's constable stood on my walls besieged by De Lacy. Once again, I stood strong and De Lacy could only stand outside looking mournfully at what was once his. A couple of years later, De Lacy was again my resident when King Henry III, who had succeeded John, restored him to the earldom. In truth, it was a different and chastened De Lacy who ruled Ulster.

During the second De Lacy occupancy, my resident completed the final extension of my fortifications resulting in an exterior that looks much the same today as it did in 1242. De Lacy effectively fortified the entire peninsula by constructing an entrance with two large drum towers, each of which is forty feet in diameter, where the Rock of Fergus first juts into the sea. These towers guarded the gate and any attempt to attack them would meet with heavy fire from archers who had a clear shot at the area in front of the gate. De Lacy then added fortified walls running back from the drum towers to where they joined those walls constructed on the orders of King John. This final phase of my construction doubled the size of the area within my fortifications. With the sea and the rocks on three sides and the imposing entry towers and the fourth side, any remote chance that I might be breached was effectively ended.

During De Lacy's second residency, he too took a wife, called Rose, and the couple had one child whose name was Maud. While I recognise the need for children in the continuation of the human species, this child seemed to serve little purpose. I am sure that in some of my brother and sister castles, a child like Maud would live an idyllic life but, within my walls, she seemed to be forever suffering from a fever or a dripping nose. I suppose my lack of comfort was the reason Rose and Maud spent most months away where I hope they were comfortable. At the end of the day, Maud was an important part of my existence because she married another Norman knight called Walter De Burgh.

Hugh De Lacy was permanently parted from my walls when he died in 1242. Because his daughter, Maud, was still a minor and not married, De Lacy's earldom was forfeited to the crown and for some years I was administered by constables appointed by the king.

Ultimately, some twenty years later, Walter De Burgh married Maud De Lacy and, as a result, was named Earl of Ulster.

Even though I was his principal fortress in Ulster, I was to see very little of Walter De Burgh for two reasons. The first was that Walter was already an important landowner with substantial holdings in Limerick and Tipperary. Unlike my walls, which were not only very well fortified but in a location that could be quickly reached by water, those counties were far less accessible and Walter spent much of his time fighting battles to preserve and expand his holding. His enemy in these battles were native Irish clans like the O'Connors and Norman-Irish like the Fitz Maurices and the reports that made their way into my walls were that he was not always successful. Whatever about his other campaigns, no one would dare to take the battle to my walls.

The second reason I saw little of Walter was that he died in 1271, only eight years after becoming the earl, and his son, Richard De Burgh, who was to become known as the 'Red Earl' because of his red complexion, succeeded him. Because Richard was only twelve at the time, I was once again administered by a constable acting for the king.

A few years after Walter's death, the native Irish, emboldened by their success against the Normans, did sack and burn several towns in Antrim, including the town of Carrickfergus outside my walls but, as you would expect, they made no attempt to breach my fortifications. Throughout the later part of the thirteenth century, until the Red Earl reached his majority, I was a totally reliable safe haven for the Normans and the crown. My role was simply to provide protection from the turmoil of warring Irish and Norman-Irish factions. I cannot say that I faced any significant challenge in serving my residents but then no one appeared willing to challenge the might of my walls.

The end of the thirteenth century found England under the rule of Edward I who may never have set foot in Ireland but was well known within my walls. My own resident, the Red Earl, reached his majority and was to rule Ulster from my walls for forty years. During those years the combined power of the Red Earl in Ireland and Edward I and his son in England, were to propel me to the forefront of disputes over the control of Ireland generally and Ulster specifically.

II Dominating the North of Ireland (1280–1320)

After he reached his majority in the 1280s, Richard De Burgh, the Red Earl, became the master of my walls but, like his father Walter, he spent little time within the security I provided. Richard took up where his father left off and he waged war against the native Irish on behalf of the English crown, held by Edward I and subsequently by his son, Edward II. The reports that reached my walls made it clear that he was far more successful than his father had ever been.

Richard was only twenty-seven when he led an expedition from Carrickfergus to conquer the Isle of Man, which he then ceded to Edward I. After that, he turned his attention to the native Irish chieftains in Connacht who had been waging war against the Normans for thirty years. I recall a great celebration after Richard had conquered Magnus O'Connor because the O'Connors had defeated his father at the Battle of Ath in Chip in County Leitrim shortly before Walter died. My resident had redeemed the family honour but, more importantly, he had defeated the native Irish in Connacht and had established his authority in that province.

By the time Richard was thirty, he controlled half of Ireland and had recruited a great army of Norman-Irish soldiers. Edward I took full advantage of the Red Earl's military might by summoning him to fight the king's battles in France and Scotland. It seemed that the only time Richard found his way into my protection was when he prepared to sail off in response to his king. Although I heard some of his allies complain about these ventures, including one cousin called William who refused to go at all, Richard responded without hesitation insisting that loyalty required his participation.

I will admit that I began to feel a bit redundant during the early years of the Red Earl's residency because, while I was an impregnable fortress, I was well within the area subject to the earl's absolute control. As a consequence, I was not required to demonstrate my prowess and since I offered little by way of comfort, only the gossip of my constables and caretakers kept me updated on the adventures of my earl. I also saw little of the earl's family because he had established them at some far more comfortable castle that he controlled. Nevertheless, I knew that the day would come when my particular strengths would be required, so I remained vigilant.

The event that caused the greatest stir among the tongue-waggers within my walls was the marriage of the Red Earl's daughter to a Scottish noble called Robert Bruce in 1302. Some years earlier Bruce had pledged loyalty to Edward I, making him a likely prospect in the eyes of my resident. However, that loyalty was short lived and Bruce took up arms against the king. The matter merited discussion because the Red Earl fought beside Edward I against Bruce and his forces in Scotland and so was the father-in-law to his sworn enemy. I suppose in retrospect it is not surprising that this conflict would eventually find its way to my walls.

I remember well the triumphant return of the Red Earl and his forces late in the year 1303. They had successfully campaigned against the Scots at the side of King Edward and sailed into Belfast Lough to the pier not far from where I stand. As usual, my walls came alive in anticipation of the visit as the constable in charge assured that the top-floor accommodations were spotless and ready to receive the earl. In the great hall, the floor was swept of the rushes used to absorb grease and dirt and new rushes were put down. The hall was set for a feast and the high table, at the top of the room, was laid with white tablecloths, napkins, knives and spoons. Several days were spent in preparing the great feast and, when the Red Earl and his officers arrived, they were treated to one of the greatest feasts ever served within my walls.

The first course included a variety of breads, eggs and light fowl. The birds prepared in a grand style were capon, swan, heron and crane and each was first presented to the earl on a silver platter for his approval. After he agreed that the dish appeared satisfactory, a small portion was served on his plate in deference, no doubt, to the many dishes which would follow. A servant sampled a small bit of the earl's food to be sure that it was not poisoned.

Between courses, dancers and jugglers appeared for the entertainment of the guest and fresh wine from France was poured. The second course included a wide range of meats, more fowl and pastries. These dishes were pork, rabbit, venison, chicken, peacock, pheasant, pigeon, gulls and curlew. Each dish was presented with great ceremony to the earl and the head table and the choicest cuts were laid before him.

The third course included many of the meats and poultry previously served but prepared in different styles, although new dishes were also added. They included, beef, quail, snipe, partridge as well as jellies, cheeses, pastries, fruit and cakes – all washed down with copious quantities of wine.

When the meal was over toasts were presented congratulating everyone on the success of the campaign against the Scots. During the toasts, however, the word went around my great hall that the earl's well-liked brother, Theobald, who had been languishing in one of my upstairs apartments, had died of wounds he had received in the fighting. The atmosphere in my great hall was suddenly sombre, although one of the jesters attempted to revive the party by offering another toast to the victory. At the mention of the victory over Bruce, the Red Earl's normally red complexion turned a shade approaching purple and he snarled to the entire gathering that in victory or not, the name of Robert Bruce was never again to be mentioned in his presence.

The name of Robert Bruce may not have been mentioned in the presence of the Red Earl but it was frequently on the tongue of others who served within my walls. Scotland is not far from Ulster and commerce with that country ensured that the news reached me quickly. Bruce, it seems, had declared himself the King of Scotland and had continued to wage war against Edward I and his successor Edward II. Although he was frequently beaten, it was clear that Bruce was not defeated.

Over the next few years the Red Earl continued to wage war in Connacht and Munster where he became embroiled in a feud between factions of a family called the O'Briens over a castle called Bunratty. The battles over this castle were also a source of continuing speculation within my walls because the castle changed hands on more than one occasion. The Red Earl was defeated when he backed the wrong chieftain but then his own supporters killed that man so the Red Earl's man became the chieftain. The Red Earl's O'Brien ally then retook Bunratty, or what was left of him as he had been burned before he was abandoned.

The only information I have about my brother castle Bunratty came from the gossip I overheard, but it is difficult for me to imagine a castle that could be so easily overrun, not once but several times. I suppose

I should have been happy that I was made of stronger stuff. I still looked forward to an opportunity to prove my worth and it was not long before such an opportunity arose.

In the year 1314 Robert Bruce, with the assistance of an Irish army from a castle called Blarney in Munster, finally defeated Edward II in a major battle at Bannockburn in Scotland. As King Robert and his queen, Elizabeth De Burgh Bruce, were now in complete control of Scotland and northern parts of England, they looked across the Irish Sea for new territories to conquer.

Less than a year after Bannockburn, Robert commissioned his brother, Edward, to invade Ireland and, in May 1315, Edward landed not far from my walls with an army of six thousand veterans of the Battle of Bannockburn and a fleet of three hundred boats. Native Irish chiefs joined the army and the combination was enough to defeat the English army under the command of the Red Earl himself in a major battle at Connor to the west of my walls. Part of the English army, including De Burgh, retreated to Dublin while the remnants fled to the security of my walls with Bruce's army in pursuit.

I remember well the meeting between a Lord Poer, who commanded the regiments of the English army who made it to my walls, and Henry of Thrapston, the storekeeper at the time.

Lord Poer began by thanking Henry for accommodating the troop which was gracefully acknowledged as Henry's duty to the Red Earl and his king. Then Lord Poer said, 'You appreciate, my good man, that the blighters are right behind us and will be knocking at your walls within a matter of days, if not hours.'

'I do indeed,' Henry replied, 'but I dare say that they won't have an easy task with Carrickfergus. The city might go quickly, mind, but this castle . . . that is another thing altogether.'

Poer spoke gravely, 'I should hope not because if Carrickfergus fails to hold, Ulster and most probably all of Ireland will fall to the Scots and their Irish rabble.'

'Carrickfergus will not fall,' Henry said with a confidence that inspired me.

'In that case,' Poer responded, 'I trust that you are well provisioned for a long siege.'

I was not so provisioned but, over the next several hours, hundreds of pounds of food and grain were stockpiled and final preparations were made for the defence of my walls. Edward Bruce's army could be heard in the distance when my gates were finally closed and bolted and the bridge across the pit at my entrance was raised. The first major test of my defences commenced in September of 1315 and I am proud to stay that I stood firm against the Scottish army.

In vain the attackers shelled me with their catapults but the rocks bounced off my walls. An attempt was made to batter a hole in a portion of my walls but I was too thick and too strong. Several attempts were made at the front gate but heavy bombardment from the drum towers discouraged those attempts. An amphibious landing was also attempted, but the Scots found that my seaward walls could not be breached. Months passed until Bruce must have conceded that I could not be taken by storm, which left only the possibility that my occupants might be starved into submission. Although my walls were served by an independent, fresh-water well, which provided abundant water, it was clear to me that human beings do require food and nourishment and so, at some point, my occupants might surrender despite my efforts.

Although I heard of Bruce's proclamation that he would take my walls at all costs, he decided to leave enough troops to maintain the siege whilst he himself campaigned in other parts of Ireland. He returned to my walls in the spring of 1316 but still I stood firm. My occupants, however, were getting weaker from lack of nourishment. Finally in April of that year an attempt was made to land provisions and resupply my walls but was not successful. I well remember the remnants of the would-be rescuers fleeing for my gate only to have it closed in their faces because the Scottish army was too close behind them. Those soldiers were butchered just beyond my walls as my occupants howled in protest and disgust.

Edward Bruce now had full control of the town of Carrickfergus but he knew, beyond question, that my walls would not be breached. The only way he would see my interior was if my occupants opened the gates and allowed him to enter.

In time, several of my occupants died of starvation and many others were seriously ill. Soon there was hardly anyone left to stand on my ramparts but, still, I would not be taken. Finally Lord Poer had little choice but to open negotiations because it was clear that the siege would not be lifted until everyone was dead. In the years that followed, I was to hear discussion about my occupants murdering and eating Scottish negotiators but I hope to put that rumour to rest. Horseflesh, leather hides and everything imaginable was eaten, human beings were not.

On September 21, 1316, over a year after the siege had begun, my gates were thrown open and my English occupants surrendered, it having been agreed that they would not be killed or mistreated. Edward Bruce the self-proclaimed 'King of Ireland' entered my walls and declared me to be his royal residence. He announced to his entire array of soldiers, administrators and labourers that I was to be the base of his operations and that Ireland would be ruled from within my walls.

As it is not my position to judge my occupants, only to provide unmatched security, I was flattered that I should now house the King of Ireland and, in that regard, I was to hear much about the political dealings of those times. I remember well the day in early October of that year when Robert Bruce, the King of Scotland, joined his brother in the apartment on the top floor of my keep.

The two embraced each other, as I have often seen brothers do, and sat down to a light meal and several bottles of wine. In time, the conversations turned to their exploits.

Robert began. 'A few years ago, we were hiding in a cave on Rathlin Island talking about what might have been.'

Edward laughed, 'Ah yes my brother. But remember the spider . . . remember the spider.'

'I do indeed,' Robert replied raising his glass. 'I remember him battered by the wind and rain and every time he started on his web, the wind would destroy what he had done. But then, in the morning . . . there he was in the bright sunlight with a fine, fat fly for breakfast.'

Edward picked up on the story, 'And then we talked about what could be if we did not give up. Remember that Robbie, remember that?'

Robert replied, 'I do remember. Scotland and then Ireland and then we will topple London itself. We're on our way Eddie, we're on our way.'

'To spiders.' The two raised their glasses in toast.

The two kings spent some time within my walls planning a campaign that they hoped would make them masters of all of Ireland. I knew little about what was beyond my walls but from everything I had learned about the activities of my former occupants, I suspected that the plans were a little optimistic. Between native Irish chieftains protecting their own interests, Norman lords with strong armies, other Norman-Irish clans and the English still strong in the area around Dublin, unifying Ireland under a Scottish flag would not be an easy task. Loyalties, I had learned, are transient matters depending entirely on time and circumstance and my Scottish occupants may not have realised that one day's ally was another day's enemy.

In the course of those planning sessions, I recall a remarkable discussion concerning my former occupant, the Red Earl, Richard De Burgh, who one might have thought would not have sat idly by while his stronghold was in the hands of a person who he had maintained was his sworn enemy.

The occasion was a reunion between Elizabeth De Burgh Bruce, now the mistress of my walls, and her sisters, Katherine and Joan, who had both married into the Fitz Geralds, powerful Norman earls. These later marriages had solidified an alliance between the Red Earl and branches of that family which held power in Kildare and Offaly.

'And how is Daddy?' Elizabeth asked. 'I do miss him terribly.'

'Nothing changes,' Joan remarked. 'He is always the same, flying into a huff over the smallest thing.'

'By the way, he sends his love and his fondest best wishes,' Katherine added.

'Does that mean he isn't annoyed with Robbie any more?' Elizabeth asked.

'Silly girl,' Katherine said. 'Did you not know that Daddy and your Robbie are the best of friends?'

A look of total surprise came over Elizabeth's face as she stammered, 'But . . .but Robbie never said a word.'

'Twas meant to be a secret, and maybe they thought it might not be if they told you,' Katherine replied with a smile. 'You know how you have a tendency to talk to just anyone.' This revelation brought a giggle among all three sisters.

'But Daddy . . . and Robbie . . . they hate each other. How?' Elizabeth asked.

Joan answered quickly, 'You know the way of things. It was only a few years ago that the Fitz Geralds killed two of our cousins and held Daddy in prison on bread and water in Laois. He might still be there if it weren't for that big meeting in Kilkenny Castle. And yet here we are, Fitz Geralds.'

'But Robbie was Daddy's sworn enemy,' Elizabeth protested.

'*Was* my dear, was,' Joan replied patting her sister's arm. 'You see they met soon after Bannockburn. Daddy never did have any use for Edward II although he was completely loyal to the first Edward and, when Robbie beat junior, Daddy not only agreed to the invasion of Ireland but also provided money and boats. Daddy found reasons to be occupied elsewhere, like Dublin and Kildare, so that was the reason he wasn't around to fight against Bruce.'

'But what of Connor, when Robbie beat the English, and Daddy?' the girl asked.

Joan waved her hand dismissively, 'Oh that . . . the battle was only for appearance's sake and Daddy pulled his men before any serious damage was done on either side. It was all a bit of a put on.'

'I suppose he figured that, if he supported the Bruces, he would have control over all of Ireland because Edward will need someone who knows what is going on. And if Robbie and Edward fail, no one will know that he was involved . . . unless you tell,' Katherine added.

The girls laughed and agreed to say nothing to anyone. Part of my ego was restored because I had wondered why the Red Earl had not fled to the safety of my walls when his army was defeated. At least I now knew that it had nothing to do with his assessment of my ability to protect.

Soon after Robert and Edward marched south to establish their claim to Ireland but the native Irish did not particularly welcome them and they met strong resistance from the English as they approached Dublin. Eventually they retreated back to my walls to consider their options.

A few months later, in 1316, Robert and Elizabeth returned to Scotland because they had their own country to rule and had no more time for the conquest of Ireland. Edward remained within my walls for a time but eventually decided that if he were to truly be King of Ireland, it would be necessary for him to march out and assert his authority. Early the following year Edward Bruce marched out of my walls with great ceremony and campaigned through the midlands and as far west as Limerick. He returned to my walls in May of that year and I would have to say that he was certainly discouraged. I recall one meeting in which Edward made his report to a representative of Robert's court in Scotland called MacVie.

'I'm afraid,' Edward began, 'that nothing seems to be going as planned.'

'Certainly your army is far better organised and equipped that anything you face,' MacVie responded.

Edward replied, 'Of course. That is not the problem. The O'Neill assured me that we would find support for our efforts to drive out the English, but that does not seem to have been the case. Instead of being hailed as liberators, we were forced to fight and burn out those who attacked us.'

'No doubt making you very popular,' MacVie replied with a scowl. 'What about our friend, Richard De Burgh?'

'Ah, the Red Earl. I'm afraid the Mayor of Dublin has imprisoned him, apparently to stop him from joining our cause, but if you ask me, it is just a bit too convenient. I think that De Burgh allowed himself to be taken because he is losing interest in the whole thing. By spending his time imprisoned he can avoid the fight until he see who is successful. If we drive the English out, he will say that there was nothing he could do because of his imprisonment. If we end up back in Scotland, he can prove to the English that he wasn't involved and insist that he never supported us in the first place. It seems our friend the Red Earl has acquired a bit of Irish statesmanship in his years among the Irish.'

'So what are your plans?' MacVie asked.

Edward pondered the question for a moment as he looked out toward the sea. 'I suppose I shall make another attempt at Dublin before the English are completely reorganised. They already seem to have taken back control of the Irish Sea and if I don't move quickly I will have not a chance.'

'So why don't you just hold Ulster?' MacVie counselled. 'Surely it will be a long time before the English can move against you here and in the meanwhile you can fortify the entire north.'

Edward replied grandly, 'Because I am the King of Ireland, not just Ulster.'

Those words were to be the downfall of Edward Bruce. A few months later in October of 1318 he marched out of my walls for the last time. A short time later he was defeated and killed at the Battle of Dundalk, and the Scots were driven out of Ireland.

As for my walls, I no longer housed the King of Ireland but a short time later I reverted to the control of the Red Earl, Richard De Burgh, who insisted that, despite his daughter's marriage, Robert Bruce was and continued to be his sworn enemy and any suggestion to the contrary was a misunderstanding.

Upon his return, the Red Earl inspected my walls from top to bottom and decided that the latest in castle technology required that my entrance should be further fortified. Inner and outer portcullises were constructed just inside of my drawbridge. These gates were massive iron structures that could be quickly lowered if the entry were breached. I saw little purpose as I couldn't imagine an attacker getting past my entry gates but I was certainly prepared to accept any addition that would make me even more secure.

The departure of Edward Bruce concluded a remarkable century of my existence in which kings of Ireland, England and Scotland not only sat on a throne within my great hall, but also issued orders and edicts by which their countries were ruled. I should think that there are few other castles who could say as much, certainly none of my brother and sister castles to the south and west of me in Ireland.

III A Centre of Government (1320–1650)

The years following the departure of Edward Bruce were peaceful, at least within my walls. Edward II reached a truce with Robert Bruce in Scotland so, to the Red Earl's delight, he could now proclaim friendship with both his king and his son-in-law. The De Burghs were fully restored to their lands, although I was never again to house Richard De Burgh. The Red Earl died shortly thereafter and was succeeded by his grandson, Walter, who became known as the 'Brown Earl', again in deference to his complexion.

In 1328, Robert Bruce returned to Ireland, this time with the blessings of the crown, and escorted the Brown Earl back to the safety of my walls. The entourage included Elizabeth De Burgh Bruce and a number of children who were, of course, the Brown Earl's cousins. As I would never be a proper venue for parties and celebrations, the group only spent a short time within my walls before moving off to some other castle where, no doubt, there were green and grassy fields and other distractions that might be of interest to a child. And I suppose those other castles would have great halls and sleeping accommodations that were warm and comfortable. As much as I was disappointed that I would not host another great feast, I knew that, should danger threaten, they would quickly return to the safety of my walls.

For several years after, I was once again a stronghold on the edge of Ireland, well removed from the battles and wars that raged throughout the rest of the country. I was generally aware of these matters because the constables, who ensured that I was prepared should my gifts be required, would discuss such things. I heard, for example, that the Brown Earl had murdered a relation and had himself been murdered which set off a war among the De Burghs (who subsequently changed their name to Burke).

War did reach my walls on a couple of occasions towards the end of the fourteenth century as first the Scots and then a combined army of Scots and Irish attacked and burned Carrickfergus town, but they clearly knew better than to try to take my walls. It seemed that burning the city even within the shadows of my walls was popular sport for those who warred against the English crown. Although a larger ditch and earthen mounds were installed to protect it, it was many years before any significant work was done to protect the town. As a result, whenever there was a threatened attack, prominent citizens scurried to the shelter of my walls bringing whatever treasures they thought were particularly important.

Throughout the fifteenth and into the sixteenth century, I stood alone against a rebellion that saw nearly the entire province turn against England. I well recall one occasion in 1513 when the Earl of Arran, James Hamilton, not only captured the town but also many smaller villages in the vicinity pillaging and plundering as he went. Finally, during the reign of Henry VII, England responded.

Fitzwalter, the Earl of Sussex, together with his brother-in-law, Sir Henry Sidney, the Lord Deputy to the crown, were sent to my walls with orders to assess my defence take whatever measures were necessary to reinforce my walls and secure the town of Carrickfergus. Using me as his base, the earl waged war against the Scots and Sidney commissioned the construction of a stone wall which encircled the entire town putting yet another obstacle between myself and attack. Sidney also ordered that my entire keep be re-roofed and storehouses were built along the northeast wall of the outer ward. In addition my walls and parapets were modified so that cannons could be swivelled to command a wider field of fire from the gun ports. This was done by modifying the outside edge of the gun ports so that they splayed outwards.

For over fifty years blood ran freely outside my walls as Scots, like James McDonnell and Sorley Boy MacDonnell, and Irish chiefs, like Phelim O'Neill, brutalised the countryside. In response, Sidney and Essex attacked in reprisal, sacking and plundering strongholds as far away as Rathlin Island.

Eventually Sir Arthur Chichester was appointed Governor of Carrickfergus and he ordered that I should always support a large garrison of English forces to protect both myself and the city. At the turn of the seventeenth century, Chichester rode out from my walls and decisively defeated an Irish chieftain called Brian McArt O'Neill – this served to pacify the territory around me, at least for the time being. He then conducted a campaign to eliminate the remaining native Irish from the vicinity of my walls and replace them with loyal English subjects. This policy naturally caused resentment among the Irish and they frequently fought with Chichester's soldiers. From time to time I held these combatants as prisoners within my walls.

One such culprit came from the O'Neill family who, in fairness, ruled Ulster long before the arrival of the Normans. That family had fought against the Normans and Norman-Irish and so it should probably have come as no surprise when, in 1603, Con O'Neill found himself imprisoned within my walls. Apparently his men had attacked and killed some soldiers after a dispute concerning the ownership of some wine and he was imprisoned for waging war against the crown.

Under normal circumstances escape would have been impossible because I was certainly as impregnable from within as I was from without, but the human element made the difference. I remember well the intrigue that led to the escape as it involved a romance between Annas Dobbin, the daughter of the castle provost, and Thomas Montgomery, the captain of a small trading vessel that brought grain to my walls.

'Ah, my one and only true love,' Thomas began as he stroked her hair in a quiet corner of my inner ward. 'How I dream of spending my life in your presence.'

Annas was a fine, big girl who, while quite pleasant, was not the most beautiful woman I ever saw. Obviously smitten, she cooed, 'If only it could be . . . I would do anything to be away from this cold and damp rock.'

'Perhaps there is a way,' Thomas continued as his hand passed onto her massive left breast. 'If you will prove to me that you truly love me and are not just playing with my affections.'

'Anything you ask my love,' she replied in wide-eyed innocence.

'Well you see, lovey,' Thomas whispered softly into her ear, 'I have a great friend called Con O'Neill who is being held captive inside Carrickfergus even though he is totally innocent of any crime. I am deeply indebted to O'Neill and I have vowed to set him free. Perhaps you have seen him because he has the run of the castle although he cannot leave, and I fear his life may yet be in danger. To prove your love for me, I want you to help him escape.'

The long and the short of it was that Thomas convinced Annas to smuggle a rope into Con O'Neill which she accomplished by wrapping it around her waist a number of times. Because of the size of her chest, the rope was not noticeable under her loose-fitting dressing gown and she was able to deliver it to O'Neill. He then went over my walls to a waiting boat commanded by Captain Montgomery and made his escape to Scotland.

Proving, perhaps, that judging human nature is yet another ability that had escaped me in my quest to perfect my service as a castle, Captain Thomas Montgomery did return and in time made Annas Dobbin his wife. Con himself was subsequently pardoned for his indiscretions and was returned to his lands to the northwest in Castlereagh.

Throughout the first half of the seventeenth century I was little more than an administrative centre for the English government in the north. The advantage I gained from this status was that I was fairly well maintained because funds were available for necessary construction and repairs. I was certainly well garrisoned because the crown had enough problems in the rest of Ireland without being concerned about the security of Ulster.

Looking back on those days I suppose it would be fair to say that I was experiencing the calm before the storm. Northeastern Ulster was relatively peaceful but turmoil, not only in the rest of Ireland but also in England, soon ended all of that. And the reason, in my opinion, was most peculiar. I am only a castle so I neither know nor care about this human preoccupation with religion. I know it is obviously a matter of some import because kings were dethroned or even beheaded in its name. My own walls became a pawn in these disputes and, although I was never breached, my occupants changed with whomever was succeeding at the time. The first indication that my world was about to change came in 1641.

It was in that year Phelim O'Neill rebelled against the crown, apparently because he was tired of decades of doing nothing while his clan was dispossessed from land it had held for centuries. I know that, beginning with Chichester and continuing for some years, soldiers would ride out driving the native Irish further and further away from me. They would then award the vacated lands to whatever English or

Scottish Protestant might be available, including the soldiers who evicted the natives. Phelim O'Neill retaliated by killing any Protestant he encountered. As a result thousands of Protestants sought protection behind the city walls of Carrickfergus.

In response, General Sir Robert Monro with a large troop of Scottish soldiers took over the defence of the town. Monro established his command post within my walls and proceeded to put down the rebellion by sending his Scottish troops into the field to kill Catholics and plunder their holdings and soon Monro himself controlled Antrim, a position he held for nearly six years.

Since the cure for the O'Neill rebellion had become worse than the disease, the government sitting in Dublin sent Sir Robert Adair to sort out Monro and that led to the first change in my occupants. Monro, confident in my ability to withstand any siege, had not bothered to fortify my walls with heavy cannon. In addition, he sent his nephew, George Monro, with two thousand infantry and two hundred horse to assist King Charles I, who was fighting his own battles in England against Oliver Cromwell and the Parliamentarians. This left my walls without a strong defensive force and so Adair was able to march through my gate and take control without a struggle and, in fact, he surprised Monro literally in his bed.

'Whatever are you doing here?' Monro enquired pulling his blanket up to his chin.

'I have orders from the parliament in Dublin to take this castle,' Adair replied.

'In whose name?' came the indignant response.

'Why the crown, of course,' Adair quickly answered.

Monro was obviously confused and struggled to control his anger, 'But I hold this castle in the king's name. My own nephew is fighting at his side, even as we speak. I assure you that you will pay a stiff price for your insolence.'

Adair smiled stiffly and responded, 'Did it ever occur to you that your king and the requirements of England may not be the same thing. I suggest you prepare for your departure before I put you in irons.'

I understand that Monro sailed off to England to join his nephew in Charles' cause against Cromwell but, before he left, he vowed that he would return and Adair would be the one facing the irons. I was to discover that Sir George Monro was not successful in his defence of Charles I. The London parliament had appointed Cromwell to rule as Lord Protector (which really meant king) and he had beaten Charles in battle and assumed the leadership of England. After England was lost, Monro returned to Ulster determined to fight for the Royalist cause in Ireland. His first thought was naturally the strength of my walls and he must have decided that I would be the stronghold from which he would conduct his campaign. At any rate, Monro appeared at my walls with his army intent on retaking me.

The officer in charge of the garrison was one Major Edmund Ellis who, it must be said, was not the most courageous commander ever to serve within my walls. I recall the discussion he had with his aide De camp, one Henry Moore.

'They are requiring our surrender,' Moore stated.

Ellis pondered his fingernails and replied, 'I should think that would be a good idea.'

'But surely we can hold out until Cromwell arrives,' Moore argued. 'He's in charge now and will surely turn his attention to Ireland within a matter of weeks.'

'I suppose you have a point,' Ellis replied. 'But we are not exactly provisioned for a siege and Monro does have those guns. I know this place is strong but who knows how it might fare against a bombardment. I think that I would prefer not to find out. Have they offered terms?'

And so it was that Major Edmund Ellis and his troops marched out under full colours to be replaced once again by General Sir George Monro who then held my walls on behalf of the Royalist cause.

Shortly thereafter, word came that Charles I had been executed in London and Cromwell had launched his expedition to retake Ireland. Once again, I was under siege, this time by a Cromwellian force led by one Colonel Robert Venebles. On this occasion I felt the sting of these iron balls propelled from cannons and, although I will admit that I didn't like the feeling, they were not strong enough to breach me. General Monro, who had been campaigning in the west, marched to relieve the garrison but he was defeated along the way and on receiving the news, my gates were thrown open and I was now in the hands of Cromwell.

Oliver Cromwell called on my walls only once during his brief stay in Ireland, but I remember him well. He was a man of average height with long hair that was thin on top. He had a large nose and hard eyes that seemed to be missing their lashes. I recall him sitting in my great room listening to the grievances of the townspeople many of whom told similar stories.

'And then, Your Majesty,' one man stuttered hat in hand, 'he killed my brother and his wife.'

Cromwell replied, 'And who was that?'

'I don't know, Your Majesty. But I think he was with that Catholic Phelim O'Neill.'

'When?' was the terse reply.

''Twas in 1641, eight years ago.'

Cromwell dismissed the man with a wave of his hand and called for the clerk. 'I've heard enough,' he announced. 'Any Catholic you find within the city walls is to be presumed a traitor and executed outright.'

I can only presume that the orders were carried out, because, in a short time, the word within my walls was that there were no Catholics living within the town walls and none were known to be in residence for miles around. After Cromwell's departure in May 1650, I continued to serve as an administrative headquarters for his government until 1658 when he died and the monarchy under Charles II was restored to the throne.

I suppose there was no real transition when Charles II was crowned and I would not have known there was a change in my residents were it not for the discussions within my walls. As far as I was concerned, a new king had succeeded a dead king and I was merely the property of whoever happened to wear the crown. Unfortunately, I had not heard the last of religious fights over the English crown as a few years later word reached my walls that another war had begun.

In the mid-1680s England was again in uproar because the reigning monarch was a Catholic called King James II who had succeeded his brother, Charles II. English Protestants supported the invasion of the king's son-in-law, called William of Orange, who soon deposed James in an unusually bloodless revolution forcing him to flee to France just as his brother had done when Cromwell came to power. In February of 1689 William and his wife Mary were jointly crowned King and Queen of England. But while England was quick to accept William, Ireland remained true to James, primarily because the Earl of Tyrconnell, a Catholic called Richard Talbot whose family came from my sister castle Malahide, controlled the English army in Ireland.

That army included, of course, the garrison which occupied my walls. Despite the efforts of the predominantly Protestant population of Carrickfergus town, and other Protestant forces that backed William of Orange, the garrison held out for James. With no cannon at their disposal there was obviously little those local Protestant forces could do to take me. Despite the ease with which my walls were held, the Jacobite forces supporting James, frequently discussed a pending invasion of Ireland by William. After all, they reasoned, William was unlikely to allow a strong and independent country at England's back while it faced regular threats from Europe. Those conjectures would have meant very little to me, except that my occupants also agreed that the logical place for William to begin his campaign was on my doorstep where he had a great deal of support from the Protestant population.

Their assessment was, in fact, accurate as William sent Frederich, the Duke of Schomberg, to take my walls and provide a stronghold from which he would begin his campaign to secure Ireland. I remember well the day in August of 1689 when a great fleet of some one hundred vessels sailed into Belfast Lough. The duty officers on my parapets sounded the alarm and final preparations were made to withstand the impending siege. I myself experienced a glow because I knew, once again, that I would be tested but I also knew that, this time, I would be required to withstand the most powerful guns available to man – I was confident that I would stand strong as I had always done. The commander of my garrison, one Colonel Thomas Maxwell, felt no such confidence and he fled for his life leaving McCarthy Mór and Cormac O'Neill with their Irish regiments to face ten thousand well-trained English soldiers.

The Duke of Schomberg quickly surrounded the walls of the town of Carrickfergus and established trenches and placements for his guns and mortars. The bombardment began shortly after and the guns on my parapets responded in defence. I withstood several blows, particularly from the four guns that concentrated their fire on my main gate between my two drum towers, but I did not fall. The greatest damage from the shelling was in the town itself and came not from these guns but from mortars located on Windmill Hill, which lobbed shells into the town. It seemed peculiar to me that the duke would batter so vigorously a town that housed people who were almost completely loyal to William but I suppose he assumed that only by taking the town would he have a realistic go at my walls.

In time, the town walls were breached and my defending garrison retreated to the safety of my walls. The duke then sent ships to shell my seaward-facing walls, assuming that they would not be as stout as my northern gate. He was wrong, of course, and I absorbed blow after blow while my defenders responded with cannon mounted high on my walls. For six days the assault continued but, when my defenders ran out of ammunition, they had little choice but to run up a white flag and surrender my walls.

Once again, I had withstood the might of the English army and the finest artillery available had not brought me down. Possession of my walls changed with the holders departing and the attackers entering through the front gate and so I had become the foothold from which William of Orange would launch his campaign against the Jacobite forces in Ireland.

With his stronghold secured and the north no longer a threat, William sailed from England and I saw him land on the dock close to me. As he stepped from his barge, the guns on my parapets fired a salute, trumpeters sounded a welcome and church bells rang continuously. It was a most noisy occasion. In honestly reporting my history, I must say that William of Orange never entered my walls but the welcoming ceremony was conducted on June 14, 1690 within the shadow of my eastern wall and I well remember the occasion.

William was a small fellow with a hunched-over back and there was nothing particularly regal about his appearance. He wore a long wig of black curls covered with a black hat, heavily plumed with white feathers. His red coat ended just below his waist, and his outfit was completed with dark-blue, knee-length britches, white knee socks and shoes with large silver buckles. He carried a ceremonial sword at his side and he rested one hand on its hilt. After the initial greeting, William was seated on a throne of sorts beneath a canopy to shelter him from the warm sun. After several speeches, Mayor Richard Dobbs presented William with the key to the city, which was promptly returned. The king then took a short stroll through the city's streets, probably to stretch his legs, after which he returned to his barge and was gone.

I have heard it said recently by historians meeting within my walls that the defeat of the Catholic King James II was assured when Schomberg took my walls. With complete control of the north, it was said, victory was inevitable and my capture was the key to that control. Whether or not that assessment is accurate means little to me because what *is* important is that I stood strong and did my job. Whatever about my occupants, I did not surrender. And when control of my walls passed to William, I served him as I had served my prior occupants, with all the strength and character of my centuries.

As an administrative centre and primary supply depot for William's continuing campaign, I discovered that, two weeks after landing at my walls, William took his army to a river called the Boyne. There, on July 1, 1690, he finally confronted King James who had arrived at the other end of Ireland near my brother castle Blarney. I know that a battle was fought at which the Jacobite army, with soldiers from other castles including Blarney, Kilkenny and Malahide, fled the field leaving William of Orange victorious. William's forces were not without their own casualties as the Duke of Schomberg was killed. Many would say that is where and when the conflict truly ended.

The Jacobite Wars brought a close to a long and storied part of my existence and I was happy to see peace again. The battering I took from Schomberg led me to recognise that men's ability to create weapons of destruction was far superior to my ability to place my five-hundred-year-old walls between the guns and the occupants I am honour bound to protect. I realised that the days of the unassailable stronghold were over and, if I were to continue to serve mankind, it would have to take some other form altogether. That is not to say that I never again faced conflict, because the day came when I was again at the centre of a battle, but I knew that I could never again withstand an artillery bombardment.

When I heard about the way other castles were reduced to ruins, I was thankful that I was removed from the conflict before the guns roared one more time. As a result, I can now say that I was never breached and that I stand as strong today as I did at the close of the twelfth century. My service to my occupants, however, would never be the same.

IV New Jobs to Perform (1650–present)

In the decades after William of Orange defeated James II, I continued as the administrative headquarters for English rule in the north of the country. Since the north was at peace, particularly during the first half of the eighteenth century, there was no need for the security that I had been proud to provide. As you would no doubt imagine, the reason that many castles face siege and attack is because the attackers think that the walls can be breached. As I was known to be impregnable, no attackers came forward. In truth it was a boring and mundane existence for a castle of my history and heritage but I carried on, providing shelter for clerks as I had once provided shelter for soldiers.

Unfortunately with all threat of conflict ended, my once proud gates were seldom closed and, in time, were incapable of providing security in the unlikely event of an attack. One of my curtain walls had even begun to crumble as no attempt was made to maintain the stones and mortar that held me together. In addition, most of the guns that had once graced my parapets had been removed and the only ammunition in my stores was to provide training for the garrison that operated from my walls. In short, sixty years after my days of glory in withstanding Schomberg's siege, I was a sorry excuse for a stronghold.

I was angry with my occupants who clearly did not appreciate the service I had provided but if they were not willing to perform the most basic maintenance, there was little I could do. I remembered the last occasion on which I had become an administrative centre under Sir Henry Sidney over two hundred years earlier. In fact, Sidney commissioned my last major repairs but castle fortresses, even as powerful as me, require a bit more than maintenance every two hundred years. I hoped that someone like Sidney might again appear and remind everyone of what I was and could be.

Only a few years later, however, the English were to pay a heavy price for allowing me to deteriorate. Between 1756 and 1763 England was engaged in a war against France, which was not an uncommon occurrence in those days. I had not participated in this war except that a large number of French prisoners of war were being held in my dungeons.

At a crucial point in the conflict, the French apparently decided to invade the south coast of England. To distract the English they also planned to invade Scotland and Ireland, more as feints than actual invasions. I discovered years later that the whole plan went disastrously wrong because the English blockade prevented most of the French fleet from leaving Dunkirk so, in the end, the whole plan was abandoned. Five frigates did escape the blockade but, in those days, before humans could communicate over long distances, they did not realise that they were on their own. This force was under the command of Commodore François Thurot and, although they lost two ships to storms at sea, the remaining French forces landed not far from my walls intent on carrying out their mission.

I remember the reaction of the garrison commander Colonel John Jennings when the landing was reported from a lookout on the roof of the keep.

'My God,' he exclaimed, 'we are sitting ducks. No guns, no ammunition, and a garrison of young boys who are still wet behind the ears.'

'What shall we do?' a nervous young lieutenant asked.

'Prepare to defend as best we can, of course,' was the terse reply. 'And one more thing, organise a detail and march those French prisoners from the cells down to Belfast. The last thing we need is for them to get loose and turn on us as well.'

Jennings orders were carried out and the garrison was deployed to the town of Carrickfergus to meet the initial assault. As they had little ammunition, the defence did not last long and the garrison retreated to the security of my walls, such as they were.

In fairness to the young boys who manned my walls with little powder and even less shot, they had only a small chance of success but still they fought bravely. Jennings ordered that half charges of powder would be used with the remaining shot. When all the shot was expended he ordered that the boys use their tunic buttons instead. And when the buttons ran out, the boys threw stones and bricks from my drum towers onto the advancing French. Eventually, the attackers reached my gates where they were greeted with another barrage of rocks pushed through the murder holes, which were openings in my battlement floor directly above my entrance.

Finally the gunfire ceased and the French charged my main gate with drawn swords. The years of neglect now haunted the defenders because they were unable to properly secure the gate and the French entered the outer ward. The battle raged at my entrance with soldiers from both sides engaged in hand-to-hand combat with knives and bayonets and, in credit to my defenders, the French were driven back out my front gate.

I was particularly proud of my valiant defenders because, although it was human neglect that allowed me to deteriorate, I am a proud fortress. The idea of attackers actually making their way into the sanctuary of my walls had been inconceivable some years earlier, yet the French almost succeeded. When they were driven out, my proud record remained intact.

While Colonel Jennings believed that he could defend the front gate, he was concerned that the French might discover the part of my wall which had been allowed to crumble and he was in no position to defend multiple points of entry. As a result he asked for terms and Commodore Thurot, impressed with the valour of the defence, accepted. My English inhabitants marched out and down to Belfast with their colours flying. The French then occupied my walls and, for the first time in my history, I was no longer under English or Irish control.

Thurot was not long in occupation when a messenger arrived from Belfast shortly after Jennings had reported his failure.

'I'm afraid your effort,' the emmisary began, 'while undoubtedly successful was rather foolish. Here you sit completely alone on these islands, whilst your nearest support is far off in France.'

'*Sacre bleu,*' Thurot exclaimed. 'What you say cannot be true. What of the invasion?'

The emissary replied with a smirk, 'I have no idea what you are talking about. The only invasion has been your little effort here in Carrickfergus and I can assure you that a proper response is not far behind me.'

Thurot looked sceptical, 'I don't know whether I believe you, Englishman. What if you are telling me lies?'

The emissary laughed, 'Then you would look like a fool. However you would be a live fool and not a dead or captured fool. You do whatever you like, but the army will be here in a matter of hours and whatever you hoped might have happened with this so-called invasion, it will not reach here soon enough to rescue you.'

Thurot thought about that for a time and then replied, 'All right, Englishman. Suppose I believe you. What terms will you give if I agree to surrender? After all, troops or no troops, this is as fine a fortress as I have seen and it will not be easy to take. Of course you could destroy it, but then you will have lost a valuable property.'

This time the Englishman scratched his chin, considering the statement. After a moment he replied, 'What terms would you like?'

Thurot smiled and responded quickly, 'If you provide me with provisions for my ships, I will sail out of here on the next tide.'

The emissary rose and looked out one of my defence windows, 'Well, that's not exactly what I had in mind. However, as you fought well and treated Jennings with honour, we will do the same. Your terms are accepted.'

The two shook hands and orders were given to implement the agreement. When his ships were equipped, Thurot departed my walls and set sail for France. Of course he threw all the remaining gunpowder into the sea and spiked the few cannon that still graced my parapets. Once again, I was in the control of the English.

I am confident that the French would never have occupied my walls if I had been maintained to any standard appropriate for a castle of my strength and character. The French did not have the guns necessary to bring me down and they would have been unable to breach my fortifications. The English also recognised this and shortly after retaking my walls they began the repairs that were so long overdue. My walls and gate were repaired, and the guns on my parapets were unspiked. The munitions stores were restocked and a trained garrison replaced the young lads who had so bravely defended my walls. In consequence, I was never again seriously threatened, although both my occupants and myself never again allowed ourselves to become complacent concerning my defence.

Some time after the French departed and my refitting had begun, I realised that the nature of my service had also changed. Because of the

Controlling Belfast Lough, I rise above the port. Carrickfergus in the eighteenth century.

power of cannon, a sustained bombardment would ultimately reduce me to ruins and so any protection I might provide to occupants within my walls would be temporary. On the other hand, fitted with the proper long-range guns, I could become a defensive force serving a much larger area, all the way to Belfast Lough.

In 1778 a naval encounter, literally in the shadows of my walls, clearly demonstrated my potential and indirectly caused my armaments to be further improved. I well recall the day in April of that year when a small ship flying a strange flag with thirteen red and white stripes and thirteen white stars in a circular pattern with a blue background in the upper left corner confronted His Majesty's ship *Drake* as she sailed out of Carrickfergus Harbour. After an ensuing exchange of broadsides, the *Drake* struck her colours. The attacker, which I subsequently discovered was the American ship *Ranger*, captained by the Scotsman John Paul Jones, took the *Drake* as a prize. The *Ranger*'s crew was released into lifeboats and rowed ashore just north of my walls. My garrison stood helplessly by their guns, which had neither the range nor the accuracy to participate in the action, while Jones boldly sailed out of Belfast Lough with the *Drake* in tow.

A full report was prepared and the manufacture of guns to defend Belfast Lough was commissioned. Soon after, more works were commissioned to transform me into this new kind of stronghold. My keep was repaired and transformed into a barracks to house not only troops but also gunners who could best utilise my armaments. A new well was also commissioned because a wide range of junk was discovered when the old well was being cleaned. My walls were further reinforced, as much to provide suitable ramparts for the guns as to improve my fortifications and more guns were added. Soon, I began to feel my old self again, strong as well as useful.

Although there was little to threaten me, I was not without an occasional crisis. I recall, for example, an occasion in 1795 when a soldier of the Royal Irish Regiment and Fifeshire Fencibles was taken before Colonel Leslie, then in command of the garrison.

'I believe you have something to tell me,' Leslie began as the soldier grimaced in pain from the shackles that bound his arms.

'Am I to be spared?' the soldier asked.

'That is the agreement,' was the reply.

'It's the United Irishmen,' the soldier whined, 'There are eighteen in the regiment that I know about who have taken the oath and I think that they plan to take the castle.'

'Go on,' Leslie said. 'Just how do they propose to do that?'

'I don't know,' the man cried, 'I really don't know. Maybe take the late watch and capture the arms store. Most of the regiment is Irish and maybe they would join up. Please . . .'

'Take him away,' Leslie ordered, 'he disgusts me.'

Shortly thereafter reports came to Leslie that the United Irishmen were massing for an attack but, as their support within my walls had been discovered, the whole plan was abandoned. The closest I got to the United Irishmen was that I was used as a prison to house insurgents. I found it ironic that my walls were now being used to keep people in rather that to keep people out but that was yet another adjustment I made in providing service to my occupants.

The nineteenth century found yet another new use for my walls when I became the principal armoury for the northern part of Ireland. Old granaries and stables were reinforced and new rooms built so that guns and ammunition could be stored in bomb-proof lockers. My keep was refitted with gun racks and there were times when I held in excess of ten thousand rifles. I was also outfitted with the long-awaited long-range guns to guard Belfast Lough, particularly during the Napoleonic Wars early in that century. During those days I saw very little action, or activity of any kind for that matter, other than a stream of wagons removing or replacing my stock. Lookouts vigilantly patrolled from my ramparts but I suspect that the French knew of my prowess so Belfast Lough was not challenged.

As I had become an important part of the defence of Belfast and the lough as well as an armoury, more effort was given to ensure that I remained a state-of-the-art defensive citadel. Throughout that century, it seemed that every few years new guns were mounted on my parapets, each one more powerful and accurate than the one it replaced. In 1889 a tunnel was cut from my inner ward to the sea so that armaments could be transferred to warships in the harbour. In addition, a crane was constructed to ease the loading process and many thousands of tons of guns and ammunition were transferred to waiting ships in this manner. This eliminated the need to transport weapons by wagons in and out of my front gates so it also improved security.

It was during the middle of the nineteenth century that I acquired a more or less permanent resident in the person of one Billy MacBean who was a drummer in a Highland regiment garrisoned within my walls. Billy had the misfortune of falling down the abandoned well shaft and, as he banged his head on the way down, he drowned before he could be pulled to safety. I suppose Billy regretted that his untimely death had prevented him from serving his time, and his spirit has remained within my walls from that day to this.

Billy would appear whenever there was a commotion, recognising that it was his duty to alert my occupants to the possibility of danger and muster a defence. Because his tam-o'-shanter had a button on the top, those who saw his ghost referred to him as the button-top boy. For some reason Billy's rare appearances cause a great deal of discussion among my current occupants. Of course, there has been very little commotion, particularly in recent years, so very little is seen of the Button Boy. As for me, Billy provides a level of comfort knowing that, day or night, I always house a human presence, in spirit if not in body.

As I entered the twentieth century, it occurred to me that man's ability to create weapons of destruction had improved to such a degree that, in the event of an attack, my walls would be so completely ineffective and redundant that two good blasts would reduce me to ruins. While this caused me some concern, I was no different to the soldiers who manned my parapets realising that their lives were always in jeopardy. I certainly understood that risk of destruction is all part of my service as one of Ireland's strongholds.

During World War I my duties included protecting Belfast Lough against German submarines. My ramparts were commissioned with high-powered telescopes to search the harbour constantly, as well as special artillery capable of blasting an invader out of the water. As it happened that was the last active service I was to provide and, like the old soldier I had become, I was retired to a more peaceful existence.

A few years after the end of that war, my seven hundred and fifty years as a military fortress came to an end. In 1928 my occupying garrison marched out for the last time and I was transferred to the Ministry of Finance in the interest of maintaining me as a monument to the centuries of my service. I recognised that I had reached the age and stage when I was no longer capable of providing the protection for which I had been created. Then too war and weaponry had changed to such a degree that even my more recent service had been rendered redundant by balloons and aircraft. To be honest, I didn't mind retiring because I knew that, were I to attempt to withstand even one modern bombardment, I would be reduced to rubble. When I was young and invincible I might have said, 'Bring it on'. Being older and wiser, I preferred to remain standing as I had throughout the centuries.

Having said that, like many old soldiers I was recalled to active duty once again during the early 1940s. When Winston Churchill called for the defence of Britain, I was happy to accommodate the people in Northern Ireland as a bomb shelter and lookout post for aircraft. Thankfully, I never did feel the pain of German bombs but I was confident that anyone within the basement of my keep would survive if a bomb ever came.

I suppose it was during those war years that it first became recognised that my walls and their history might have some interest to visitors from around Ireland and the world. During those years, a regiment of the United States Army Rangers was stationed in Carrickfergus town and on several occasions American soldiers toured my walls listening with great interest to the information provided by my custodian. Unfortunately, the custodian was not particularly familiar with much of my history and some of the information he provided was not exactly accurate, but he was enthusiastic and a great storyteller. The young Americans quite enjoyed climbing on my ramparts and on many occasions I heard them discuss what it must have been like to be a knight when I was at the height of my power and strength.

After those visits, I began to entertain hopes that I might become a living museum in which visitors might learn about the history of Ireland by understanding my centuries of service. It seemed to me that such a role would not only be useful but a pleasant way to spend the next few centuries.

Fortunately, that was the future envisaged for me by the Ministry of Finance as gradually modern facilities were added to accommodate the needs of modern visitors. All of the gun racks and other paraphernalia from my days as an armoury were removed from my keep and it was returned to a reasonable replica of the days when I served John De Courcy and Hugh De Lacy.

A great deal of work was performed in early 1961 when it was announced that I would have one more royal visitor. I well remember the day in August of that year when Queen Elizabeth II, accompanied by the Duke of Edinburgh, Prince Charles and Princess Anne walked through my gates. The visit was the first by a reigning monarch in nearly six hundred and fifty years and it reminded me of the days when I was, literally, the seat of English power.

Queen Elizabeth was a welcome change from the prior monarchs who had found shelter in my walls as she was quite attractive with a warm smile and wave for all the well-wishers who came to see her. Her two children were well behaved until they saw my towers and parapets and then, like children anywhere, they demanded to be taken to my highest point so that they could look out over the sea and countryside.

The queen did not issue any edicts from my walls nor did she make any proclamations concerning the governance of the kingdom, but she did comment on my condition. 'This is truly a remarkable castle. Nearly eight hundred and fifty years old you say.'

'Like the empire,' the duke replied with a smile. 'In good hands and looking very fit.'

'I have little doubt,' Her Majesty graciously replied, 'that our friend Carrickfergus Castle will be here for at least another nine hundred years.'

In parting, the duke added, 'I think it is important that this castle be fully restored as a landmark historic sight. I can think of no castle on these islands that wears its years so well or is as perfect a representative of the age in which it was built and served the empire.'

As you would guess, that was among the proudest moments in my history and I am sure that anyone standing within the proximity of my walls could feel a glow that nearly eclipsed the sun's warmth. I had been publicly recognised for standing strong throughout the centuries. I had also been given an important task for continuing to provide service to humankind into the future. I was to become a living museum, who would welcome visitors from Ireland and around the world. Within my walls modern men, women and certainly children would find a link with my historic past and, hopefully, understand what it was like to stand on my walls one hundred, five hundred or even eight hundred years ago.

And so, I am now a historic museum and nearly every day visitors walk within my walls viewing my keep that has been fully restored to the same condition as I was in the days of De Courcy. Nearly everyone walks on my parapets looking down the barrels of the guns that defended my walls during the Napoleonic Wars. Staff and volunteers who are friendly and enthusiastic about me and my history greet the visitors. Some of them, like myself, are retired from the wars they have fought, either literally or in the commercial world. Fortunately they have taken the time to know and understand my story. In truth, I enjoy my current position and look forward to providing this service for many centuries to come.

And so it is that I come to the end of my story. I trust that I have accomplished my goal in describing my history and service as one of Ireland's strongholds. I hope you understand that I have never tried to be anything other than a castle fortress, providing security to those who sought protection and a strong wall against anyone who would attack my occupants. When it was required, I spread the blanket of my security to larger areas around my walls, always in service to my occupants. While I may now have taken a different role, I do so, not because I failed as a stronghold, but because the modern world has made my methods of providing safety and security redundant. In a manner of speaking, I have retired as a true castle. However I am most proud to state that I retired having never surrendered, and now I never will.

KILKENNY CASTLE

~

I How I Came into Being (1180–1390)

You are all very welcome to my walls that everyone knows as Kilkenny
Castle. At the risk of appearing to be vain, I'm sure you have noticed
the manner in which I rise majestically above the beautiful River Nore
in what is now called the city of Kilkenny. Although you surely will not
believe me when I tell you, I am over eight hundred and twenty-five
years old. Like all Irish ladies, I have aged gracefully and I know that I
am remarkably well preserved for a castle of my years. When you hear
my story you will be even more impressed because, unlike my sister
castle, Malahide, my existence has not been all wine and roses.

You see I am one of Ireland's strongholds providing both security
and comfort to my human residents. Like my brother, Bunratty, I have
felt the wrath of fire, rock and ball and have seen my walls shattered
and scarred, but I have always risen from the ashes of human dispute.
Like my brother, Blarney, and sister, Malahide, I have provided
comfort for many generations of the same family who, in my case, were
called the Butlers, the earls of Ormond. And today, in the peace and
tranquillity of modern Ireland, like my sister, Malahide and my
brother, Carrickfergus, I provide a living history dating back to
Norman times as I welcome guests from all over the world. I am
delighted to tell you my story because I believe that it reflects not only
the history of my country but the resilience its people.

Although I am well over eight hundred years of age, I will admit that only parts of my foundation remain from my earliest days in the late twelfth century when Richard De Clare, first chose this site for a castle. I began my existence in Norman times as a motte and bailey castle constructed primarily of wood. My first existence was a fortified wooden tower called a keep and I was built on a hill of earth and rocks called a motte. A narrow passage led down the hill to an enclosed area called a bailey, which held many smaller buildings. The mistress and master of my walls lived in the keep with their family and domestic servants, while the buildings in the bailey housed soldiers and other staff. A wood and stone wall enclosed the entire motte and bailey beyond which was a ditch, called a moat. I discovered that many of my brother and sister castles from those days trace their origins to such simple beginnings because the design suited the Norman conquerors.

As you probably know, Richard De Clare, more famously known as Strongbow, was sent to Ireland by Henry II to subdue the native Irish chieftains and bring Norman organisation and structure to the land. The first step in that process was to establish a number of castles, which could be easily defended, at important locations. My site, at a bend in the River Nore, was considered just such a location. Like several of my brother and sister castles, a location on the edge of water was preferable because it provided extra defence on the side that faced the water. These motte and bailey castles were easily constructed and readily defended, so they served the Norman's purpose until permanent structures could be completed. I have few memories of my days as a wooden castle as I was just a child, and the wood has long since returned to the earth. My stone base remains, however, because it has become part of my foundations, particularly on my northwest and southwest sides. I have undergone many changes over the centuries but those few rocks and stones remain part of me and they always remind me of my beginnings.

I share a further common Norman heritage with my sister in Malahide because, while Strongbow was granted authority over most of Leinster, a small part was granted to Richard De Talbot who, in turn, built that castle. As a result, our initial grants came directly from the crown. These Norman origins and our status as lady castles are among the very few things we have in common because, while Lady Malahide was to enjoy a pleasant and secure existence within the Pale of Dublin,

Pax Britannia did not come quietly to most of Ireland, particularly Kilkenny.

I suspect that, in her early days, Malahide was able to communicate freely with the motte and bailey castle she replaced, but I had no such luxury. Within a very few years of my construction the O'Briens of Thomond, who were later to occupy my brother castle Bunratty, came east and burned my wooden walls to my foundation. The O'Briens, of course, were native Irish and they were not particularly pleased that the Normans had come from England intent on conquering Ireland and taking their land.

My location on the River Nore was so important, however, that a few years later in the early days of the thirteenth century, Stongbow's son-in-law and successor, William Marshall, the Earl of Pembroke, promptly rebuilt my walls using the rocks from my motte and bailey foundation to construct an enclosed trapezoid with drum towers on the corners, three of which survive to this day. As you will see, these towers do not appear today exactly as they did those many centuries ago, but you will certainly understand that a lady must keep in style with the times.

I know that many of the other Norman castles of my vintage began with a fortified tower house which is a further development of a keep. Once the tower house was completed walls were built enclosing it to provide further protection. However, after Marshall rebuilt my walls I became a 'keepless' castle, which means I did not have a fortified tower house. At a meeting among the remnants of my motte, I recall Earl Marshall describing his plan.

'I appreciate your advice,' Marshall said to his construction foreman, 'but we need more than a tower house for my stronghold.'

The foreman countered, 'But this is the way we have designed and constructed our castles in England and Ireland for the last hundred years. It is a design that has been proven to be most successful.'

Marshall sighed, his patience strained, 'The locals had little difficulty in overrunning our bailey and this time I want a castle that sends out a message that we are here to stay. If the O'Briens think that we are an easy mark for their future endeavours, they have another think coming.'

'But it won't be very comfortable for her ladyship,' the builder remarked.

'Don't worry about that,' was the reply. 'I am well aware of her ladyship's needs. The drum towers are large enough to provide for comfort as well as security and we can always build out from the connecting walls. Since the river side is the most secure from attack, we can build back from that wall. Whatever about the fortification, I can assure you it will be comfortable enough for my wife.'

And so it was that I rose above a crossing on the banks of the Nore with walls and towers that were to last for centuries, or at least until humankind's ability to destroy created weapons that no stone wall could withstand.

I certainly recall my first mistress and a wonderful woman she was. Really, I have no idea why her husband and his builder should have had any concerns about her comfort because, while Isabel may have been Strongbow's daughter, she was no dandified Norman princess. Rather, she was a strong-willed Celtic queen who knew as much, or more, about power and authority as her husband. On the other hand, Isabel also showed a remarkable tendency to recall small details about those who served her. She might, for example, enquire as to the health of a serving girl's grandmother who had been ill, which made the young one feel welcome. This combination of talents made Isabel not only well respected, but also well liked.

In time I discovered that, while Isabel Marshall's father was Strongbow, her mother was none other than Aoife, the daughter and heiress of Diarmuid MacMurchadha, the Irish King of Leinster. I suppose that Strongbow had quickly realised that, if he were to be successful in subduing Ireland, he would require the co-operation of at least some of the native chiefs and the best way to accomplish that was to marry strategically just as the Irish clans had done for centuries. By marrying the heiress of the King of Leinster, Strongbow had hoped to confirm his own power in the province. When Isabel, the child of that couple came to reside within my walls, even as they were still rising, she came as an Irish queen, well able for the rigors of life beyond the Pale and truly in charge of her household.

In truth, it was Isabel who oversaw much of my construction, particularly my interior detail. After all, since I was to provide a comfortable home, I would certainly have to meet her requirements. More importantly, for some of those early years, her husband, William, was off in some remote part of the world fighting the Crusades leaving Isabel to organise her home. As a result the various attachments which grew from my interior walls were neat and orderly. They included a grain storage, a blacksmith shop, open-air kitchens, a butchery and sleeping quarters for the soldiers and staff. When my construction was complete, I was an imposing stone fortress at once able to provide security from attack and a comfortable home for the Marshalls.

I wouldn't want to give the impression that Isabel was in permanent residence as she was often absent attending to other duties. You see, as the sole heiress of Strongbow, as well as the daughter of the Irish king, Isabel was an important person so her responsibilities did not allow her the luxury of establishing herself in one location to the exclusion of others. When she was not in residence, I was occupied by a caretaker called a constable and a force of soldiers to ensure my security.

While in residence, Isabel lived in my northeast drum tower overlooking the river. My southeast drum tower was also well furnished as it was used for housing and entertaining the various guests and dignitaries who would call on her. In 1207 William Marshall eventually returned from the Crusades and was reunited with his wife. William certainly recognised the quality of my construction and decided that he would administer his wife's vast inheritance from my walls. As a result, for the next six years William and Isabel were in more or less continual residence.

There were times when William would be gone for a time on some duty to the English crown. Perhaps he felt that those duties were more important than his life in Kilkenny because they were to eventually result in his final departure from my walls. I do remember the domestic discussion that resulted in that move.

'I'm afraid, my dear wife, that I have been summoned to court once again,' Marshall announced.

Isabel looked up from her needlepoint with resignation, 'How tiresome this has become. No sooner do you settle down than you are called off again. How long will it be this time?'

Marshall, his hands behind his back walked over to a window overlooking the Nore, 'I'm afraid I have no way of knowing. King John is not in the best of health and his son, Henry, is only a child. As I am the executor of his will, I can only imagine what might happen if he were to pass on. It may be a rather long assignment.'

'I see,' Isabel replied. 'I trust that you don't expect me to accompany you on this errand.'

'But of course I do,' Marshall replied turning quickly toward her, 'Your place is at my side.'

Isabel replied sternly, 'That is as may be, however, you know that I despise court. Everyone fawning all over each other when it suits and stabbing each other in the back when it doesn't. I gave this matter a great deal of thought the last time I was there and I have decided that I have made my last trip to London.'

Marshall returned his gaze to the river and said nothing for a long time. Finally he replied, 'I know you well enough to know that there is little I can say to that but, you see, I have a duty, an obligation to the crown.'

'Yes, I do understand that,' she quickly responded. 'But I also have a responsibility to my own crown, and I think it best that I remain within these walls.'

Shortly after in 1213, William Marshall did leave my walls and return to England. News of him made its way back to me from time to time as he wrote or sent messages to Isabel. From those communications, I learned that Marshall was one of those who signed a document called the Magna Carta, by which King John granted rights to some of the people of England. He also served as the executor of King John's will and was the Regent of the Realm until Henry III reached his majority. William Marshall died some six years later having never returned to my walls.

Isabel, meanwhile, lived within my walls with her five daughters. In fairness to Marshall, my configuration was certainly a deterrent to further attempts by the O'Briens or any other clan to bring me down. Looking back over the centuries, I suppose I was then at the height of my prowess as a stronghold because there were few castles that were more secure. Those who would dare challenge my walls were

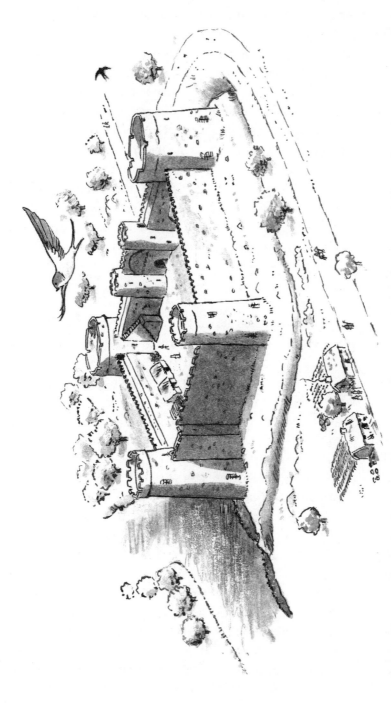

My early days in the late twelfth century soon after William Marshall built me. You can see that my drum towers and curtain walls, later destroyed by Cromwell's guns, are intact.

confronted with a great fortress with massive drum-shaped towers on each corner. The towers rose some sixty feet and each had a diameter of thirty-five feet. The curtain walls between the towers created an irregularly shaped rectangle completely enclosing the central courtyard. At the top of the walls wide parapets allowed defenders to repel any attack by shooting down on the enemy as they made their way forward. Within the courtyard various buildings had been constructed to meet the needs of a busy castle, including a chapel and reception hall. I was truly *the* stronghold in the south centre of Ireland.

On the death of Marshall, his vast estates were divided among his daughters and my walls were assigned to Isabel, the eldest of the girls and namesake of her mother. Isabel married into a family called the Despencers who did not reside in Ireland and so, for many years, I was not a family dwelling. That does not mean, however, that I sat vacant in the hands of minders – throughout the thirteenth and fourteenth centuries I was second in importance only to Dublin in Norman Ireland.

I'm sure you understand that travel was difficult in those days and the Normans had spread their conquest throughout Ireland. I suppose I was closer than Dublin to other parts of the country and so parliament often met within my walls. In consequence, I became well acquainted with the Norman rule in Ireland.

Another reason I was chosen for this responsibility was that I was a formidable stronghold in those days and the country around me was generally at peace. The same could not, however, be said about the rest of Ireland and I remember many discussions about the continuing wars between the Normans and the Irish.

In the mid-1300s the king's justiciar was a man called Thomas Rokeby and he frequently called on my walls as he was coming to and from his various campaigns. Rokeby had established himself in Bunratty Castle, over in Clare, while he tried to pacify that part of the Ireland. As the king's representative and an accomplished soldier his information was always interesting not only to me but also to the Norman leaders meeting within my walls. The principal difficulty Rokeby faced was that, no sooner had he put out one fire of rebellion, than another arose in some other part of Ireland.

I remember well the report that reached my walls concerning his own castle. While Rokeby was campaigning in Leinster, Bunratty was sacked and Thomond, as north Munster was called at that time, was lost to the Normans. Incidents like that caused a great deal of concern among the Norman settlers and the parliament decided to act.

I well remember two parliamentary debates during which the state of Norman Ireland was discussed. The first was in July 1360. Many members rose to discuss the dire state of affairs, which was made more serious by the plague and famine that was ravaging the country. On a unanimous motion, it was decided to send a message and request to Edward III. In it, the Norman colonists told him of the desperate conditions in Ireland due to plague, impoverishment, bad government and the failure of Norman knights to defend the lands they had been granted. It also warned that, unless something was done, the Irish might overrun the entire county. (I must say I thought that a little rich in that the whole country was Irish long before the Normans arrived.) Anyway, they petitioned the king for the appointment of a strong leader with an army and all the resources necessary to secure the country. Without such support, the petition warned, the Normans could never live in a proper English style.

The plea was successful as Edward sent his son Lionel of Clarence with an army that immediately began to campaign in Wicklow. Over the next few years, the reports reaching my walls indicated that Lionel was campaigning with varying degrees of success. I also heard that Lionel had married the only daughter and heir of William De Burgh from Carrickfergus Castle, so he had his own interests in Ireland particularly in Ulster. Ultimately, Lionel decided that the reason the Normans could not subjugate the Irish was as much the fault of the Norman landowners as it was the natives and so he called for another session of parliament to be held within my walls.

When the parliament convened, Lionel proposed a statute that angered many and was hotly debated by the members. It ultimately passed but only after dire threats by the king's son. I remember well parts of the speech that Lionel delivered and the debate that followed.

'You petitioned my father,' he began, 'to provide the necessary military support to ensure that you could live on your estates as proper

English gentlemen lest you be overrun by the Irish. And yet, many of you are not the slightest bit English. You have become, in my opinion, at least as Irish as the natives. Look at you. You speak Irish, your women wear Irish cloaks, you wear moustaches. You have married Irish people and you live as the Irish live. First and foremost, this has got to change.'

When the roar of protest settled, an older member rose, 'My friend,' he said, 'I appreciate that you have only been here for a few years, but while we would certainly like to live as English lords, Ireland is not England and adjustments must be made. Why, Strongbow himself married an Irishwoman and this noble castle is owned by a descendant of that marriage.'

Many 'here, heres' rang out and another man, very rotund with a bushy moustache rose. 'Do you not realise how cold it is here? An Irish cloak is just the thing to keep a woman warm and moustaches also help fight the chill. What do those things have to do with our being proper Norman landlords?'

Another complained, 'How can we control people if we can't speak their language? They are hardly going to go to the effort of learning ours.'

Others rose in protest reminding Lionel that the Normans had adopted English language and customs and had married English women after conquering England and that did not seem to affect Norman control, so why should it be any different in Ireland. When my meeting hall became quiet, I was sure that whatever Lionel had in mind would be defeated by the sitting parliament but I was wrong.

After everyone had had his say, Lionel rose again, withdrawing a parchment from a satchel. 'Nevertheless,' he said, 'as you know I have just returned from England where I reported my progress over the last few years. My father, your king, is not pleased with the way that many of you have adopted Irish customs and he has ordered that this stop. It is his strongly held belief that the reason you have so much trouble controlling your estates is that you have forgotten the Norman ways. Therefore, he has ordered that you shall pass this statute putting an end to all this Irish nonsense. These are his orders: "It shall be treasonous for any Norman holding title to property from the crown to speak

Irish, dress like the Irish, ride horses without a proper saddle, marry Irish people, allow poets, musicians or bards to provide entertainment at banquets, or to participate in Irish sports, particularly hurling." These are the king's orders and I expect you to endorse them by passing a statute to this effect.'

A long debate followed after which the parliament broke up while various members discussed the matter in private. It was clear to me that few of the Norman lords agreed with all of the mandates but the consensus seemed to be that the statute would be passed to satisfy the king and the Norman lords would continue to do whatever was expedient in ruling their lands.

When the parliament reconvened, the Statute of Kilkenny was passed despite several protest votes and Lionel left my walls with his mandate. A few months later he left Ireland altogether. Over the next several years, reports to my walls made it clear that about the only place where the statute was strictly enforced was in a narrow strip of land on the east coast including Dublin and several miles to the north of Dublin, which became known as the Pale. This would, of course, have been where my sister castle, Malahide, was located and I have little doubt that a word of Irish was never heard within her walls.

As for my walls, and I suspect the remainder of the country, the statute was observed more through breaches than in compliance. Reports continued to find their way to me so I knew that, beyond the Pale, the wars between the Irish and the Normans continued and, for that matter, the Normans were not above fighting between themselves. It also transpired that Norman sheriffs, appointed to keep order, were a particular target of both the Irish and disgruntled Norman-Irish. This dangerous state of affairs caused more and more magistrates to sell their land and return to England. The land did not revert to the Irish because there was no shortage of other Normans who were more prepared to confront the problems.

The Irish did not threaten the Despencer family, who held title to me, because they did not live in Ireland and the area around my walls was generally peaceful. Despite this, I am sure the Despencers were influenced by stories about the problems in Ireland, which they undoubtedly assumed would depreciate my value. As a result, in 1391

I was sold by Hugh Despencer to a family called the Butlers.

For nearly two hundred years, I had been the stronghold of direct descendants of Strongbow himself, beginning with his daughter and son-in-law. Admittedly, I had not been a true residence to them for many years but my value was apparent to all of Norman Ireland. While I had not really been tested by arrow or rock, my strength and character made me the most important castle in Ireland outside the Pale. As a result, I was well informed on all measure of matters from serious issues affecting Norman control of the country to the gossip of the courts both in London and in Dublin. I couldn't have been more pleased with my status and I was particularly proud of my service to humankind and to Ireland.

It was strange, therefore, to consider that all this might change as a new owner, one who had already lost castles in Nenagh and Roscrea to the native Irish, would soon move into my walls. I well understood, however, that a castle's job is not to question human decisions or to judge its occupants and so I embraced the chance to begin an entirely new chapter in my history. Little did I know that my new occupants would stay with me for nearly six hundred years.

II How I Acquired Power and Prestige (1390–1640)

In my role as the host for the Norman parliament, I had heard of my new occupants but I knew very little about them. I quickly learned about their history because they frequently entertained and were proud to relate their path to wealth and power to anyone who might listen. My new resident owners, the Butlers, were also a Norman family who had arrived in Ireland during the days of Strongbow, but they did not acquire power through military conquest or marriage. Rather, the Butlers became involved in the alcoholic beverage trade, which was apparently a lucrative business in Ireland even all those years ago.

You see the Butlers were originally called the Walter family but soon after their arrival in Ireland Theobald Walter managed to acquire the title of Ireland's Chief Butler to the Crown. This title was primarily ceremonial but it established Theobald as the toastmaster at coronation ceremonies. According to tradition, the chief butler would offer the new king his first cup of wine and present a toast for a long and prosperous reign. The true advantage of the position was that it included the right to collect an import duty on all the wine that made its way into England and Ireland and that duty made the family very wealthy indeed.

To mark their new title, and perhaps to ensure that no other family would challenge its rights, at the beginning of the thirteenth century the Walters changed their name to Butler. In the decades that followed, the Butlers acquired vast tracts of land primarily in the south centre of Ireland and they were already quite wealthy and powerful when they acquired the title to my walls in 1391. Having said that, some of their property in areas where Norman control was not so strong had been taken by native Irish and other properties were also under threat.

The Butlers' acquisition of my walls undoubtedly provided them with not only a secure estate near enough to Dublin, but also the power and prestige associated with owning a castle of my impeccable reputation. At the risk of appearing vain, it must be said that I was the crown jewel in the acquisitions of James Butler, who quickly made me his principal residence. Thereafter the Butlers, the earls of Ormond, became the most powerful family in and around Tipperary and Kilkenny – and indeed, in all of Ireland.

From their first days with me, the earls of Ormond were staunchly loyal to the English crown and, as the generations passed, the Butlers came and went with little change or effect to my walls. In truth I seldom saw a great deal of the earls themselves because they spent more time off on crown business then they did within my walls. I did hear a great deal about their exploits and at times I felt like a mother anxiously waiting for news about her children who were far away. When they were at home I made a special effort to provide the finest security, warmth and comfort available.

The first of the Butlers entrusted to my care was James, the third Earl of Ormond, a title that would remain in the family, with an occasional confusing lapse, for all succeeding centuries. James was a big man with a long, thin nose and large, heavy-lidded eyes, a trait that seemed to be inherited by all his descendants. As one would expect of a man of his size, James loved his food, not to mention the wine, women and entertainment that would accompany his meals. He was certainly not a proponent of the Statute of Kilkenny because he spoke fluent Irish, which allowed him to improve relations with various clans in residence near my walls including the O'Neills, O'Briens, O'Connors, McMurroughs and O'Kennedys.

In a short time James Butler was well established within my walls. After he had made some modest improvements, his rather large family joined him in residence. All the children, of course, intrigued me and I enjoyed the sounds of laughter and delight that accompanied them. While I have no objection to sheltering troops of soldiers, I found the play of children far superior entertainment than men practising their swordsmanship.

The children were not long with me when it became clear to me that, while James sired all of them, their mothers were not all the same. In addition to the children born to his wife (two boys called James and Richard after himself and his king) he had several other children, many of whom were born to his favourite mistress, Katherine. All the children seemed to enjoy each other's company so their parentage mattered little to me, or to anyone else as far as I could tell.

Among the first guests to be greeted by James as my resident, was none other than Richard II, the King of England, who earlier had landed in Waterford with the largest army ever sent to Ireland. Richard was a tall man with a long, sharp nose and his large, clear eyes certainly appeared to reflect a strong intellect. His brow was creased in a most peculiar fashion with wrinkles rising from the bridge of his nose at an angle up over his eyebrows giving him the appearance of one who was continually surprised. As you will see, Richard was the first of many English kings and queens to be welcomed to my walls but, being the first, he was perhaps the most memorable. In fact, when I think about all the monarchs who followed, I would be quite surprised if any of my brother or sister castles in Ireland could match the number of these royal visits.

Anyway, Richard was intent on straightening out the Irish, once and for all. His job, quite simply, was to subdue the native population and bring about a state of peace and harmony not unlike that enjoyed in the south and southeast of England. Richard made this clear during the course of his visit when he remarked, 'We have enough problems in Europe and Scotland without having another thorn in our backsides.'

Richard's visit was, as you would certainly expect, one of the highlights of my early years as the residence for the earls of Ormond. I remember the meal that was prepared for Richard and it *was* certainly a feast fit for a king. In typical Norman style there were four courses, each of which included at least seven dishes. Every type of meat and fowl imaginable was served at one or more of the courses including venison, beef, pork, lamb, mutton, swan, capon, pheasant, duck, pigeon and chicken. The meal also included a wide range of breads, sweetmeats, cheeses, fruits and vegetables, all of which were washed down with large quantities of the finest of French wines.

Between courses, the king was entertained with music, poetry and dance but, most interestingly, the entertainment included Irish acts in clear violation of the Statute of Kilkenny. The king himself pointed out this infraction. 'I know you are not a proponent of the statute,' he began, 'but one would think that at least you should have enough sense not to flaunt it before us.'

'Indeed,' was the reply, 'but you see, I know you to be far more enlightened than some of your predecessors and it would be hypocritical for me to pretend one thing while you are here and act differently when you are not. Believe me when I say that the statute causes far more problems than it solves.'

'In what way?' the king enquired.

James responded promptly, 'I suppose the first is communication. If we can't communicate with those who live in our estates, there are bound to be misunderstandings. These Irish are quick to settle their differences on the battlefield and it is a waste of all our time and energy to be fighting over something that might not have been a problem in the first place if we understood one another. We can't expect the Irish to immediately learn to speak our language although I would certainly hope that, in time, they will learn. In the meanwhile, it only makes sense to speak theirs.'

'And the other things?' the king asked.

'As you well know, we adopted many customs and practices from the natives in England when William went over there, so what difference?' James replied. 'The Irish have much to offer. Why even that hand towel you are using is made of Irish linen, which, as you have probably noticed, is far superior to anything available in England. Are we to deny ourselves such luxuries merely because they are Irish? I believe we should take the best of what the Irish offer and give the best of what we have.'

I think that the king might have been impressed with the argument because he seemed to enjoy the remainder of the entertainment. I did notice that he frequently considered his linen table napkin and took it with him when he left. Years later I heard it said that Richard had popularised the use of the handkerchief, as opposed to wiping one's nose on the back of one's sleeve, and I often wondered whether the idea for this innovation came from the linen he used within my walls.

James died soon after the turn of the fifteenth century and was succeeded by his son, also called James, the fourth Earl of Ormond. James was known as the 'White Earl' and if there was one thing he inherited from his father, it was a love of food because he was as corpulent a man as I ever housed. Despite this, he was a seasoned soldier and had served under King Henry V. This association with the court in London was to serve succeeding generations of Butlers well because they, like James, were well known and well respected in

London. Of course, the consequence of this association was that the second of my Butler residents (and others that followed) did not spend nearly as much time within my walls as had his father. In 1420 James accepted the appointment as lieutenant, the king's principal representative in Ireland, and much of his time was spent fighting the enemies of the crown and trying to bring English peace to Ireland. As it transpired, the native Irish were not the only adversary.

When James was within my walls, his main preoccupation seemed to be a dispute between himself and a man called John Talbot whose family occupied my sister, Malahide Castle. The very mention of Talbot's name caused James to erupt in the most amazing litany of profanities and he announced on any number of occasions that the man was his sworn enemy and some day he would see him dead. It was never particularly clear to me why my resident would hold such feelings although they were both powerful men in Norman Ireland. My own suspicion was that the dispute was little more than a difference in personalities and, perhaps, petty jealousy over who curried the most favour with Henry V.

From what I could learn, Talbot had preceded James as the Lieutenant of Ireland and was only twenty-nine when the king appointed him to that post. Talbot had been successful in forcing various chieftains to submit to the crown, including a family called the O'Mores. Talbot's brother, Richard, was also the Archbishop of Dublin and so that family was as strong and influential as my own residents. John Talbot had resigned the post claiming that he had not been provided with the finance necessary to consolidate those successes and was succeeded by Butler.

When Talbot left the post, some of the families he had subdued, including the O'Mores, broke faith with their submission and returned to the field. My resident thought that John Talbot was behind this change of heart and, to make matter worse, my resident was defeated in battle by the O'Mores in May 1421 and forced to sue for peace. Shortly after that, James left his position and travelled to England at which time many more clans, some of which had been subdued in Talbot's time, also rose.

Over the next several years the competition between the two

intensified as Talbot was appointed justiciar at the same time as James returned to his post as lieutenant. The two took opposing sides in a dispute between two factions of a family called MacMurrough that ultimately led to bloodshed on each side. I will be the first to admit that much of what I learned about the feud was from rumours circulating around my walls because it was difficult to keep track of who my resident might be supporting and what effect that might have on Talbot. I do know that, whenever the White Earl was present in my walls, he spent a great deal of time raging about 'that (well the word isn't suitable for use by a lady) Talbot'. I suspect that the discussions in Malahide Castle probably took on a similar tone.

For over twenty years, the feud raged but I am delighted to report that it ended in a rather romantic fashion and about this I know a great deal. It seems that, in the early part of 1440, Elizabeth Butler, my occupant's daughter, fell in love with Peter, the son of John Talbot. The White Earl was furious with his daughter and, as you can well imagine, I witnessed a great deal of shouting and crying over the entire affair. Fortunately Joan, the earl's wife, was more concerned about her daughter's happiness and wellbeing than she was about her husband's feud. When he erupted with temper, she calmed him with soft words of endearment. When he was in good humour, she cajoled him with tales of their daughter's unhappiness. Finally Joan's efforts were successful and the marriage was approved.

Although I have no direct information about the wedding that took place at St Canice's Cathedral in Kilkenny town, I believe it was beautiful. I do know that the wedding feast held within my walls was as impressive as the feast held for King Richard fifty years earlier. I suspect that the bride's father decided that it was most important to impress his daughter's father-in-law with a show of wealth and hospitality the likes of which he had never seen. It apparently worked, because Talbot and his entire family marvelled at the condition of my walls and the grandeur of the feast. In time, and after several bottles of wine, the two old enemies were soon laughing and chatting like old friends. John Talbot and James Butler obviously worked out whatever disputes had caused their falling out and finished the evening discussing the possibilities for grandchildren from the union of their children.

Having found peace with his old enemy, James Butler spent a good deal of his final ten years on this earth pursuing his hobbies, which included collecting antiques and studying history. He was also quite generous to St Canice's and spent many a pleasant evening discoursing with bishops from that cathedral. Unfortunately, he contracted the plague and died in Ardee in 1452, when he was only sixty-two.

James, the fourth Earl of Ormond, had three sons but, as it transpired, none of them was to succeed him as my resident. As I had known all of the boys when they were very young, I was certainly interested in their lives. I did hear a great deal about them because the agents who were responsible for managing their many estates in Ireland, including myself, were in residence with me.

All three sons moved to England at an early age and there they met remarkably different fates. One (the fifth earl) picked the wrong side in the War of the Roses and, in consequence, the poor boy was executed as a traitor and his head, once topped with curly, blond hair, was set on a spike on London Bridge. A second (the sixth earl) gained great wealth in England as a favourite of Edward IV but died young and the third (the seventh earl called the 'Earl of Wool') was one of the wealthiest men in England. As it happened, he was also the grandfather of Anne Boleyn, which made him the great-grandfather of Queen Elizabeth I. With all due respect to my brother and sister castles in Ireland, I doubt that any of them can claim so direct a connection to the English crown.

Since none of the three sons of James left a male heir, the title of eighth Earl of Ormond skipped over to one of his grand-nephews, called Piers, who was the first earl to reside within my walls as a permanent occupant, not spending months on end engaged in the king's business. I remember little of Piers but I well remember his wife, Margaret Fitz Gerald, who was the daughter of the Earl of Kildare.

Because Ormond and Kildare were among the most powerful family estates in Ireland, women from less important families eagerly sought her patronage. Margaret was certainly not shy about granting or withholding that support. To be invited to a chat within my walls was to gain entry into the very fabric of the highest levels of Norman society, and Margaret was the key. My mistress was, I suppose, an early example of a woman who was 'larger than life'. She was large, loud and opinionated and everyone from her husband to those who called on my walls cowered in her presence.

For all her strength and character, Margaret was a loving mother, particularly to her eldest son, who inherited none of her stout physical constitution. James, who would later become the ninth earl, was known as 'James the Lame' as he had a pronounced limp because one of his legs was shorter than the other. I well remember her agony when James was shipped off to the court of Henry VIII to be polished for the diplomatic roles he would later assume. Although she certainly knew that the move would further advance his career, which could never include the military, Margaret made a great show keening as if he had passed out of this life.

Her sacrifice paid dividends because James became a favourite of the king and was appointed the Lord High Treasurer of Ireland. He ultimately returned to his mother and myself and, from my walls, undertook his responsibilities to the crown with steady, if not particular, distinction. Within my walls he was certainly productive as seven sons were born to his wife, Joan, and himself.

In 1546 James was succeeded by his eldest son, Thomas, as the tenth Earl of Ormond. He led a far more remarkable life in the court of Elizabeth I who was his fourth cousin. From his few appearances within my walls, I remember Thomas as a tall, slender, fine-looking man with large, dark eyes and a full, black beard. It is little wonder that he was known as 'Black Tom' and he was a particular favourite of the queen.

Apparently Thomas was a strong leader and excellent general and he was often called on to protect the interests of the crown. I certainly don't believe in passing on idle gossip, but the queen, popularly known as the 'Virgin Queen', was fond of calling our Tom her 'black husband', and she may have had one interest that he did not protect. The talk within my walls was that this 'husband' was quite probably more than just an endearment.

You see Thomas produced only daughters from his marriage but he also sired at least twelve illegitimate children by various mistresses both in England and in Ireland. To one of these extra-marital sons he was most generous both in life and through his will. The boy was called

Piers of Duiske and his descendants became the viscounts Galmoye. (Coincidently, for a time some years later, one such Viscount Galmoye managed my walls.) Apparently the young man not only resembled Thomas but also looked a great deal like the queen and when her diary included an extended illness at the time Piers was born, certainly conclusions were reached . . . need I say more.

When Thomas died leaving no legitimate male heir, his title and lands could not be passed on to his illegitimate sons. In addition a legitimate daughter could not inherit either, a tradition that made absolutely no sense to me at all. In my experience, it was usually the women who organised life within my walls and ensured that other great houses and castles were well maintained. Certainly they were well able to manage property and they had the added advantage of managing from the actual castle as opposed to some battlefield hundreds of miles, or an ocean apart.

Thomas left a widow and three daughters each of whom would be perfectly able for the management and operation of my walls and I well remember his wife attempting to explain the inheritance law to her daughter when she was only a girl.

'Because that is the way it is love,' the mother softly said. 'If Daddy dies we will have to move out because someone else would own Kilkenny.'

'But if I were a boy we could stay because I would own Kilkenny. That is so not fair,' Elizabeth replied.

'No love, it isn't fair, but it is the law and we must abide by the law.'

Elizabeth thought about that for a moment before declaring, 'Some day, Mammy, some day I will do something about that.'

Her determination was such that it did not particularly surprise me when she did just that. On the death of her father, Thomas, a number of years later, the Ormond title and my walls were passed to his nephew, Walter, who became the eleventh earl. Walter was a devout Catholic and was known as 'Walter of the Beads' for his incessant praying for deliverance from the blows that life had dealt him. These would have included the death of his son, called Thomas. Unfortunately, all this Catholic praying did not sit well with King James I, who was a Protestant.

The king, exercising his own power over the earls, all of whom held title through him, arranged the marriage of Black Tom's daughter, Elizabeth, to one of his friends, Richard Preston, and then designated Richard the Earl of Desmond. I know that Elizabeth was not an idle pawn in this match because she was hardly the type of woman who would allow a marriage with which she did not agree. Now that she had a properly titled husband, King James then awarded Elizabeth most of the Ormond estate. Young Elizabeth had succeeded in her vow and remained in my walls as the mistress of Kilkenny. In years to come, her own daughter was to take a similar stand, with equal or perhaps even greater success, which I think should confirm that indeed this archaic principle of primogeniture, or succession by the male heirs, should have been abandoned years ago.

In time, I heard that Walter had managed to compound his problems in London. It seems he protested strongly at the injustice of the king's award of Ormond land because he claimed that it violated the basic principals of fairness upon which the earls held title from the crown. It was reported that he argued that if every estate was subject to the whims of the crown, the earls could not be expected to remain loyal. To the king's ear this sounded a great deal like treason and Walter paid the price. For his troubles, the king put him in prison for eight years and his grandsons were made wards of the crown.

While Walter languished in prison, no doubt praying for deliverance from this latest injustice, his grandsons benefited greatly as wards of the crown. The boys were educated as Protestants, much to Walter's further shame, and became great friends with kings and future kings.

As a result, when Walter died his grandson, James, became the twelfth earl of Ormond and, with the title, the ownership of my walls was returned to that Butler line. While the crown had no difficulty punishing Walter, it rewarded his grandson for the young man's continuing friendship and loyalty. This was to cause some confusion over the title to my walls because Elizabeth Butler Preston was not about to relinquish her claim but even that matter was eventually sorted out in a most agreeable manner.

III How I Survived War and Retribution (1640–1700)

When James returned to me as the newly designated Earl of Ormond, and apparent owner of my walls, he encountered Elizabeth Preston Butler. Elizabeth had not changed her position from that which she had declared to her own mother those many years ago and certainly had no interest in being shifted just because the king had decided to give the same property to two different people. What might have been the cause for a difficult confrontation was soon sorted, however, because James Butler took an immediate shine to Elizabeth Preston, the daughter of Elizabeth Butler Preston and grand-daughter of Black Tom, the tenth earl. Soon after the two married, making the new bride Elizabeth Preston Butler, the daughter of Elizabeth Butler Preston . . . I think. By making this marriage, James brought together the two factions of the family that had disputed the title a generation earlier and they all lived in harmony with all the comfort I could provide.

Like her mother, the second Elizabeth was herself a remarkable woman who had very strong views on her entitlements and her country, not all of which coincided with her husband's. In the earl's absence, my new mistress contributed her significant wisdom and common sense to the operation of my walls. Quite apart from everything else, you might be interested to know that Elizabeth Preston Butler, through her own daughter, also called Elizabeth, was a direct ancestor to the current English monarch, Queen Elizabeth II!

In the two hundred years that the Butlers had occupied my walls, there had never been a question about their loyalty to the English crown. The crown had placed them in a position of power and despite their growing wealth and influence, they never forgot the origins of their success. I respected that virtue and, when news of various events reached my walls, I often pondered how the residents of some other castles, like Blarney or Bunratty, could change loyalties as easily as a shift of the wind.

As the seventeenth century progressed, however, I was to discover that the rewards for loyalty to the crown are only as permanent as the crown itself. If, perchance, the crown were at risk, so would be the wealth – and indeed health – of those who so loyally supported it. James Butler, my then occupant as the twelfth Earl of Ormond

Here I am in the seventeenth century, still bearing the scars of Cromwell's cannon. You can see how James Butler, recently returned from France where he was in exile with Charles II, remodelled me in French chateau style.

continued this tradition of loyalty in no small measure because he had been educated in London and was a personal friend of both King Charles I and his eldest son, also called Charles. Upon returning to Ireland, he had been rewarded with the position of Lord Lieutenant and Commander of the English Army in Ireland. As a result, he spent very little time within my walls, which were then managed by an agent, the earl's cousin, the Viscount Mountgarret.

While the earl was absent conducting matters in the king's name, a large group of Old English Catholic property owners met in my great hall to discuss the difficulties that Catholics were facing in England and the effect those problems might have on Ireland.

'It appears,' Viscount Mountgarret began, 'that the English parliament has decided that, among other things, Charles is too accommodating to Catholics and therefore must go. Charles, of course, believes that the parliament must go. As for me, I know nothing good will come of it.'

A bishop in attendance then addressed the group, 'I trust that you all understand that as the London parliament goes, so goes Dublin. It should be abundantly clear that there is a very real possibility that your lands will be at risk if London and Dublin decide that the best way to keep you under control is to require that you lose your faith. You would undoubtedly lose your lands because I know that none of you would risk your immortal souls for the riches of this world.'

This pronouncement was met with several shouts of 'Never . . . never . . .'

I thought this speech remarkable as it was delivered in the castle of a Protestant but it seemed that everyone liked to believe that, in the privacy of the confessional, James was a Catholic and that public rumour to the contrary was only an expedient way to ensure the support of the crown.

The meeting progressed and, after additional speeches emphasised the detail of the difficulties faced by Catholics in London, Mountgarret rose once again and addressed the gathering.

'Gentlemen,' he began scanning the group in an attempt to catch each man's eye. 'I recommend that we establish an alternate parliament, here in this fine castle, and pass whatever measures are necessary to protect our interests.'

'But what of the king?' one man shouted. 'It is the king who established the Dublin parliament. Is that not treason?'

Mountgarret responded quickly, 'Not at all. Our first loyalty is to the crown, of course. We will sit and govern this country in trust for the king, taking whatever measures are necessary to defend our lands and castles, all in the name of the king. But we can't allow a parliament sitting in Dublin to do to us what London is doing to the Catholic landowners of England.'

And so it was that the Confederation of Kilkenny was born. A Supreme Council was elected and a bureaucracy was established to administer the civil, legal and military affairs of the country. For six years – from 1642 until 1648 – the council met in my great hall to make decisions about the governance of the country and, as a practical matter, I was the capital of Ireland.

James, the twelfth earl, was not pleased with my being used in this way because, while the confederates protested that they were loyal to the crown, he regarded their action as a breach of trust with the king. Soon after, he met with many of the landowners, including his cousins, within my walls. While James voiced his disapproval, the support for the confederation was so strong that there was little he could do. James held legal power from the crown but, without the support of his family, including his wife, he would lose practical control of his many estates, including myself.

When the discussion had concluded, James announced, 'Well now, you realise that I cannot endorse your confederation regardless of my sympathies. On the other hand, we don't want to fall out again over this and end up at each other's throats like the O'Briens in Bunratty. I will continue in service to the crown and attempt to impress on the king your own bona fides. With the problems in London, I suspect that our interests may meet at the end of the day.'

In the years that followed, I was to see very little of James as he continued to campaign in various parts of Ireland. I did hear reports which made it clear that he was not altogether successful in gaining the crown's acceptance for the confederation but then he did broker a peace which held for a few years.

One person who did call on my walls in 1645 was Cardinal John

Baptist Rinuccini, the Papal Nuncio, who had been sent by Pope Innocent X to rally the Confederation of Catholic Landowners. The cardinal spent a pleasant couple of days enjoying the best hospitality I could offer while he discussed the group's successes and failures. I do remember that several confederation council members suggested that the cause might be best helped if the Holy Father could see his way clear to assist with the funding of the cause.

The cardinal responded with a shrug of his shoulders and upraised hands, 'Ah . . . but you see, I have no authority to speak of such matters.' Soon after he continued his journey and I understood that his next stop was to be Bunratty Castle where McCarthy of Blarney was laying siege on behalf of the confederation.

Unfortunately for both the Confederate cause, and my earl James, who was leading the Royalists as the king's Lord Lieutenant, Oliver Cromwell took power in England in 1648. King Charles I was promptly executed and, a few months later, Cromwell invaded Ireland. The word soon reached my walls that Cromwell was massacring Catholic garrisons and townspeople throughout the eastern part of the country and no one seemed willing, or able, to stand in his way. As the earl had predicted, the cause of the Confederation of Catholic Landowners and that of the Royalists were now one and the same but neither side had the strength or the will to continue the fight. Cromwell marched unhindered toward Kilkenny.

I well recall the day in 1651 that Cromwell's Roundhead army appeared at my walls. As there was no army to protect me, my gates were bolted and the meagre force defending me took to my ramparts. I was cautiously optimistic that I could withstand a siege but at the same time I feared the worst because I had never really been tested. I also knew that in many respects I had become more a mansion than a stronghold but I still had my drum towers and my curtain walls.

My fears turned out to be far more justified than my optimism and I was shocked when Cromwell's big guns roared and a massive breach suddenly appeared in my east curtain wall. Then they roared again, and the top half of my northeast tower was blown off. They roared one more time and another hole appeared in the same tower. Even now, three centuries later, it is difficult for me to describe how I felt.

Surprise, shock, pain, amazement and disbelief were all mixed into the cocktail of my emotions. It should come as no surprise, that Cromwell and his troops needed no siege because the battle was over in a matter of minutes. When the dust had settled, a Colonel Axtell ruled from my walls as military governor.

I remember little of the days under Cromwell's control except that the colonel was one of the cruellest human beings I have ever encountered. He had decided that the earl must have a hoard of riches secreted on my grounds and that this treasure would be his reward for his efforts. When an initial search did not disclose the location of the hoard, Axtell took an ancient retainer called George, who had once been the earl's manservant, and demanded that he produce his master's treasure and when George was unable to deliver, Axtell tortured him. Since the earl had long ago removed his wealth from my walls, there was nothing the old man could disclose but his denials fell on deaf ears, and soon he was dead.

Following the defeat of the Royalists by Cromwell, my James Butler went into exile in France with Charles II, who had succeeded his father, and others who had also supported Charles including McCarthy of Blarney and Talbot of Malahide. Cromwell ordered that the estates of all his enemies, which certainly included myself, be forfeited to himself as Lord Protector of England. Enforcing this order was another thing altogether, however, because Cromwell did not count on the iron will of my remarkable mistress, Elizabeth Preston Butler.

'You will surrender title to this castle and vacate within the fortnight,' Axtell snarled. 'Your husband who held these lands is a traitor and, by royal decree, his land is forfeit to the crown.'

'Your are mistaken,' Elizabeth replied. 'I hold these lands by my own right as heir to Thomas Butler, the tenth Earl of Ormond. I did not rise against Cromwell and it was he that destroyed my castle totally without cause. I require compensation.'

'You what?' Axtell roared. 'Your husband is a traitor and Cromwell demands reparations. This land is forfeit.'

Elizabeth calmly responded, 'If you have a complaint against my husband, I would suggest you confront him. I believe he is in France. As for my property and me, what he did or did not do is none of my affair nor does it impact on what I hold in my own right. I have personally written to Cromwell to make this perfectly clear. I would suggest that you tread softly for he will surely see the justice in my case.'

I do not know whether her appeal to Cromwell was favourably received or whether, perhaps, he had better things to attend to but Elizabeth remained in residence within my walls throughout the years Cromwell was in power. I discovered that my brother castle, Blarney, and my sister, Malahide, were not so fortunate and passed into the hands of Cromwellian Roundheads. This is not to say those were pleasant years for Elizabeth and her family because Axtell took possession of the earl's apartment, but neither did she have further difficulties with him. From time to time Elizabeth received correspondence from Cromwell or his administrator indicating that her claim was under investigation. Whenever Axtell caused problems, she would display the letter and warn him of the dire consequences he would incur when her claim was allowed.

Within a decade, Cromwell was dead and the Royalists were restored to power in England and subsequently in Ireland. When Charles II was proclaimed king in May 1660 there were great celebrations within my walls and my earl James returned in triumph. While exiled in France, Charles had anointed James as the first Duke of Ormonde, which supplemented his title as twelfth Earl of Ormond. His wife, Elizabeth, thought that the addition of the *e* to the identification was 'just plain silly'. However, subsequent generations bore the new spelling in respect for the years James spent in exile.

While James was more often in residence within my walls after the restoration of the monarchy, I saw little change in day-to-day life because Elizabeth continued to govern the household affairs. I do not recall her ever again asserting her personal claim to the estate but as she had successfully defended the land and ensured the children of James and herself would inherit the estate, perhaps it made no difference. What did make a difference to Elizabeth was the condition and status of my walls.

Since she had so nobly defended me in those troubled times and had lived with few of the comforts to which she had become accustomed, Elizabeth determined that, with my restoration to the Butler family, I would lack for nothing. I would be totally remodelled as a permanent reminder of the couple's wealth and success. Workmen soon arrived to transform my walls, but this time I was to become the most elegant French chateau imaginable.

My eastern wall, which had been destroyed by Cromwell's guns, was removed in its entirety, completely eliminating my fortress aspect. I understood that similar work was undertaken by the mistress of Malahide as neither woman wanted to see their treasured castles subjected to future siege or assault. An attempt was made to restore my northeast tower but it had been too badly damaged so it was removed and replaced with two smaller drum towers to enclose the eastern wall.

Perhaps my most impressive additions were a vast collection of expensive furnishings, including intricately carved furniture, expensive mirrors covered with inlaid stones and silver, a number of Chinese and Japanese porcelains and beautiful French tapestries and wall hangings. Elizabeth then commissioned the finest French chefs from Paris who completely changed my kitchen and prepared food of a quality that had never before been presented in Ireland.

The earl himself completely supported the project and took a particular interest in the gardens and grounds outside my walls. He imported a wide range of exotic and interesting trees and plants and the grounds soon became the talk of the county. James also paved the courtyard adding magnificent gates and fountains. Finally the duke began to collect family portraits and other works of art that were of interest to him and installed them in a gallery he had constructed for that purpose.

When the work had been completed, my residents entertained in grand style and everyone marvelled at my transformation. Of course this entertainment was an important part to the duke's continuing duties to the crown because it was a demonstration of his wealth and political power. There were times when as many as two hundred gentlemen gathered within my walls and they were not only easily accommodated but treated with the most gracious hospitality.

The duke served another term as Lord Lieutenant of Ireland which ended in 1682 when, at the age of seventy-two, he retired to my walls, having never faltered in his loyalty to English kings. When he finally died, six years later, his remains were removed for burial in Westminster Abbey.

Shortly before the duke's death, word reached my walls that King Charles II had died and had been succeeded by his brother, James II. James was a Catholic and his determination to restore the rights of English Catholics meant that the parliament in London treated him in a similar fashion to that accorded to his father. The English Protestants again overthrew their king, this time in favour of his son-in-law, William of Orange. When, in late 1688, William landed in England with an army of fifteen thousand, James escaped into exile in France, fortunately with his head still on his shoulders.

I can still hear the collective groans of the older retainers and staff, as the news was a constant topic of conversation. 'Not again,' they said. As for my own reaction, I had only just recovered from the first of these disputes and had finally begun to enjoy the chance to provide unparalleled hospitality to my residents. The last thing I wanted was another war.

The second Duke of Ormonde was also called James and succeeded his grandfather to the title and ownership of my walls. His father, Thomas, who died before the first James and so did not succeed to the title, had been a sailor and bore the title Duke of Ossory. In the early days of his ownership, my second duke James added to my grounds with the erection of a handsome gatehouse in the classical style, but he soon tired of the life of a country gentleman and returned to his first love, because, first and foremost, James was a soldier.

In the years that followed, the second duke James, like his grandfather, spent very little time in my walls because he was fighting primarily to defend English causes in Europe. Like his father, the second duke was a personal friend of William of Orange and had served with him in Europe. In those days William had been a strong ally of King Charles II and the future King James II and he had married James' daughter, the Princess Mary. Because of the Butlers' personal loyalty to William, it was not surprising that duke James would continue to support him when William returned to England and assumed the crown.

Meanwhile, the duke's cousin, Lord Galmoye who was not only a Catholic but also a strong supporter of King James, administered my walls. Galmoye, you may recall, was a descendant of Black Tom (and perhaps Queen Elizabeth). On several occasions, Lord Galmoye met Richard Talbot, the Lord Tyrconnell, within my walls so I heard a great deal about the inevitable conflict. Tyrconnell came from the family that owned Malahide and was in charge of King James's army in Ireland. Since this army was overwhelmingly Catholic, Tyrconnell was confident that he could hold Ireland for James and, hopefully, assist the king in the retaking of his kingdom. Of course, he made it clear that anyone who supported the king would be well rewarded.

Although Galmoye knew well where my title owner's loyalties lay, he was prompt in pledging his support for King James. When his wife questioned his decision, Galmoye assured her that, when James was successful, he would take permanent control of my walls as Duke of Ormonde. Shortly after, in 1689, King James came to Ireland and made his way up to my walls.

I remember King James as a shortish man with a long nose and stylish wig. He was, of course welcomed to my walls with all the hospitality my occupants could provide. At the meal which was presented, he marvelled at the excellence of the food remarking that he had not tasted the equal of it even during his years of exile in Paris. After the meal, the business of the upcoming battle was the topic of conversation.

The king himself said very little but leaned back in his chair, one arm draped over the back, fanning himself with a kerchief. Tyrconnell did most of the talking assuring Galmoye and the other Butlers who had attended that all was in proper order and the battle would most certainly be won. A massive army had apparently been assembled from clans, Norman and Irish, all over the country and they would all converge on William and destroy him before he could establish himself in Ireland. After arranging for the recruitment of troops from in and around my walls and confirming their presence when the time came, King James, Tyrconnell and their large complement of retainers continued on their way to Dublin.

In June of the following year, 1690, Lord Galmoye marched out with great ceremony at the head of his troops to join King James in his fight against William. Like many of the troops that marched from my brother and sister castles around Ireland, Galmoye did not return, although a few stragglers made their way to my walls and were able to tell what had happened.

As you probably know, King James and his forces were defeated on the banks of a river called the Boyne and the powerful force that had so confidently ridden out was now crawling back to their homes. William, the King of England, was now in nearly full control of Ireland as well because all challenges to his crown had died at the Boyne.

While I was certainly distressed that misfortune should fall upon any of my residents, I was not concerned about my own position because my titleholder, James Butler, the thirteenth Earl of Ormond and the second Duke of Ormonde, fought gallantly with King William and it was to him that the spoils were due.

Despite this, I must admit that I was surprised when, a few weeks later, the duke arrived at my walls in the company of King William himself. The feast that was laid on for the king was, without question, the greatest celebration that I ever saw. All of the finery that had been acquired by the first duke was displayed to its greatest effect and the French chefs created a feast of no fewer than ten courses, each of which was more impressive than the last. Only the finest of wine was served and, in time, the entire group was dancing and singing.

Like King James II, William was a smallish man who wore a stylish black wig, but he was remarkable in that he appeared to be slightly hunched over. Although he did not join in the dancing, it was clear to me that he genuinely enjoyed himself. It was also obvious that the duke and himself were fast friends who, after months of campaigning, could finally enjoy themselves.

As I think back on those days, I take particular pride in the fact that I provided the most gracious of hospitality to two English kings in a matter of less than a year and both left, marvelling at the beauty and grace of my walls. In some respects, the visit of King William was the last event in the golden years of my greatest glory. Little did I know that it would be nearly three hundred years before I would again approach the glamour of that day, fit enough to host the king of the British Empire. And yet I knew I should be thankful because, while other castles were reduced to ruins after the Jacobite Wars, I survived and never again knew war or destruction.

IV How I Became a Modern Showpiece (1700–Present)

For some years, James the second Duke of Ormonde served King William III and William's successor, Queen Anne, first in Ireland and then in Spain. Queen Anne appointed him Viceroy of Ireland so he was often within my walls because, I am proud to say, he particularly enjoyed the comfort I provided. In fairness, James himself had a great interest in my condition and he frequently ordered works by way of repairs or improvements. In time he returned again to England and served as Captain General in the queen's forces fighting in Spain. His long and loyal service was not, however, to be rewarded with a quiet retirement in Kilkenny.

Queen Anne gained the throne in peculiar circumstances. As often happened during those days the succession to the English throne was never particularly clear. The most recent Stewart to hold the throne was James II and he claimed its rights as did the line created by William and his queen, Mary. As the Catholic problem was a thing of the past, the English parliament was no longer enamoured with William, so they also took a view on the succession. In 1701 they passed a law that the crown must be held by an English Anglican, so neither William III nor James II qualified. When William died, the crown went to Anne. You see she was also the daughter of James II through his Protestant marriage, but she had supported her sister (King William's wife, Mary). Parliament had no difficulty returning the throne to the Stewarts, because she met the standards set in the 1701 law.

I would not pretend to understand all of the various interests and claims but it did affect the ownership of my own walls because, as you have seen, title to the land on which I stand was held at the pleasure of the English crown. Therefore, if one of my earls chose the wrong side, he would find himself without a title, without land and potentially without a head.

As the crown jewel in the Ormonde empire, matters of succession and control were a constant topic of conversation among the administrators and occupants of my walls so I was well informed on what had transpired. My second Duke of Ormonde, James, who had fought with King William and hosted him within my walls, fell afoul of the crown when he chose the wrong side after the death of Queen

Anne in 1714. In choosing to support the Stewarts, as descendents of King James II, over George I, he was judged to be a traitor to the crown and fled into exile where he died in Rome some years later.

Meanwhile his title and property, including my walls, were forfeited to the crown. By rights of succession, they could have been claimed by James's brother, Charles, who was the Earl of Arran. However, after considering the delicate balance that had landed his brother in disfavour, Charles decided he was happy enough with the title and lands he had. As Charles declined the Ormonde title, although legally he became the third duke whether he liked it or not, he passed the lands on to his sister, Amelia, who was a threat to no one. On her death shortly after at the age of ninety-nine, my walls passed to her son, John, who was no spring chicken himself. When Charles died without heirs, the title of Duke of Ormonde was extinguished. As for my walls, I remained in the Butler family and was now in the ownership of a John Butler.

John lived in a place called Kilcash far south of my walls, over the mountains and nearly in County Waterford. As a result, he spent very little time as a resident of mine and, I am sorry to say, the agents who did occupy me, spent very little effort in maintaining the beauty and comfort which was my pride. In time, my furnishings no longer shone brightly and the dampness began to creep into my brick and wood, especially when the fires that used to burn in every room were no long tended. Because I had watched so many of my residents grow old, particularly women who had once been so strong, I believe I understood what was happening to me. As little pains became bigger pains, dampness caused small cracks that became bigger cracks. As skin wrinkles and paint peels, the beauty and vitality of youth is exchanged for the wisdom of age – albeit with no shortage of aches and pains.

I had seen a great deal in my years of splendour and I well understood the people who lived in my walls. Unfortunately, I had no more control over my own destiny than humans would have over the passing of time. Without human interest and concern, a building will slowly disintegrate in the same way as time slowly takes its toll on the human body. I must say this was particularly depressing for a lady who had so recently, in terms of my age, been at the prime of her existence.

I also can certainly understand that money is an important commodity to human beings and it takes a great deal of it to maintain me in the style to which I had become accustomed. I suppose, at the end of the day, lack of money was the biggest cause of my deterioration.

When John died, his cousin Walter became the fifteenth Earl of Ormond. Not believing his good fortune, Walter immediately moved from Garryricken to occupy my walls. Walter was sixty-three years old and spent a great deal of time wandering around my walls talking to himself. I was never quite clear on what he mumbled about but it sounded remarkably like, 'This is mine, and this is also mine.' Walter had some money so he made modest improvements and, since he was a staunch Catholic, the first of his projects was my chapel. Walter enjoyed running his dogs through the grounds outside my walls but, as he grew older, he paid less and less attention to my condition and I continued to deteriorate.

When he died eighteen years later in 1783, my next earl – his son John – had the good fortune to marry an heiress named Anne Wandesford, the daughter of Viscount Castlecomer and Earl of Wandesford, and the two moved into my walls. Anne was plump and homely but, in addition to her money, she was remarkably good humoured and a wonderful wife and mother. John recognised the importance of the family title and had the old family dignities restored assuming the mantle of sixteenth Earl of Ormond.

I was delighted to see that I was, once again, a home for a family, which eventually included eight boys and two girls. I was also pleased that my occupants could afford to return me to good health. Over the next few years much of my mistress's fortune was spent in not only restoring my walls but in building a stable and dower house. They also spent a considerable amount of money on the gardens and courtyards beyond my walls and, for a time, the splendour had returned.

With the restoration project well underway, John and Anne entertained friends and acquaintances and my walls rang out with the sound of laughter and music and the tinkle of crystal at dinner parties carried on well into the night. With Anne in charge of the feast, entertainment and libations, each party seemed to be an amazing success and John soon became known as Jack o'the Castle. I found it remarkable that Anne, with all of her children, could manage such affairs because, although she did have an extensive staff, my mistress attended to every detail.

John, on the other hand, when not assuming his seat in the House of Lords or entertaining in his own home seemed to have acquired a reputation for enjoying himself in various establishments in London, Dublin and Kilkenny City. This reputation did not always serve him well. I remember one guest who called to my great hall about ten years after John had been installed. The man, who was called Jonah Barrington and who was, I must say, particularly impressed with my condition, had not been invited for entertainment.

Barrington was a sharp-featured man, clean-shaven with closely cropped hair and no wig, as was the style of the day. Barrington was a barrister of some skill and later I was to hear reports concerning his career as a politician and writer but for the moment he called in a professional capacity.

'And what, pray tell, am I being accused of?' my occupant enquired of his guest.

Barrington responded, 'Outrage, as it happens. You will recall sending a glazier to repair the windows of one Doctor Duffy.'

'Of course I do,' John replied, 'because it was the proper thing to do. I was in company with a number of associates at an entertainment establishment operated by the Widow Madden, and Doctor Duffy became the subject of one young man's attempts at humour. I was long gone at the time but my son told me that someone in the group, having had far too much to drink, threw a stone through the good doctor's window. I thought it best to address the matter promptly.'

'Well, it seems the good doctor has named not only your son and his cronies but yourself as well. Are you confident that you were not in company when the incident occurred?' Barrington enquired.

John paused for a moment considering the question before replying, 'I was certainly not present when any such conduct occurred. I would not have tolerated it.'

'Yes, I thought as much,' Barrington replied. 'Duffy has apparently taken your gesture in paying for the repairs as an admission of guilt and is claiming in the courts. I will certainly handle the brief and I have little doubt your reputation will remain unsullied.'

Barrington's word was good and I discovered that the matter ended to my resident's satisfaction. It seems that, in those days, people made claims for the silliest reasons but when I discovered the size of Barrington's statement for services, it was clear that the legal profession had no difficulty with that practice.

The succession of Butlers that followed throughout the nineteenth century were generally well heeled and, although I suffered from the maladies of ageing, I never returned to the derelict state in which I had found myself seventy-five years earlier. Most of my residents were educated among the elite of England and were well known to the royal family. They took their seats in the House of Lords and assumed all of their honours including Earl of Ormonde, Marquess of Ormonde, Earl of Ossory, Viscount Thurles and, of course, Chief Butler of Ireland.

Their wealth came from tenants who rented ground on the hundreds of acres they owned in Kilkenny and Tipperary. Having said that, Walter of the stone-throwing crowd supplemented his wealth by selling off the family entitlement to a duty on wine that had been in the family for nearly five hundred years. It seems that the estate income was not enough to meet his entertainment expenses so he accepted two hundred and sixteen thousand pounds to relinquish this entitlement.

These earls returned to my walls for rest and relaxation and to entertain their well-born friends from London. Because the purpose of this entertainment was to impress friends and associates, I certainly benefited from the money that was spent to ensure that I always looked my best. At one point in the mid-nineteenth century, my resident earl, called John, decided that, if I were a medieval castle, I should look more like a medieval castle rather than a French chateau.

I recall the earl discussing the matter with his builder when the plans were being drawn. 'You see, Edward, this baronial style is the rage of London and it just won't do for us to be seen as old fashioned.'

'But you do understand,' Edward replied, 'that this will entail removing the chateau roofs from all of the drum towers. I can't imagine what that might cost. You can't just go out and order people to build castle like they did when this place was first constructed.'

John stared at his builder, 'Never mind the cost. Does Windsor

Here I am today with open walls to welcome visitors from all over the world.

Castle have a chateau roof? I should say not. What I want is a castle that will speak of chivalry and knights in shining armour from the days of old. I want this castle to look like it jumped right out of a Walter Scott novel. Do I make myself clear?'

Apparently Edward understood and the construction work began. I can't say I was particularly pleased with the result but, of course, I had little to say about it.

The work included building up the height of my towers and castellating them so that one could envisage the knights who once stood in those same towers shooting arrows onto their attackers. Machicolations, or platforms that overhung my walls, were added so that one could imagine the knights dumping boiling oil down murder holes and onto attackers below. While the effect might have been to create romantic memories of times past, I found the additions rather distasteful, rather gruesome in fact. But then, I can remember what those days were truly like. Other additions included constructing rather peculiar balconied windows along the north front of my walls presumably to provide guests with more interesting vistas of Kilkenny City.

In fairness, my interior was also modernised so that I could present a more hospitable environment for my guests and I certainly had no complaints about that. After all, I had long ago ceased to be a defensive stronghold and my sole purpose as a castle was to provide comfort to those would call to me. A beautiful white Cararra marble chimney piece was added to the long gallery and many fine works of art were acquired to grace my walls. A beautiful Moorish staircase gave access to my upper floors and many other details were added to my walls and ceilings. All of these additions cost a great deal of money but certainly made me a favourite destination for the wealthy people of England.

I trust that you will not think that, during those days when my walls were being lavished with the wealth of the Butlers, I knew nothing about the people who supplied that wealth. As an Irish castle, I cannot say that my occupants were blameless for the suffering and death that accompanied the years in the middle of the nineteenth century when the potato crop failed. Certainly the matter was discussed within my walls and I have no doubt that my residents could have done much more had they chosen to. After all, their expenditures on my walls made it clear that they were not impoverished as so many Irish people were.

The labourers who worked on the estate constructing walls and maintaining my buildings were paid more than just the price of a meal, although it was hardly a living wage. I also know that, in many cases, my occupants or their agents reduced or waived rents for their tenants and arranged passage for tenants who sought a new life in America. When my resident earl, called John, died suddenly in 1854, the Bishop of Ossory said that he did not leave an enemy behind him, which was certainly a testimony to his popularity even among his tenants.

Among the guests who were welcomed to my walls at the turn of the twentieth century were King Edward VII and his wife Queen Alexandra who were entertained by my twenty-first earl, James Butler. I do generally recall the fine banquet that was presented to honour my royal guests but I specifically recall a moment at the end of the meal when James rose and knelt at the side of his king's chair.

With tears in his eyes James offered the king his cup and said, 'Sire, I am still your loyal and faithful butler. Please take my cup.'

The king put his arm out and after resting it on my occupant's shoulder for a moment thanked him for the gesture, 'I am truly moved my dear James. Your are more than our butler, you are our friend.'

A few years later Edward's successor, George V, and his queen, Mary, also visited my walls, impressed no doubt by the story of the earlier royal visit. On that occasion, the earl and his guests spent many pleasant hours shooting on the grounds beyond my walls but they returned for the hospitality my kitchen and dining room was proud to provide.

As the king and the earl relaxed over port and cigars, King George remarked, 'Most extraordinary James, most extraordinary indeed. I must say we never dreamed we would see the likes of this grand castle in the wilds of Ireland.'

'My family has served the crown from these walls for six hundred years,' the earl replied, 'so I raise my glass to the crown that has indulged my family for all these years and to my family who have built this castle as monument to the crown.'

'Here, here,' the king replied raising his own glass.

Those visits were perhaps my last opportunities to provide a grand scale of hospitality to the families that owned and occupied my walls. The twentieth century not only brought changes to the way in which people lived, but it also brought changes to the country in which I have so proudly stood. While the Butlers were Irish to the extent that they were occasionally born in Ireland and had owned property in Ireland for hundreds of years, their loyalties were always to the English crown. The Butlers, for all their wealth, were perfectly content that Ireland remain a part of England, a sentiment not shared by the majority of Irish people.

In fairness to my residents, they were not particularly affected by the disturbances that many landlords experienced because, as a rule, they were fair and well respected by their tenants. Nevertheless, they recognised that their lives would never be the same as they had been in the past. Nearly every day, I heard them discuss Irish leaders who were demanding a total reform of the land system so that tenants would own their own land. They also discussed arguments that were being made for Home Rule and even total independence from England. Most importantly, the Butlers realised that these leaders did not represent a small minority of the Irish people, but a majority.

My occupants' response could be best summarised by a statement made by my then resident Arthur Butler one morning, 'We shall continue to live as we have always lived. We shall respect our tenants and neighbours and do nothing that might cause them to do us harm. Beyond that, whatever happens is in the hands of God.'

And so my occupants lived a quiet life during the first two decades of the twentieth century. There were no great parties and the royal visits were the last I saw of dignitaries from England. A number of my rooms were closed and the furnishings either removed for safekeeping or covered with protective cloth and the Butlers resided only in the rooms they needed to be comfortable, when they were in residence at all.

I do remember a day in May of 1922 when the troubles caught up with my walls. George, my current earl's brother, was sleeping peacefully when his butler knocked urgently at the door, 'I do beg you pardon, sir,' he said, 'but it appears that the Republicans have taken the castle.'

'Indeed,' George replied, quickly donning his dressing gown and hurrying down to the reception hall. Confronting the leader of the attackers he said, 'I say, my good man, whatever do you think you are doing?'

The Republican smiled at the sight of the proper British gentleman having been awoken from his slumber and replied, 'We are claiming this castle in the name of the Irish people. We will provide you with a receipt for everything we take and, if you do what you are told, no one will be hurt.'

'What is it that you want?' George asked.

'Guns and ammunition,' was the prompt reply. 'Do you have any about?'

'Goodness no,' George said scratching his balding head. 'Whatever use would we have for guns and ammunition?'

'Hunting and shooting,' was the reasonable response.

'No, nothing like that,' George responded vaguely.

Whether or not the Republican chose to believe my resident is not clear but the group of soldiers immediately began a search of the house. In fairness although the search was thorough they did not cause any damage. Several hours later, the Free State forces arrived and surrounded the house. After a lapse of two hundred and fifty years, I was once again under siege.

The siege continued for nearly two days because the Free State troops did not want to rush my walls for fear of causing injury to my residents. The Republicans had no way to escape and not enough weapons to fight their way clear. Given the circumstances it appeared to me that the siege might go on for some time. The Butlers were gracious hosts to their captors and soon pots of tea were provided with bread and plenty of jam. The Republicans ate as if it might be their last meal and old George discussed their cause and debated the issues of the day with them. Being an old soldier himself, the young men certainly did not intimidate him and, in time, it was clear that Republicans respected their captive.

Ultimately, George negotiated a resolution in which the Republicans gave themselves up on the solemn promise to George personally that they would not be shot outright. When the Republican's left, each shook George's hand and everyone agreed that no harm had been done.

With the cessation of the War of Independence and the end of the Civil War that followed, life returned to normal within my walls. The difference, however, was that I was now part of a different country. My residents were not disturbed in their occupancy but their way of life, and certainly the massive income they once received from tenant farmers, was gone. The cost of maintaining my walls could not be supported from the Butlers' income and, in 1935, they decided to leave me.

It was a sad day for me when, after nearly six hundred years, the Butlers finally moved from my walls. What they did not take with them was sold at a massive auction conducted over eight days in November 1935. When it was over, I was vacant, stripped and abandoned, a sorry state for one who had given so much and had so much more to give.

A few years later I found myself a barracks for the Irish army during the Emergency of the late 1930s and early 1940s but, apart from that, I stood empty and derelict like so many castles dotting the Irish countryside that had outlived their usefulness. My owners, the Butlers, could not afford to pay even the most basic costs of maintenance and restoration was totally out of the question. Fortunately for me, this condition was not to remain uncorrected.

In 1976 Arthur, the twenty-fourth Earl of Ormond, sold my walls and ground to the Irish government for fifty pounds and my new life had begun. Soon after, generous contributions began to flow in as nearly everyone wanted to see my walls returned to their legendary grandeur. Although it took nearly ten years, my roofs were repaired or replaced, my brickwork was repaired and my finishes were restored to a level of beauty that I had never known. Many of the pictures and furnishings that had been sold forty years earlier were returned to my walls and I became a living museum. Within my walls, the people of Ireland and the world can enjoy my hospitality and experience what it was like to live amidst the grandeur of one of Ireland's finest castles.

And so you find me here in my present state, my dear friends. For well over eight hundred years I have been pleased to provide comfort, safety and hospitality to my residents and all who might visit my walls.

I am proud to be counted among Ireland's strongholds – different perhaps than my brother and sister castles, but how boring it would be if we were all the same. Just as I have enjoyed the past centuries, even in the hardest times, I look forward to many more years of welcome and hospitality.

BLARNEY CASTLE

~

I Early Days and the Source of my Power (1150–1600)

Well, I never thought I'd see the day when human beings might actually listen to castle walls telling our stories and yet . . . here I am. Of course, while any castle in Ireland, from Antrim to Cork or from Clare to Dublin could tell people stories, it should be perfectly clear that no castle in all the world is better equipped to provide erudite and particularly interesting information, factual of course, than yours truly, Blarney Castle.

'Why should this be the case?' you might reasonably enquire. Well now, I'll tell you now starting from the beginning. My existence began in the twelfth century as little more than a wooden hut surrounded by a wall of pointed sticks and piled rocks, which were primarily used to keep out wild animals. My job was to provide warmth and shelter to a noble clan called the McCarthys – a job, I might add, that I accomplished with unequalled skill. My life was simple in those days, the idyllic life of a small holding on the banks of the Blarney river amidst the rolling woodlands of Cork. Little did I know back then that I was destined for far greater things.

In 1118 Turlough O'Connor, acting as High King of Ireland, divided Munster between Donal O'Brien in the North and my own resident chieftain, Cormac McCarthy who became king of south Munster. (I should warn you that Cormac was a very popular name among my resident McCarthys so I hope that you will not be confused when it emerges with some regularity.) Anyway, the O'Briens ultimately took over a castle called Bunratty in what is now County Clare. Over the years I was to hear a great deal about this brother castle because the O'Briens were always warring with someone, or each other, and in such cases it is always the castle that takes the beating.

I was now also a king's castle and, over the next several years, various minor works were undertaken to strengthen my perimeter walls but very little was done with my primary structure. For all the presence of a king, I certainly did not feel any different except that there were far more people who came to live in the vicinity of my walls. Eventually that was to change but not without two generations of continuous suggestion by the wives of Cormac's sons Dermod and Donnell, who insisted, quite properly I might add, that the castle of a king should have more than wooden walls. You see, in the year 1170, people called the Normans had invaded Ireland and soon after they began to build massive stone and rock strongholds that would withstand attacks by great armies who would not be able to get inside. My mistresses thought that such a home would be far more secure and certainly more impressive that a wooden house.

These persistent recommendations finally took root when Finghin McCarthy began to construct proper stone walls in the early part of the thirteenth century. Unfortunately, Finghin only lasted three years because, while he doted on his wife, Grainne, and would willingly provide whatever she required, she did not provide much in the way of nocturnal gratification. Finghin, having heard rumours about a Norman custom called *droit de seigneur* (wherein the master of an estate was somehow entitled to deflower virgins within his demesne), decided that this was the answer to his frustration.

'You see, my dear wife,' he explained, 'the French in Normandy have apparently discovered that this practice assists in maintaining the good order of the subjects by creating a relationship between the local wives and the chieftain. In addition, the occasional child that might arise from the union assists in keeping the bloodlines strong.'

Grainne was well able to understand the true reason for the practice but she had her own agenda, 'That is all very well, dear husband,' she replied, 'but I assume that you will not be bothering me in the middle of the night with your, how do you put it, "natural male requirements".'

Finghin was relieved at her response but added, 'I hope you don't think for one second that I will actually enjoy this task. Rather I am undertaking it purely in the best interests of my clan and my people.'

'Perish the thought,' Grainne said, rolling her eyes, 'perish the thought.'

Despite Grainne's tacit approval, Finghin's people were not as agreeable and killed him and that was the end of *droit de seigneur* – in Blarney anyway. His three brothers – Dermod Cluasach, Cormac Fionn, and Donell Gott – succeeded Finghin and, by 1210, my wooden walls were replaced with stone and I had become a proper castle, although certainly not of the size I was to become.

My walls in those days were only two storeys high and I was essentially a rectangular stone hall-house but, as I was constructed high on a limestone rock, I provided a far greater level of security and comfort for my residents.

Since I was now a stronghold of the McCarthys, my residents consolidated their power and a number of forays set out from my walls to wage war against the invasion of the Normans who had conquered Britain after a battle in 1066 and were now spreading around Ireland. I clearly remember a great victory celebration in 1261 when Donell Gott's son, also Finghin, defeated the Normans at a battle in Kerry and, as a result, under traditional Irish laws of succession, his cousin Donell Roe McCarthy ruled undisturbed for forty years.

While the McCarthys consolidated their power in south Munster, they also entered into alliances with kings from other parts of Ireland and so I hosted several feasts celebrating these friendships. I recall one such celebration because the guest of honour was not Irish at all but little did I know that it would set into motion a series of events which would bestow me with the international acclaim I enjoy to this day.

My resident chieftain in the early 1300s was called Cormac McCarthy and he became acquainted with Richard De Burgh, the Red Earl of Ulster, who controlled most of the northern half of Ireland from his castle in Carrickfergus. De Burgh's daughter, Elizabeth, had married a Scotsman, Robert Bruce, much to the disgust of the Red Earl because Bruce was an enemy of the English King Edward I and De Burgh was supposedly loyal to the king. Robert Bruce sought allies for his cause and Cormac invited him to spend some time within my walls to see if some accommodation could be reached.

As you would expect from walls the quality of myself, the hospitality provided was second to none as hunting parties and sporting events occupied the days while the nights included several banquets. The final banquet was among the greatest ever presented within my walls.

As always, the feast was conducted in my great hall, a cavernous room in the centre of my domain, where my walls were covered in animal skins to keep out the cold. At one end of the room there was a raised platform for the king and his honoured guests while at the other end were massive fireplaces where the meals were cooked. Along the walls were tables for lesser dignitaries and the middle was kept clear for serving the food and facilitating the entertainment. The fare for the feast was primarily the produce of the hunt, including venison, wild boar, pheasant and rabbit but it also included fish, breads, cheeses and, of course, great quantities of mead. The entertainment included musicians, bards and storytellers and it continued until the dawn began to illuminate my walls. Finally my great hall fell into a satiated slumber and the dogs were blessed with the remains of the feast. The last conversation I recall was, of all things, Robert Bruce explaining the lessons that could be learned from the persistence of spiders.

'It wasn't that long ago,' Robert began, his eyes half closed and a goblet of mead resting on his chest, 'that I was ruined by King Eddie and hiding out with my brother Edward in a cave on Rathlin Island. I thought my world had come to an end, my wealth and position were gone and I was on the run.'

'So what did you do?' Cormac asked.

'Nothing, for a long time. Nothing but watch the rain through the entrance of the cave. But while I was doing that I noticed a spider weaving his web in one corner of the cave's entrance so I watched him for hours as I thought about my life. Funny thing, though, every time a strong and wet breeze blew, the web would be destroyed. That didn't stop the spider from continuing his task, because he just started all over again. I fell asleep after a while and when I awoke the sun was out.

I saw that the web was completed and the spider was feeding on a fat fly in its middle. That was the day, my friend,' he concluded, 'that was the day that my life began again and no matter how the gods might conspire against me, I will never give up.'

'Never give up!' Cormac replied raising his own goblet.

A moment later the remains of the cup were splashed on his robe and the two were snoring loudly. Quite apart from being allies, Bruce and McCarthy established a life-long bond of friendship that night.

Some years later, Robert Bruce called on that friendship and asked Cormac to provide troops to support him in his battle for the freedom of Scotland against Edward II, the King of England. Cormac obliged and four thousand men sailed for Scotland. On June 24, 1314, a date that for decades was annually celebrated within my walls, Bruce defeated Edward at a place called Bannockburn and became the King of the Scots. In thanking Cormac for his help, Bruce gave my resident a stone that was kept secure within my walls and some years later became part of me.

Generous, you might say. A stone in return for a kingdom . . . however, this was not just any old stone. It was half of the Stone of Scone, perhaps the most legendary stone in the human history of the world. As you would expect, we heard the entire story from the Stone of Scone herself when she came to reside with us and eventually became implanted in my walls.

'I was an ordinary stone,' she explained, 'and resided for centuries in the Middle East in what is now part of Egypt. One night a man named Jacob was resting his head against me when I felt a strange warm glow unlike anything I had experienced since my time began in the days of fire. An angel of the Lord occupied my every pore and from me created a vision for Jacob, a ladder into the heavens that in turn, gave him the power and eloquence to serve the Lord. When he awoke, I still glowed with this warmth and Jacob took me with him, as I was the conduit between himself and the angel. I was cared for by Jacob and his descendants as an honoured relic and it was I that Moses struck in the desert when the Lord told him to strike the Stone so that his people would have water.'

The Stone of Scone, who was called Jacob's Ladder in those days, told us that she never lost that angel's glow and she regaled us with the story of her life – how she travelled from Egypt to Assyria to Babylon to Italy to Spain and finally to Ireland and Tara where she was blessed by no less than St Patrick himself. Because of her ability to give wisdom and eloquence, the high kings of Ireland placed their thrones above her when they assumed power. She told us that in the mid-ninth century, King Kenneth I moved her to Scone in Scotland. And, although she moved several times within that country, she finally returned to Scone and was used to crown Scottish kings for another several hundred years. The stone explained that all this transport, and a particularly fat Scottish king, had eventually caused her to break in half. So while her twin embarked on another history finding herself in Westminster Abbey and finally Edinburgh Castle, Robert Bruce gave our stone to Cormac McCarthy as a reward for his support at Bannockburn.

For a hundred and twenty years the stone occupied a place of honour under the King's Chair in my own great hall and McCarthys were themselves crowned from that chair. There must have been some power in that stone because, despite the precarious times, my residents always seemed to make the proper alliances. Although there was great turmoil in other parts of Ireland, and my inhabitants forayed out to support their allies, I never came under attack in those years. Of course, between visiting messengers and my residents' own activities, I heard about attacks on other castles, particularly Bunratty and Kilkenny who were both razed on more than one occasion. Determined to spare me a similar fate, a decision was taken to reconstruct my walls on a far grander and more secure scale.

In 1446 Cormac Láidir (which means 'the strong') McCarthy, rebuilt me from the ground up and my walls today are much as they were when Cormac finished the job. The job took some years as skilled craftsmen and stonemasons from all over Munster descended on me to ensure that the job was properly completed. Apart from the ground floor, I was constructed from the inside out with each storey building on the previous one. I am sorry to say that a good few workers lost their lives in the effort particularly when the wind and the rain made completion of the upper floors difficult.

The stone from my old walls was used for my foundation and my configuration is rectangular in shape, sixty feet long by thirty-six feet wide. I am five storeys high reaching nearly eighty-five feet at my highest point and am twelve feet thick at my base tapering to a thickness of eight feet at my third floor. Access to the upper floors is only available by circular staircases set in my corners, constructed so that no more than one invader can emerge from the stairs at a time. My interior was fairly dark because the windows were tall and narrow allowing for archers to defend from within while presenting a small target for those outside. My battlements overhang my outside walls and, at various intervals, there is an opening, or murder hole, in the battlement floor so that defenders can shoot down onto invaders below or, perhaps dump all measure of junk on their heads.

As for the Stone of Scone, Cormac Láidir was concerned that in some future generation an invading force might capture her so he decided to make her part of my walls, locating her in an inaccessible place where she could not be damaged by attack or stolen. Cormac embedded the stone in the external side of one of the intervals in my battlements where she has become an integral part of me - no different than any other rock or stone that together create my walls. Of course, she still glows a warmth that now reaches to every part of my walls and it is from her I possess the legendary powers you may have heard about. Only today people all over the world would know her as the Blarney Stone, a perfectly reasonable name change if you ask me, as she is part of my legend.

Even though the stone had been part of me for nearly three hundred years, it was not until the late 1500s that the power it bestowed on me was officially recognised. My resident chieftain at the time was another Cormac (McTeige) McCarthy. Now this Cormac was, I suppose, what is known in the common parlance of today as a 'cute hoor', but then he would have to be considering the times.

On the other side of the Irish Sea, Elizabeth I was the Queen of England, a position she held from 1558 when she was crowned until 1603 when she died. Apparently she had inherited from her father, Henry VIII, a penchant for lopping off people's heads and it wouldn't do to annoy this queen. Elizabeth was excommunicated in 1570 so she was not popular with Catholics in Ireland, or Rome for that matter.

Cormac McTeige's first encounter with the queen ended to his advantage, primarily because my resident mistress more quickly developed a common-sense approach to dealing with the queen than did her husband.

From the discussions about the situation within my walls it seems that Elizabeth seized territories previously granted to Catholics by her predecessor, Queen Mary, which naturally angered Catholic Ireland. The Catholic King of Spain sent James Fitz Maurice with a small army of Spanish and Italian mercenaries to rally the Catholics in rebellion. Among those who joined the revolt were Sirs James and John Fitz Gerald. The queen then sent Gerald Fitz Gerald, the Earl of Desmond, to put down the revolt but, being Fitz Maurice's cousin, not to mention the brother of James and John, the earl also rose, setting off what became known as the Desmond Rebellion.

McCarthy was not particularly interested in the venture because he had recently reached an accommodation with Queen Elizabeth so he remained neutral. That did not sit well with the Desmonds and, in consequence, Sir James Fitz Gerald invaded my domain with a large force. My man Cormac defeated the earl at a townland called Aghavrin just west of my walls near Coachford in Cork and took him captive. The problem this created was what to do about James.

'Sure he was only doing what we all would like to be doing,' Cormac said, 'trying to drive the foreigners from our shores.'

'Foreigners you say,' his wife Joan Butler raged. 'He attacked Muskerry not Cork City. You should have seen to it that he was killed in battle.'

Cormac sighed, 'Now, pet, he's a likeable enough chap and the Desmond crowd is finished. I think we ought to let him escape.'

'Right so,' Joan replied, her meaty arms folded across her imposing bosoms, 'and then the queen will decide that you have conspired with Fitz Gerald and it will be your head on the block. She's a great one for collecting heads you know.'

Cormac agreed to consider the matter further and in the end, when the queen's commander called at my walls, Sir James was turned over and my chieftain's relationship with the queen remained intact. As for poor James, his head became a display on the Northgate Bridge in

Cork for a while.

Cormac McTeige's instincts were certainly sharpened by that encounter but he also developed an interesting way of dealing with Queen Elizabeth. I would maintain, with no undue modesty, that his skills did not drop from a tree, rather were the result of his extended association with the magic of my walls. It was from those dealings that my power was first recognised.

With the end of the Desmond Rebellion most of Ireland was under the control of Elizabeth I and the only clans still in open rebellion were the O'Neills and the O'Donnells far off in Ulster. Her goal was to wipe our all traces of the Gaelic culture and eliminate the clan system and she was well on her way to success. The remaining clans were not only strong but were rallying other clans to their cause.

Meanwhile, Cormac McTeige had been designated Lord Muskerry and held a great deal of land and wealth that he would lose if he chose the wrong side. Muskerry, after all, included most of east Cork as well as parts of Waterford and Wexford. While at heart he was a Gaelic clan chieftain, the practicalities of the queen's military might caused him great concern particularly because his territory was more accessible to London than western parts of Munster, Connacht or Ulster where clans were safe in their isolation. As a result, for many years in the late 1500s he remained nominally neutral despite his assurances to the queen that he would certainly declare his support for her.

It was during this time that Elizabeth I sent Lord Robert Dudley, the Earl of Leicester, to secure the submission of McCarthy and the use of my walls in her interests. I hosted many banquets and celebrations honouring the earl and his queen but my resident chieftain never quite got around to actually pledging for the crown or delivering my walls for her use.

'My dear Blarney,' Dudley said on one occasion, 'I greatly appreciate your hospitality as this banquet is splendid indeed, but I must depart tomorrow to make my report to Her Royal Highness. What am I to tell her?'

'What indeed, your worship,' Cormac McCarthy replied with a condescending smile, 'and here am I thinking that I made that perfectly clear. I know that I certainly intended to make it perfectly clear but then sometimes I lose the head on myself and end up thinking that I thought I had made my position on the matter perfectly clear and while it might have been perfectly clear in my own mind, I can understand why it might not be perfectly clear in someone else's mind. Is that clear?'

Dudley, a confused look on his face, responded, 'Not particularly. What I need, quite simply, is your written pledge to support the queen in her endeavour to bring peace to this troubled land.'

McCarthy replied, 'But of course. And here I certainly thought that I had made it perfectly clear and indeed that the queen understood that I fully intend, that is to say, that it is my clear intention to not only provide her with a pledge of my support but to place my facilities at her disposal once I have been granted the privilege – and I want you to make it perfectly clear to Her Most Royal and Gracious Highness, that I do indeed consider it a privilege of the highest magnitude – the privilege, or dare I say honour, perhaps honour would be a better word, of providing her with whatever she, in her sole discretion, believes would be in the best interest of me, her humble servant, my people and indeed all of her people here in Cork. I hope that makes my intention perfectly clear.'

'Yes of course, but the written undertaking . . .' Dudley said.

McCarthy replied, 'Of course, of course but the middle of a feast is hardly the time to be drawing up such documents. I would hate to think what the queen would think of me if some paper were delivered to her dripping in goose grease. Why she might have my head. We will have plenty of time for that tomorrow but meanwhile, I think you will find the spring lamb to be most succulent.'

Lord Dudley apparently resigned himself to the inevitable and assumed that he would obtain the undertakings before he departed. Unfortunately, at dawn, McCarthy was urgently called away to deal with a problem arising with the O'Sullivans, a lesser clan under McCarthys in the far southwest of the county, and was unable to sign any document. Dudley once again returned to London frustrated in his attempts to obtain the public support of my resident chieftain with only their conversations to report.

With the power of my famous stone, I take particular pride in this most adroit and expeditious statesmanship that finally resulted in the queen's public acknowledgement of the gift I bestowed on my resident. The 'Virgin Queen' (now, from the talk within my walls at the time that is a good bit of fiction) frustrated with my smooth-talking and elusive resident, reportedly muttered the immortal words, 'This is all Blarney. What he says, he never means.' And so it was that 'blarney', a pleasant way of speaking which is intended to deceive without offending, was born into the English language.

I was sorry to see the death of Cormac McTeige McCarthy in 1583 because he was not only a leader of some substantial charisma, but an entertaining character as well. After all, it was his facile tongue through which I became legendary. Fortunately his successor, Cormac Dermod McCarthy, learned a great deal at his old man's feet and continued the same policies with some success.

The problem facing my resident a few years later in the first days of the seventeenth century was that this habit of dancing a cautious jig with the queen was coming to an end. Hugh O'Neill had travelled to Munster to seek the support of Cormac Dermod and the other chiefs in finally confronting the English and another war was imminent.

II Home, Fortress and Community (1600–1650)

I remember well the meeting within my walls at which the clan and its freeholders met to discuss the alliance with the Ulster clans in revolt against the crown. After everyone had gathered, all the leaders were given a chance to present their case. Donogh O'Leary, who had recently been elected the chieftain of the O'Learys, a clan of freeholders but subject to McCarthy, gave a rousing speech in which he extolled the history and culture of the Gaels and vowed to give his last drop of blood in fighting the heathen swine. Other sub-chiefs added their voices to that of The O'Leary and, before long, my walls were shaking with the stomping of feet and banging of fists and the entire clan worked itself into a blood rage. Cormac Dermod remained quiet, thoughtfully considering the whole matter and eventually silence descended and he addressed the gathering.

'My brothers,' he began. 'You all know that Clan McCarthy has ruled south Munster for well over five hundred years. Our right comes from the high kings of Ireland who granted us this power in 1118 and we have ruled in strict compliance with the Gaelic laws and tradition. These very walls will attest to our strength and character in fighting invaders from across the sea. However, we have seen the strength of the enemy who comes in unending waves, and much of our province lies in ruins. I say that there comes a time when we must look beyond the might of our arms and that time has arrived. I propose therefore to declare for the queen.'

Shouts and roars of disbelief shattered a moment's silence. Cries of 'never', 'Munster Abú' and 'treachery' filled the air and I thought for a moment that Cormac Dermod McCarthy would be killed outright.

He stretched out his hand for silence and, when the shouting stopped, he continued in a commanding voice that echoed to the back of the hall, 'And . . . we will fight.'

Immediately my hall fell into silence as the sub-chieftains exchanged puzzled looks. When he had regained everyone's attention McCarthy concluded, 'The official position of the clan and its freeholders will be loyalty to the queen so that, if she is successful, our lands will be protected. Any pledges we have to make or any fighting we have to do to demonstrate our loyalty to the queen will be for public show only.

The strength of our arms will be with O'Donnell and O'Neill although not under the banner of the McCarthys.'

After some further discussion, it became clear that, although a fight to the death was certainly honourable, living to fight again also had a certain appeal so Cormac Dermod's plan was agreed and my residents declared for the queen.

Some weeks later, Sir George Carew, the English President of Munster and the queen's representative, arrived at my door to confirm the terms of the declaration. It was clear to me that Carew had been well briefed about the McCarthys' propensity for dispensing blarney.

When presented with the written undertaking so long sought, Carew said, 'This is all well and good, Lord Blarney, and I must say that the queen never doubted your sincerity.'

'I am greatly relieved to hear that,' Cormac Dermod replied, 'because, as you will know, no one has been more loyal and supportive to her policies than my family and I look forward to continued service.'

Carew stroked his beard, perhaps trying to keep a straight face, 'Yes of course, my good man. But the queen realises that you have many responsibilities as clan chieftain and she has asked me to require your attendance at Shandon Castle in Cork on a rather permanent basis so that you will be able to concentrate your efforts on her behalf at least until the current difficulties with our friends from Ulster have been resolved.'

Since Cormac Dermod was unable to find a way to avoid this direct order, he replied, 'But of course. As I have always made it perfectly clear, I am at the queen's disposal.'

And so it was that Cormac himself was not available to fight when the native Irish chieftains made their last stand against the English crown, which, as it transpired meant that my own walls continued to serve as a home for the McCarthys for another hundred years.

Some years later, when Cormac Dermod returned to my walls and the matter was discussed in some detail, I learned that, in 1601, O'Neill and O'Donnell and their allied clans were soundly defeated at the Battle of Kinsale, a town on the south coast of Ireland. Despite the best efforts of McCarthy kinsman, including the O'Learys, the English under Charles Blount, Lord Mountjoy, took advantage of confusion among the Irish armies and ensured that England decisively broke the power of the Irish clans. The clan chieftains, native earls, fled Ireland into exile.

To prove his loyalty to the crown, Cormac Dermod McCarthy was forced to personally parade his troops below the walls of Kinsale where the Spaniards, who had landed rather late in support of the Gaels but proved to be of little assistance, were encamped. Cormac did so with some aplomb, rattling sabres and exchanging taunts with very little threat to the wellbeing of either side. Of course Cormac Dermod McCarthy and his clan, saved from the queen's retribution by his 'loyalty', enjoyed telling the story at feasts within my walls, to the great good humour of all involved.

I particularly appreciated those celebrations because I will be so bold as to suggest that the McCarthys, before and after Cormac McTeige and Cormac Dermod, would not have been able to so adroitly navigate the stormy waters of Normans, Saxons and Gaels were they not blessed with inspiration provided by my walls, and particularly by the most famous stone I possess, the Blarney Stone. Would that all wars were handled in this way, with smooth words instead of angry deeds. The castles and buildings of this world would be far better off. Unfortunately, I was soon to discover, the power bestowed by the Blarney Stone is of a gentle persuasion and it did not always protect me from the ravages of time or the angry slings and arrows of those who warred against those I sought to protect.

Although my importance as a military stronghold may have ended several hundred years ago when cannons replaced catapults, no castle in Ireland or indeed around the world can boast, humbly of course, of an ability to transcend violence by bestowing on human beings the gift of eloquent speech. It is a gift I cherish and I fervently hope that I will continue to provide it to humankind for many centuries to come.

In my years of association with humans, I certainly know that all castles don't serve the same purpose. Such matters were among the first subjects of discussion when chieftains like the O'Briens of Bunratty or the queen's representatives like George Carew, called to talk to my resident lord. As a result, I know that some castles, like Carrickfergus, offered defence to the exclusion of comfort while others, like Malahide couldn't defend themselves against a stiff breeze but certainly provided the greatest of comforts.

Quite apart from that special gift I possess, I am most certainly one of Ireland's strongholds. I was not only invincible, at least until the big guns came along but, for over seven hundred years, I was a comfortable home for the McCarthys and much more to those who lived in my shadows. In my time I was the refuge in whom the people of Cork could depend and, in addition, I have always been a centre of culture. You see, in my years as an active castle, I believe that I provided a rare combination – I was at once a strong fortress, a warm hearth and a place for an entire community to grow and prosper.

I am situated on top of an isolated limestone rock that rises majestically over the junction of the Blarney and Comane rivers. In the millennia before my existence, the elements created their own set of natural caves and passages through the rock. This network not only served as my dungeon, kennels and barracks, but also provided secret access in the days when my walls alone were not enough to withstand attack.

Within my protective walls and ramparts, a massive banqueting hall hosted many lavish parties and functions. Below the banquet hall was the great hall from which the family and guests could access my many bedrooms, offices and living quarters. A special corridor provided access to the women's rooms, which allowed them additional privacy. The earl's rooms were on the ground floor together with a chapel and rooms for resident priests. There were also rooms for house guards and, of course, a massive kitchen to service my residents. My walls were hung with pictures and tapestries and the floors were covered with rugs, which provided warmth, both physical and aesthetic.

Spread under my protective shadow were many other buildings that housed tradesmen, labourers, shop owners and all the people that you would find in any small town. In times of trouble, my doors were opened and they would find refuge within my walls.

As a family home, I became comfortable with the relationships between the McCarthys, their spouses and their large and generally happy families. While The McCarthy may have been the chieftain, the spouses controlled many decisions even in matters of some importance.

As you will recall the McCarthy's handling of the Desmond Rebellion is certainly testimony to the counsel and good sense of my mistresses.

And so you see during all the years I housed the McCarthys, I was first and foremost a family home providing warmth and comfort to my residents and, for this service, I am most proud. I also witnessed all the trials and tribulations that, I suspect, one would find in any home. Beyond my role as a home and a castle, I also provided a greater gift to the entire community and, indeed, to Ireland itself.

I suppose that, since the Blarney Stone is part of me, it is not surprising that throughout the many years that the McCarthys lived within my walls, I was also the home for one of the finest bardic schools in Ireland. These noble poets, musicians and storytellers were always welcome at my door, as they would have been at any self-respecting castle the length and breadth of Ireland. Within my walls, however, the McCarthys realised that, without schools to pass on the skills acquired over many centuries, there would be no more bards. For this reason, throughout my existence, the McCarthys supported and maintained schools where promising young people not only learned the history of their race but also acquired the special skills necessary to pass on the bardic tradition and create works of their own.

The Bardic School was located in a secluded garden not far from my walls very close to the banks of the Blarney river. The building that housed the school was about sixty feet long by thirty feet wide, but very low to the ground so that a tall man would have to bend down to cross the portal. It had no windows to let in the daylight and contained a common room and several small apartments that held only a bed, table and a couple of chairs. Since the school was my nearest neighbour, I got to know her quite well and learned much about what transpired within her walls.

'And why are there no windows?' I asked her one day.

'It is the way of the bards,' she told me. 'The professors teach my scholars in absolute darkness because light distracts a student's focus by allowing him to consider the objects that he sees. In the darkness the student sees and feels only the words and how they relate to each other in syllables, rhymes and verse. After the lesson, each student retreats to his room and ponders what has been learned and creates his own poetry on the subject of the lecture.'

'Have they no light at all?' I queried.

The school replied, 'Only candles, which are used by the student in his room to commit what he has created to paper so that it can be scrutinised by the master.'

Students spent many years in the Bardic School and, throughout their training, they would always be welcome with their masters at dinners and feasts held in my great hall. Because the feasts always included recitals and entertainment by the bards, promising students were occasionally allowed to demonstrate what they had learned. I particularly remember the effort of one such young bard during the last days of Cormac Dermod McCarthy because he created verse as if it were I that was speaking.

> I have taken many forms
> The rocky cliff, the moonless night
> The lion's roar, the dragon's might
> The river's rage, the eagle's flight
> And yet to those who shelter seek
> The warming hearth, the welcome spit
> The honeyed mead, the child's smile
> The bardic tome, the harpist's song
> And all of these I will become
> For master strong and facile tongue
> To save my stones from Norman bed
> From Saxon blast and foreign wed
> So that a rock I will long reign
> And never let this power wane.

I suppose that young man's effort defined my role as the stronghold of the McCarthys for all those years. Little did I know, however, that five hundred years of unbroken service to that family were coming to an end.

The problems began soon after the English, under Lord Mountjoy, defeated the Irish chieftains at Kinsale in 1601. As you might well imagine, the vanquished in that battle were not particularly pleased to see that, while they lost everything, my chieftain retained his lands and wealth and actually prospered. Apparently word was planted in appropriate ears that my chieftain's assaults against the Spanish were not quite as enthusiastic as they might have been. Since George Carew, the President of Munster who also fought at Kinsale, never did quite trust Cormac Dermod McCarthy, he sent a spy by the name of Blake to gather evidence of his insincerity.

Blake was welcomed as a guest because it was thought that he was associated with O'Sullivan, a chieftain from the far west who was still in rebellion against Queen Elizabeth I. In truth O'Sullivan's rebellion was little more than a nuisance as all he really did was evade capture whilst declaring boldly that he was still in rebellion. At any rate, another of McCarthy's sub-chieftains had attested the spy's bona fides but I knew he was a blackguard because I heard him conspire with his retainer in the privacy of their room. There was little I could do, however, except watch the treachery unfold.

'So Mr Blake,' Cormac Dermod asked, 'how are things going in the west of Cork?'

Blake responded, 'Well now, our friend O'Sullivan has gone to ground and it is unlikely that he will be rooted out very soon. I trust that I am not being presumptuous in referring to him as your friend as well as my own.'

'But of course I'm his friend,' Cormac answered. 'Why, didn't I send the O'Learys to stand with him at Kinsale?'

'One can never be too sure,' Blake said. 'After all, wasn't it you who pushed back the Spaniards when they tried to break out of Kinsale Castle?'

McCarthy roared with laughter holding up his goblet, 'But of course my good man. And that is why you are enjoying this fine Spanish wine courtesy of their commander Don Juan del Aguila. 'Twas all a bit of a charade to impress the queen. You don't really think that the Spanish had any real interest in breaking out of the comfort of Kinsale, now, do you?'

'Ah yes, but not everyone knows that now do they?' Blake replied returning the toast.

'And let's hope it stays that way,' Cormac answered.

Of course it did not stay that way. Blake had been gone for less that a week when Sir George Carew arrived with a substantial force to arrest

Cormac Dermod and take him away charged with consorting with the Spanish. Fortunately, the imprisonment did not last long primarily because Queen Elizabeth, in the final doddering years of her reign recalled the pleasure she had taken from 'Blarney' and having decided that Kinsale was all 'water under the bridge', ordered that he be released. Cormac Dermod returned to my walls but for the first time allowed his temper to interfere with good common sense.

'Your are going to declare for who?' the wife roared.

Cormac shouted back, 'O'Sullivan – and don't take that tone of voice with me. I will decide what's best for the McCarthys.'

'You're daft do you know that?' she replied. 'O'Sullivan has even less of a chance than O'Neill and O'Donnell did at Kinsale.'

Over the strong protests of virtually all of the sub-chieftains, Cormac marched out of my walls one late summer's day intent on joining Donall Cam O'Sullivan in west Cork. Apparently he came to his senses rather quickly and surrendered at the first opportunity. Since he had done little damage, he was quickly pardoned and returned to his family, a chastened man. In fairness, his wife was most supportive of her fallen hero and he, in turn, announced that since further rebellion was useless, he would henceforth serve the queen. When Queen Elizabeth died less than a year later, a feast was held in my great hall in her honour. For the next forty years, my McCarthys virtuously served the crown and, for their service, the titles of Viscount Muskerry and Lord Blarney were bestowed on Cormac Dermod's son, Cormac Óg.

Unfortunately Cormac Óg was succeeded in 1640 by his son, Donogh, who not only chose to support one side in a dispute, but chose the wrong side. Although I would not pretend to understand all the intricacies, a group of Catholic landowners, both English and Irish, met at my sister castle, Kilkenny, and established a Catholic confederacy, (called the Confederation of Kilkenny). It was intended to administer Catholic controlled parts of Ireland on behalf of the English crown. This was seen as necessary because the English parliament had taken strong measures against Catholics in England and the confederation could see a similar situation developing in Ireland.

Donogh not only declared for the confederation but was among the military commanders who fought on its behalf. Although there was nothing particularly sinister about the group that espoused continuing loyalty, the crown was not pleased with this independent parliament and battles were fought with Royalist forces. Donogh himself laid siege to Bunratty Castle and ultimately captured it for the confederation.

Since 1642 the English Parliamentarian forces had been fighting a civil war with King Charles I over the way England should be run – Parliament wanted more power and a strongly Protestant government while Charles wanted absolute power and religious tolerance. Charles was particularly tolerant of Catholics (he had married one) and this further angered Parliament. A man called Oliver Cromwell was the leader of the Parliamentarians and saw this civil war as a crusade against Catholics which was of grave concern to Catholic Ireland. In January 1649 Charles had his head lopped off and Cromwell, having secured power in England, turned his attention to Ireland. Donogh McCarthy and the confederation could hardly support this new 'king' so they pledged their support to Charles II, who had formally succeeded his father although he was the king in name only and had fled to Scotland and then to France.

Oliver Cromwell and his army, who became known as Roundheads because of the helmets they wore, did not hesitate to move against the confederation. Because they were weakened from fighting, the confederation offered little opposition. Donogh, realising that he could not hold the castle against Cromwell's army, quickly departed Bunratty, leaving it to the Roundheads. A short time later in early 1650 Donogh returned to the safety of my walls.

Although I had been the subject of several sieges during the two hundred years since my reconstruction by Cormac Láidir, I had never succumbed. As a result, I believed that I was invincible, at least from external attack. From the discussions in my great hall, I knew that once again I was facing an assault and I also knew that it would be my duty to stand strong against the rocks and arrows of those who would threaten my residents. I could see the enemy who were gathered on Card Hill on a precipice above the lake. All of this seemed normal, but I should have known that, this time, nothing was the same.

First, the Roundheads did not come with a large force of soldiers, certainly not enough to either overrun my walls or lay siege to them for an extended period. More importantly, they did not haul catapults into place – rather the enemy wheeled some strange iron tubes into a row with gaping mouths facing my walls. Were this not enough, my residents were behaving in a most peculiar fashion as they gathered in my great hall.

'They have artillery,' Donogh McCarthy stated to the gathered clan.

'What can we do?' was the question that came from several mouths.

I thought to myself, *What a foolish question. You do what you have always done and that is barricade the portals and trust the strength of your walls. You are well provisioned for a siege and they will soon tire of the wait.*

The McCarthy looked around at the anxious faces, 'We abandon Blarney and make our escape through the rock tunnels. We will carry the fight for another day, a day that can bring us victory.'

What? I screamed to myself. *Seven hundred years of McCarthys are spinning in their graves. Where is the strength? Where is the honour? Where is the courage? You lot are not worthy of the name! Not worthy of the proud name Blarney.*

And yet I watched in total disbelief as the entire household, save only a couple of old men, under cover of darkness disappeared into the rocks on which I was built, into the Badger's Cave and away to the west. They took away all of the gold and treasures that had been amassed over the centuries. I had been abandoned without so much as a 'McCarthy Abú'.

Be damned, the lot of you, I thought at the time. *Sure the gates are barred and the enemy doesn't know I have been abandoned. I will stand strong for the generations who never ran.*

Imagine my surprise on that sunny summer's morning in 1649 when I felt a blow from an iron ball propelled by some force far greater than any catapult. The first such blow thundered against my walls, repelled by my thickness at the point of impact, but the second one hit a less fortified stone and drove all the way through. I had been breached and I was no longer invincible. It didn't take long for Cromwell's general, Roger Boyle, known as Lord Broghill, to destroy my external fortifications and, soon after, his meagre army stormed my walls.

When they entered my keep, Broghill's army realised that there would be no defence so they had no difficulty breaking down my wooden portal and invading my tower house. To the disgust of the invaders – who expected to loot the family treasures and capture valuable prisoners for ransom and glory – only the silent echoes of my great hall greeted their arrival.

All they encountered were the two ancient retainers who stood straight, swords in hands, ready to fight to the death . . . God love them. The Saxon captain laughed and the two were quickly disarmed and taken before the general who had entered my walls when he realised there was no threat to his person. The old men said nothing except that they had been abandoned.

'So you have nothing to say?' Broghill sneered and the two men stood before him as straight and proud, as their years would allow. He considered the two for a moment, the scowl never leaving his face.

'Kill them!' He shouted at an officer and the two were dragged out into the courtyard where they were chopped down.

To this very day, I honour the memory of my two last defenders whose time, like my own, had long passed. The two faced death, not cowering or pleading their age and infirmity, but with a mocking smile and courageous contempt.

While I had been damaged, I survived but those iron balls did more that just batter my walls, they destroyed part of my essence and that was my greatest shock. I thought, perhaps, that my two defenders took the better course because, when their time came, they embraced their destruction. I, on the other hand, had seen over five hundred years of service rendered redundant in less than an hour. I could no longer be considered a fortress because I was no longer able to protect my residents, standing impregnable against an assault by those who would threaten their lives.

My shock at this turn of events was further aggravated by the presence of strangers within my walls, the very people who were the cause of my downfall. I will admit that it took me some time to accept my plight but I vowed to dedicate myself to the service I could provide, rather than dwelling on what I could no longer do. I discovered, however, that that was not an easy task.

III Descent into Ruin (1650–1800)

As a reward for his services in taking my walls, Oliver Cromwell, the Lord Protector named Lord Broghill the Protestant Administrator of Cork. Although he was not continually in residence within my walls because his principal office was in the city, I saw a great deal of my captor. I remained, after all, a comfortable residence with spacious quarters in a beautiful location. It was from Broghill that I discovered that Donogh McCarthy lost everything, eventually surrendering to Cromwell's forces at Ross Castle in 1652. Donogh fled to France and the protection of Charles II, also in exile, where he was created the First Earl of Clancarthy. Just as King Charles II proclaimed his right to the crown in countries over which he had not power, Donogh was the earl of a clan and territories far from his actual residence.

For the next several years I was little more than an administrative office for Cromwell's people who had designated Cork for settlement by his government officials. Those were sad years and I missed the family life and the craic surrounding banquets and celebrations. I also missed the bards and the Bardic School, which was closed as soon as Broghill took charge. I felt particularly bad for my friend, the school, who was transformed into a stable. What a terrible fate for so noble a building.

As I recall those days, I suppose the administrative drudgery suited me because it took me some years to rise above the general malaise caused by the recognition of my mortality. I couldn't care less about what was happening within my walls, which was very little and that suited me well. That all changed, however, in 1660.

Once again, it was a fine spring day in May, when the combination of the sunshine and the best news I had heard in a decade brought me back to life. Broghill was meeting with some of his minions in the offices at the earl's quarters when Sir William Jephson, a prominent Cromwellian soldier, disrupted the meeting.

'What is it?' Broghill asked in a tone that was both impatient and respectful.

Jephson took a seat, lounging with one arm over the back of the chair and examined his fingernails before responding. 'Bad news, I'm afraid. The monarchy has been restored in London and Charles II has again been proclaimed king.'

Broghill did not seem particularly surprised but he banged his hand on the desk and snarled, 'Hell and damnation. I suppose it was inevitable when Oliver died. His brother Henry is a twit, no backbone at all. I suppose parliament figured that with the Catholics sorted out, they had better return the rule to an actual king. Charles II may have sympathy for the Catholics but he is no Catholic himself and he has certainly learned what happens when you cross parliament.'

'And what do you propose to do?' Jephson asked. 'You do know that Eddie Ludlow, your commander-in-chief will be lucky to escape the noose.'

'Well I certainly have not been as heavy handed as Ludlow, killing people right and left. And no one asked me to sign the execution order for Charles I, so I am not a regicide to be hunted down. I suppose I shall retire quietly to the family home in Cork and keep my head down,' Broghill replied.

'And what of Blarney?' Jephson enquired with a sweeping gesture to include my walls.

Broghill shrugged as if it made no difference to him, 'McCarthy again, I suppose. Muskerry and Charles were tight as thieves and to the winner goes the spoils.'

Lord Broghill was correct in his assessment and, several months later, Donogh McCarthy triumphantly returned to my walls. The restoration of the English monarchy included the restoration of many of those loyal to the king, however, the price to be paid was an expedient conversion from Catholicism. Charles II was married to a French Catholic and was indeed sympathetic to Catholics, but the Protestants returned him to power – something of which he was mindful – so most of the rewards were reserved for Protestants.

Donogh, the first Protestant Earl of Clancarthy, was welcomed by nearly all the residents in the vicinity, many of whom volunteered to assist in the restoration of my walls. The McCarthy was not particularly interested in restoring the fortifications because they would have little use against another bombardment but he spent a great deal of time 'removing the English taint' to use his words. When the work was completed to Donogh's satisfaction, a grand party was held and bards and poets from all over Ireland arrived to celebrate the return of the McCarthys.

The celebration that followed was a proud moment for me because, while I had finally come to terms with my frailty against the latest weapons man could devise, I demonstrated that I was still capable of providing warmth and comfort to the new generations of McCarthys. In addition, I was once again the centre of the region and my grounds came alive with farmers, merchants and tradesmen who gathered in the shadows of my walls. Unfortunately within a couple of years, Donogh McCarthy was dead and events began to unfold that would banish the McCarthys from my walls forever.

Donogh, the first earl of Clancarthy, had three sons – the elder and heir was in service to Charles II, the second studied for the priesthood and the third was in France where he was in service to Louis XIV. In 1665 both the earl and his first heir were dead within a few months of each other.

The clan gathered in my great hall and the meeting was opened by Donogh's second son and now heir, Ceallachan, the seminarian.

'As you are aware by now,' he began, 'my father, the Earl of Clancarthy, died unexpectedly last month in London after he heard the news that my older brother, Cormac, had also died. You all know how much my father loved Cormac and I can only think that he died of a broken heart, God rest him. My brother died heroically from wounds suffered in a naval engagement while he was fighting beside James, the Duke of York and brother of the king. As a Catholic, never mind student for the holy priesthood, I am not permitted by Caroline mandate to assume the mantle of second Earl of Clancarthy so we are left with the question of succession.'

A scholarly gentleman called Pindaric the Wise rose, 'The law would be quite clear; your younger brother, Justin, must be recalled from France.'

An audible 'Justin, Justin' rang through the gathering.

Ceallachan, however, had another idea and he rose slowly to address the clan. 'I am certain that my younger brother would serve the clan well. However, I believe it is equally important that he serve the King of France on our behalf. Although it is not my first choice, I see that I have no alternative but to leave the celibate monastery, renounce my faith, publicly at any rate, and become the second Earl of Clancarthy.'

From a side table, Donogh's widow Eleanor cried out, 'No,

Ceallachan. Not my holy priest.'

Ceallachan turned to her and said, 'Mother, I must do this for the family' and, after the necessary proclamations had concluded, the McCarthys had a new clan chief.

Ceallachan McCarthy eventually married Elizabeth Fitzgerald who was the daughter of some important man called the sixteenth Earl of Kildare and for the last time my walls were the site of a party that lasted day and night for the better part of a week. Ceallachan ruled as the second Earl of Clancarthy and, for several years, my walls returned to the peaceful existence I had enjoyed before the confederation and Cromwellian times.

In due course a child, called Donogh after his grandfather, was born to Ceallachan and Elizabeth. Little did I know that he would be the last McCarthy to be born within my walls and the last to occupy Blarney as The McCarthy.

This second Donogh, called Dony, was a bright little fellow and was reared with stories of the glorious history of the McCarthys. In truth, from a very early age, he looked remarkably like his great-great grandfather, Cormac McTeige McCarthy, who was the subject of many stories. I would be the first to admit that some of these stories and legends were slightly exaggerated but what can one expect when the tellers themselves acquired their storytelling gifts from within my walls. In any case, Dony was well acquainted with the long and proud history of my walls.

He was also well acquainted with the restoration of the McCarthy rights by Charles II and the death of his Uncle Cormac at the side of the king's brother James, who would himself soon become King of England as James II. (Actually, the story told Dony was that Cormac gave his life to save James, however, in typical Blarney fashion, that was a marked improvement on earlier versions told within my walls.) Dony was only about ten when his father died and he succeeded as the Earl of Clancarthy although, for the years while his training continued, Dony's Uncle Justin provided leadership for the clan, at least when he was not in service to Louis XIV of France.

During those years I heard reports about battles fought far away between James II and his son-in-law William of Orange who had been given the crown of England by parliament, who no longer wanted James. Once again, it seemed, the parliament decided that its king was being too friendly to Catholics. I suppose they were accurate in the assessment because James II actually became a Catholic himself. After being deposed, James escaped to France as a guest of King Louis where he frequently encountered Dony's Uncle Justin. Justin's reports back to my walls made it clear that James was planning to return. Dony was barely twenty when the clan gathered within my walls to make the decisions that would dictate my future.

The principal participants at the clan conference included Donogh who, in deference to the age and experience of his uncle, said little, Justin McCarthy, who had been designated by James II as Lord Lieutenant of County Cork, and Richard Talbot from the Malahide Castle Talbots. Richard was the Earl of Tyrconnell, and had been appointed by James II as the first Catholic Viceroy of Ireland in a hundred and fifty years.

I would never have taken Talbot for a soldier as he was tall, thin and very well dressed and spoke in an accent totally different to any I had ever heard. I specifically recall that his eyes seemed to 'bug out' far more than was normal. When he discussed his family home at Malahide Castle, I was less surprised by his appearance because I knew that castle, apparently like its master, had never felt a wrathful blow. Nevertheless, he was the designated representative of the king and he was treated with the utmost respect.

'Quite frankly,' Talbot intoned as the meeting began, 'the only way that our good friend James, as a Stewart, can retake his rightful place on the throne in England is to secure Ireland.'

'Do we want to get involved in this affair over the English crown?' Donogh timidly asked, albeit with a good bit of common sense if you ask me.

Justin rose in response. 'Above all else, it is a matter of honour, Dony. My own brother, your uncle, gave his life for James. You would not sit as Earl of Clancarthy were it not that Charles and then James restored our lands. You know well that the restoration was strongly contested in parliament because of our family's Catholic tradition.'

'And for Ireland, son,' Talbot added in what I thought to be a most condescending fashion. 'With James as king, we Catholics will have equal rights under the crown and all of the land confiscated by Cromwell will be returned to its rightful owners.'

Donogh considered that for a moment before replying, 'And what if we lose? The last time the McCarthys fought for honour and religion, grandfather found himself exiled to France. Aren't we better served waiting to see how the wind blows, particularly as neither my father nor I are Catholic?'

'Ah, but we won't lose,' Talbot replied. 'The entire country, save a few isolated areas up near Carrickfergus Castle, have pledged. The O'Briens and MacNamaras from around Bunratty have pledged, Thomond and I have raised tens of thousands of men from Leinster and Connaught.'

'And don't forget the French,' Justin added. 'King Louis has pledged seven thousand first-line troops.'

The discussion went on well into the night, but eventually Donogh agreed and the McCarthys were pledged to back James II. Even at the time, I thought that Donogh was well advised to resist the arguments of his elders but I suppose he eventually grew tired of standing alone.

James landed at Kinsale in March of 1690 and I remember well the cold winter evening when he called at my doors and was, of course, offered all the warmth and hospitality that I was well able to provide. James was not particularly tall but he had a long, thin face with a matching nose and, as one would expect, he was royally dressed wearing a great black wig with curls well past his shoulders. And a good thing it was, because when he retired to his bed it became apparent that not much grew up there naturally.

Donogh's Uncle Justin, who knew James well from his years in France, took charge of the evening's entertainment and it was clear that all the guests were confident that their venture would be a success. I noticed, however, that Donogh was particularly quiet and it seemed to me that, for all the banter, he was not comfortable with the decision to fight. Being the image of his ancestor, Cormac McTeige, I wondered if he were thinking of some way to talk his way out of the alliance.

Over the next several months, I saw little of either Donogh or Justin as they were off waging war on behalf of James II. Donogh, despite his age but in credit to his leadership skills and status as The McCarthy, was the leader of the Munster forces while his Uncle Justin had complete charge of the artillery. Unfortunately, the little I heard when a messenger would return to report to those left behind was not particularly encouraging.

Finally, in July 1690 an exhausted messenger arrived having ridden for nearly three days from Dublin. His report was conclusive: James had been soundly defeated at some place along the Boyne river and William of Orange was in control of Dublin and most of Ireland. The invincible forces of King James had been scattered to the four corners from which they came. Like his grandmother forty years earlier, Donogh's mother, Elizabeth, began to pack the family treasures.

Donogh returned briefly in August to complete the packing and depart my walls for Kinsale and then France. It was during that brief stay that I heard the whole story.

'I should have listened to my instincts,' Donogh told his mother. 'I should have known that something would go wrong.'

Elizabeth commiserated with her son, assuring him that he had done his best. She did ask, 'What happened? To hear Tyrconnell and James you would think that victory was a forgone conclusion.'

Donogh shook his head in sadness, 'Right. A forgone conclusion. What didn't go wrong? There were just as many Catholics fighting for William as there were for James, and William flew the Papal Banner. The French did send seven thousand troops but they required five thousand in return so off marched Uncle Justin and five thousand of our best men to serve Louis XIV in France of all places. Then, of course, James was no leader and he ran for Dublin the minute things looked a little dicey. Some battle – about fifty thousand soldiers and only two thousand casualties and most of them died of fright or heat exhaustion or some such nonsense.'

Elizabeth asked, 'Is there nothing to be done? What about Blarney?'

Donogh replied with a sigh, 'I'm afraid Blarney is finished. William and his lot are certainly not going to let us keep our lands and castles. We have no choice but to leave for France before they arrive.'

It was a sad day when the packing was done and my resident family of nearly six hundred years moved out of my walls for the last time. I assumed that at some future time another family, perhaps loyal to King William would occupy my walls but a few months later, another administrator arrived to determine my fate. Once again, the administrator set up offices in the earl's quarters while the remaining parts of my walls remained vacant.

The agent, whose name was Walfield, called the tenants in from all of the small holdings around my walls and announced that Blarney Castle and the adjoining three thousand acres had been sold to an operation called the Hollow Sword Blade Company and that all subsequent rent payments would be made to the agent for the company's account. Although the tenants were respectful in the presence of Walfield, the banter was much more interesting when they gathered outside.

'Pity about our new landlord's blade,' one man offered. 'I'd be concerned it might snap off at the first sign of any action.'

Another added, 'Well, it has to be a one-generation landlord because I don't suppose there will be any daggers coming along.'

I was also understandably curious not only about the identity of my owner but also its long-term plans so, unlike the days when Broghill was administrator, I was attentive to the business operations. It transpired that the Hollow Sword Blade Company manufactured swords for the English government, grooved in the interest of making them lighter, thus the name. The company had been granted many estates and castles including my neighbour, Macroom, for small amounts of money or in lieu of cash payments for weapons provided. As the company was not in the business of land ownership, they liquidated many grants as soon as they were able. The pundit was, therefore, correct when he said that the holding would be short term although not for the reason suggested.

A couple of years later I was sold to Sir Richard Payne, the Lord Chief Justice of Ireland for three thousand pounds. It transpired that Payne was comfortably ensconced in Dublin and had no particular interest in my walls except to collect the rents from the local tenants. Payne never did darken my doorstep because shortly thereafter, in 1703, my walls were sold on to Sir James St John Jefferyes, the Governor of Cork who did attend at my walls.

Jefferyes was delighted with his purchase and I recall him meeting with his agent shortly after the transfer had been completed.

'You won't believe it, Hamilton, but Sir Richard sold me this place for three hundred pounds,' Jefferyes announced. 'Imagine, three hundred pounds and I own Blarney.'

Hamilton was also delighted with the purchase because the more property he managed the greater his share of the rents collected. 'And how was that, sir? If you don't mind my asking.'

'Not at all, not at all,' Jefferyes replied. 'You know that when his horse stepped on a molehill and King Billy fell off and died, James II's daughter Anne took over in England. The first thing she did was declare war on France and Spain. Well England lost a couple of battles and Sir Richard got it into his head that the McCarthys would soon be back so he figured he'd better get out before it was too late.'

'So will they be back?' Hamilton asked.

'Not at all, not at all,' Jefferyes answered, repeating what must have been his favourite expression. 'Payne is just a nervous type. No faith in the crown and all that stuff.'

Although I hoped that there might be some substance to a rumour that English difficulties with the French would bring the McCarthys back, Sir James Jefferyes' assessment was correct and my walls were to remain in the Jefferyes family for the next couple of hundred years. To my disgust, Jefferyes had no particular interest in occupying my walls as his residence because, despite the comfort I might have provided to the McCarthys, he required a far more modern residence so he built a house against my walls. Apparently, as I was to discover, that was the fashionable thing to do in those days.

I had very little discourse with this structure because, to be quite honest, he was rude, arrogant and effete, not unlike his resident. He told me in no uncertain terms that I was a decrepit and useless building and, for all he cared, I could collapse in on myself. Considering that my own walls abutted his, that comment was an example of his foolishness. Anyway, I ignored him completely because I had been around for hundreds of years and I thought it far more likely that he would collapse. In that, I didn't miss the mark by much because, less than eighty years later, he caught fire, was abandoned and allowed to fall into ruin when a much grander house was built not far from my walls. All that remains of him is a skinny little tower than looks like a smokestack with windows.

A low point in the eighteenth century: my new owners move into
a fancy house built in my shadows.

Despite my confidence, I was deeply distressed by the Jefferyes' decision to abandon me as a residence. It was bad enough that my value as a fortress had been made redundant by Cromwell's guns, but now it appeared that my value as a home had also disappeared. I might have attributed this to the arrogant ignorance of my current residents, but it was clear that the Jefferyes would not occupy me and there were no other possibilities.

The only satisfaction I got from my experience with the Jefferyes was that any money they might have saved in purchasing my walls was lost through their greed.

With a castle of my standing, there are always legends and stories circulating about, particularly when my residents have acquired a particular penchant for telling tales. One such rumour was that the first Donogh McCarthy, faced with the guns of Lord Broghill, had fled my walls in a panic and had thrown all the gold and family treasures into a large lake not far away rather than let them fall into Cromwell's hands. I knew this to be untrue because that departure was organised and well planned, but then no one asked me about it. Nevertheless, the rumour persisted that there was a great deal of treasure at the bottom of the lake.

Jefferyes convinced himself that the story was true and he spent a fortune draining the lake to recover the treasure. I took some pleasure in admiring the bright-red and purple hues that came over his face when the dried lake disgorged no gold.

Although my stone walls stood strong during all those years, my floors and ceilings, most of which were made of wood, were allowed to deteriorate and collapse. Those years were the saddest and loneliest of my existence. I believed that I served no useful purpose except to house birds and animals and many's the day when I looked off into the distant Boggerah Mountains and mourned for my past glory. I was the last thing I ever expected to be – a decaying ruin.

There were times in the middle part of the nineteenth century when I nearly gave up and allowed myself to collapse entirely but part of me would not allow that to happen. Sure I was no longer a fortress or even a home, but I still had the gift, even if few people remembered. My gift, my Blarney Stone, still stood high on my battlements and she would not let the rest of us lose faith.

'Remember,' she said. 'Remember Robert Bruce and his spider. Never . . . never give up. Our day will come again as sure as the sun rises in the east. Our day will come again.'

Thankfully, we didn't give up, and our day did come again.

IV Ascent into Legend (1800–Present)

The nineteenth century found me a deteriorating spectator to developments within the shadow of my walls. I had plenty of time to ponder my past and future because nothing much happened. The Jefferyes family, who held title to the land beneath my walls, grew rich from fortuitous marriages to the likes of John Fitzgibbon, the first Earl of Cork, and Anne, the daughter of David la Touche, who was a banker and the richest man in Ireland.

In fairness, while the Jefferyes may have done nothing but allow my walls to fall further into ruin, they spent a great deal of money improving the grounds around my walls. Each year more trees and flowers were planted, walking pathways laid out and passages through the ancient rocks and boulders were cleared away so visitors could enjoy the natural beauty of the land on which I was constructed. A part of these gardens, called the Rock Close, contains formations that were apparently used in druidic times, although I will admit that was long before I came along.

The Jefferyes also brought industry and commerce to the areas around my walls developing a model village also called Blarney. Jefferyes invested in linen mills and, for a time, Blarney Village was among the most prosperous in the county. Later cotton and then woollen mills replace the linen and the community continued to thrive well into the twentieth century.

As for my own walls, the years passed and I could see less and less hope for the future. It seemed that every few months, another stone fell or another beam rotted through. One of the lowest points of my existence was a visit by Samuel Lewis in 1837 when he was preparing to write a book on the topography of Ireland.

I recall him slowly climbing my circular staircase to my parapets from which he viewed the beautiful countryside below. 'My goodness,' he remarked, 'the countryside is stunning. Too bad about the castle. Although it is picturesque in its own right, a picturesque ruin.' Picturesque ruin indeed. Me, Blarney Castle, possessing powers that few castles could ever dream of, had been reduced by scholars to the status of a picturesque ruin.

In 1846 Louisa Jefferyes, the granddaughter and sole heir of James

St John Jefferyes, married a fellow called Sir George Colthurst. The grounds around my walls were closed to the public and a reception was conducted in the gardens. Since this was the social event of the year in Blarney, the two families were the talk of the community. As the weeks passed I heard a great deal about the Colthurst family from the locals who gathered in my shadows to pass the time of day. The truth of the matter was that, while the Jefferyes were tolerated, the Colthursts were generally disliked. The reason for this distaste was that the family was an integral part of the English establishment and had become high sheriffs of County Cork and members of parliament in the years since Cromwell. In fact, more than one of Sir George's ancestors had found themselves on the wrong end of a bullet fired from rebel hands.

That was the way things were back then – the English gentry married other English gentry and the Irish were kept well clear unless servants or hard labour were required. When the potato, the staple food for the poor, failed in the mid-nineteenth century, the English gentry continued their lives without a care in the world. The Irish who were left to starve, became angry and desperate.

I well recall a conversation between two old men who sought shelter from a cold rain one October day shortly after the Colthurst–Jefferyes marriage in the middle of the famine times.

'Did ya hear now that Widow Barry was taken before the Magistrate's Court by your man Sir George Colthurst for helping herself to just one of his fine turnips?' the one fellow asked.

The other fellow sucked his pipe and shaking his head responded, 'Sure you'd think his nibs would have better things to do entertaining that young wife of his, than going after a poor widow.'

'Right you are,' the first one replied. 'I hardly think that he would miss one wee turnip for a starving woman but there you have it. Anyway, she was fined twenty shillings by the magistrate, Jefferyes, who would be your man Colthurst's father-in-law. Fine chance she had. They probably had a glass of sherry to celebrate.'

The other man nodded slowly, 'I suppose it's off to the poor house for her. If she had twenty shillings she wouldn't be pinching turnips.'

When her father died in 1862, Louisa Jefferyes Colthurst inherited the family estate and soon after began to build a grand new house in the Scots-Baronial style a couple of sliotar pucks south of my walls. I thought that this house was entirely too severe and lacked any appreciable warmth, but the Colthursts were apparently happy with it. Being a good neighbour, I tried to become friendly with this house too but, like the house she was built to replace, she would not have a good word for you on a sunny day. To add insult to injury, Louisa christened her new house, Blarney Castle House. In addition to lavishing money on their house, the Colthursts also spent a great deal more planting trees and flowers and creating a beautiful park in and around my walls. Meanwhile padlocks barred my entrance for fear that someone might cause me damage. Now that was very considerate treatment for a castle that was already in ruins.

On occasion, keys to my walls would be made available to visitors who had some particular interest in seeing what had become of me. On the one hand, I resented these visits because I was certainly not proud of what I had become but, on the other, they did provide relief from the boredom of my existence. Had I been more observant, I might have recognised in the visits signs that my fortunes were again on the rise but, at the time, I was too despondent to notice a pattern. Looking back, however, it is clear to me that, as a result of many factors, my future was far brighter than I realised.

First, there were scholars, other than Mr Lewis of course, whose studies into my history led them to realise that perhaps there was some relationship between myself and peculiarities in and around my walls. Thus they began to connect the smooth talking of Cormac McTeige McCarthy, the wisdom of Cormac Dermod McCarthy, the bardic schools that had been operated in the shadow of my walls, the courts of poetry that continued in the vicinity of my walls and the remarkable ability of Cork people in turning a phrase. Perhaps they recognised it was not mere coincidence that this gifted ability to communicate flourished in my presence.

In addition, rumour is a remarkable commodity among human beings and one rumour, that had never really gone away, was again the topic of more frequent conversation. This rumour – which was in fact the truth – was that the Stone of Scone, on which kings were crowned granting them the wisdom and eloquence needed to rule their people, was part of my walls. As a result curious visitors would often arrive for a glimpse of my famous stone and quite often kissed it in reverence.

I believe it was in September 1858 when a sombre man named Charles who was in his mid-forties with unruly, dark hair and a long beard shaved at the sides, spent an hour on my parapets admiring the scenery before he finally ventured over to my famous stone.

'I propose to kiss the Blarney Stone,' he proclaimed to his assistant, called Tim.

'Why ever would you do a daft thing like that?' Tim asked. 'You could be killed.'

Charles responded with a hint of sarcasm. 'Because it is widely known, at least among those of us who do any significant reading, that kissing this stone can bestow on one a gift of eloquence.'

With the able assistance of at least three handlers, Charles was lowered down and placed his lips against my wall.

When he had regained his feet, Tim looked curiously at his employer and asked, 'Well?'

Charles pondered the question before replying, 'On the one hand I got the fright of my life but on the other, I felt strangely exhilarated, a certain euphoria as it were. I suppose I would say it was the best of times and the worst of times.'

Charles puzzled for a moment longer and then ordered, 'Timothy, write that down.'

Although at the time he was just another interesting visitor, a surge of tourists followed and from them I discovered the bearded man was called Charles Dickens, a writer of some repute. Visitors like that fanned the rumours concerning the gifts available to anyone who would kiss my stone. I am not a great reader but I have it on good authority that my visitor's next novel, *A Tale of Two Cities*, began with the words he uttered after kissing my stone.

One young scholar was particularly instrumental in bringing rumour and history together. The young man had obtained a key to my gates and, on many occasions, he would wander within my walls speaking to me as if I could hear and understand what he said. Of course, I could understand so I attempted to respond and perhaps he heard what the walls had to say. Anyway, his name was Francis Sylvester Mahony and

Eighty-five feet tall and twelve feet thick, built on a limestone rock and rising majestically over the junction of the Blarney and Comane rivers.

he came to me in the first part of the nineteenth century.

Mahony was a Blarney boy, born and bred and the son of a weaver. He originally trained as a Jesuit, so he certainly had a scholarly background but he was ordained as a parish priest and served in the Diocese of Cork. Young Fr Mahony enjoyed writing and over the years published many poems and articles under the pseudonym Fr Prout.

It was soon after one of his visits to my walls that Fr Prout published a poem that first recognised my special power. In part, the poem read:

> There is a stone there,
> That whoever kisses,
> Oh! he never misses
> To grow eloquent.
> 'Tis he may clamber
> To a Lady's chamber,
> Or become a member
> Of parliament.
> A clever spouter
> He'll soon turn out, or
> An out-and-outer,
> To be let alone.
> Don't hope to hinder him,
> Or to bewilder him,
> Sure he's a pilgrim
> From the Blarney Stone!

The publication of this poem apparently revived rumours about my extraordinary powers that had been in circulation since the eighteenth century. Slowly but steadily more and more pilgrims began to appear at my walls seeking to partake in the gifts that I most certainly possessed. When they came, the visitors would discuss all the reasons that brought them to me, from publications in which I was prominently featured to a quiet word from a friend or associate. In this way I was able to keep abreast of my spreading fame.

Among the more famous pilgrims who visited my walls and kissed my Blarney Stone was the well-know novelist Sir Walter Scott who came in the company of Irish writer Maria Edgeworth. I am happy to confirm the accuracy of Sir Walter's biographer who wrote of the trip, ' . . .not forgetting an excursion to the groves of Blarney in whose shade we had a right mirthful picnic. Sir Walter scrambled up to the top of the castle and kissed, with due faith and devotion, the famous Blarney Stone.'

Fr Prout himself related the tale of their visit in an essay called *Plea for Pilgrimages*. In that essay, written on my behalf, he suggests in prose that were someone to kiss my stone, he or she would be blessed with 'the gift of soft talk in all its ramifications' including the ability to captivate the human heart or speak in a grosser grain – as in the House of Commons.

I will admit that I viewed with two minds the possibility that a politician might kiss my stone to acquire elocution. It was flattering that words inspired by my walls might change the course of history but on the other hand, many politicians are not to be trusted and I would hate to bestow my gift when it might be abused. Of course the truth is that I have little control over who seeks to acquire the gift, so I can only hope that it will be more often used for good than for evil.

Only four years after calling me a picturesque ruin, Mr Samuel Lewis updated his *Topography of Ireland* by telling the world of a stone in my walls called the Blarney Stone and that 'if anyone kisses it, he will ever after have a cajoling tongue and the art of flattery or of telling lies with unblushing effrontery'. My gifts were further advertised in so studious a publication as the *Cork Historical and Archaeological Journal* where, in 1912, it reported that a popular tradition attributed to those who kiss my stone was a 'sweet persuasive wheedling eloquence, so perceptible in the language of the Cork people'.

In time, the trickle of pilgrims to my walls became a stream and the stream became a river. As the twentieth century progressed, access to my walls and ultimately my famous stone became easier as motor cars replaced horses. Then, too, the Cork and Muskerry Light Railway provide direct access to my grounds and, further afield, ocean liners became fast and dependable so that Ireland and its treasures were more accessible to the world.

As word spread through published articles and reports, my

titleholders provided greater access to the many visitors who came seeking the gift that I could bestow. During those early years of my reincarnation, kissing my famous stone was not as easy or as safe as it has become. Finding one's way up my winding staircase was fraught with danger because little had been done to maintain the stairs. Not only were their false stairs intended from the beginning to trip up the unwary invader but also the only light came from an occasional slit in the tower so a visitor had to feel his or her way to the top.

My parapets, which capped my external walls, were mostly intact so it was possible to walk from the staircase around the tower. My internal construction, including floor and ceilings had been originally constructed in wood and they had long since decayed and collapsed. Looking down internally from my parapets a visitor could see my ground floor eighty feet down and there was nothing between the parapet and the void. As a result, walking the parapets was a dangerous exercise, particularly on a wet day when a slip might be fatal.

And finally, actually doing the deed required assistance because it was necessary to lie on one's back and slide down into an opening in the floor of the parapet so that the stone, located on the far side of the opening, could be kissed. At the time, there were no side rails to grasp or protective grates to catch a person who might slip from the grasp of the holder, as is the case today. I am sorry to report that a few prospective elocutionists perished in their attempts. Perhaps that was the reason that more people did not take advantage of the opportunity. However, I was pleased that slowly and steadily Ireland, and indeed the world, was learning about the power within my walls.

Lest you think that the visitors were only tourists in search of a tale to tell, even in those early days dignitaries also sought my gifts. In 1912 Sir Winston Churchill himself climbed my parapets and kissed my special stone. I would not be so bold as to suggest that the eloquence he demonstrated, particularly during the dark days of the Emergency, was the result of his pilgrimage. Perhaps it is only a coincidence that Churchill made no memorable speeches prior to that day when he embraced my walls, but made several after.

The early part of the twentieth century found Ireland engaged in its struggle for independence and, on several occasions, clandestine

A current portrait. I am topped by battlements, one of which includes my famous stone. All that remains of that fancy house is a leaning tower.

meetings were held near my walls. I know that my owners were particular targets of the rebellion because of their participation in English rule. A relative from nearby Dripsey called Captain Bowen-Colthurst began a reign of terror in Dublin when, in April 1916, he ordered the summary execution of a famous journalist and pacifist called Francis Sheehy Skeffington. The eighth baronet, and titleholder to Blarney, Sir Richard Colthurst was the High Sheriff of Dublin in 1921 and 1922.

My neighbour, Blarney Castle House, was certainly a primary target for reprisals during the Irish War of Independence, and I remember a dark night in 1921 when a group of men gathered to burn the place to the ground.

'The place is crawling with Tans,' a scout announced.

'Of course it is,' another responded. 'I can't think of any place in Cork that is a more obvious target. The trouble is that the Tans know that as well as we do.'

'So what about the castle?' a young fellow asked. There's no one guarding it.'

'The castle! You eejit. There's nothing there to destroy. Besides, the castle is more Irish than any of us,' the commander responded quickly, much to my pleasure and relief.

A third man offered, 'So why don't we just throw some torches through the window of the Castle House and hope for the best. We have to make some kind of effort.'

In the end some half-hearted efforts were made to torch my pompous neighbour with little effect. The house was usually well guarded by English soldiers who seldom ventured beyond the safety of her walls for fear they would be ambushed. As a result, I continued to serve as a meeting place for other efforts conducted in the region around my walls, perhaps because my walls and grounds provided so many different avenues of escape.

During the War of Independence and indeed the troubles that followed, the stream of pilgrims to my walls slowed somewhat because Cork was not a particularly hospitable place for tourists, at least English tourists. Occasionally, local people would venture to the gardens around my walls for a picnic so I was not totally without human contact. Looking back, I suppose those years that eventually included the Emergency in the late 1930s and early 1940s when much of the world was at war, were a bit of a lull before the storm. I am confident that my legendary status did not remain stagnant yet I was once again relatively inaccessible to the world.

In time, independence and peace returned to Ireland. Prosperity, however, was another matter altogether but some bright minister decided that tourism could become Ireland's principal industry. Government efforts encouraged the development of many interesting sites, not least of which were its castles. I know that many brother and sister castles the length and breadth of the country present the history of Ireland in a most unique and interesting manner. I, however, had something entirely different to offer. I am proud to say that my walls have been embraced, literally as well as figuratively, in a way no other castle can claim.

As the years have passed, the river of tourists who come in search of the gift available only from my walls has become a raging torrent. Tens of thousands of visitors kiss my famous stone every year making me, I would suspect, the most kissed object, animate or inanimate, in the world. Since most of the kisses are directed at one stone in my walls, you might think that a bit unhygienic, however between the rain and sanitary efforts of my minders, the only thing anyone really catches from me is the gift of eloquence.

Because no one knows more about the stone and the powers it contains than me, I am happy to explain a few things to those of you who might one day seek its gifts. You should know that the stone does not bestow her favours lightly, nor does everyone who presses their lips to her cool face actually receive this power of elegant and persuasive speech. A person who kisses my stone for a lark, without a true belief in its powers, will usually be disappointed. Occasionally, she will bestow the power anyway because there is nothing so powerful as a reformed sinner. Generally, however, her gifts are reserved for the true believers.

The power of the Blarney Stone is limitless and no amount of kissing will diminish her supply. The reason for this as you will remember is because an angel inhabited her allowing Jacob to ascend into the heavens and communicate with the Lord. One can only wonder about the power and eloquence of that communication. During this process, a window was opened to eternity and from that window the gift flows. Since eternity has no end, neither do the gifts that flow.

And finally, the Blarney Stone herself has asked me to pass on a soft word to those who, having received the gift, might use it for totally immoral or improper purposes: 'Don't.'

And so I continue to welcome pilgrims from Ireland and all over the world, rich and poor, famous and not so famous, old and young. I am amazed at the variety of interesting people who have called, which certainly keeps me amused in my late middle age. I even recall one man who was the image of my original builder Cormac Láidir McCarthy, a little thinner perhaps but the same sardonic smile, inverted *V* eyebrows, and able to spin a tale with the best of them. Remarkably, I discovered he was Cormac 'the Lean' McCarthy and came from some place in Wexford called Kilmore Quay. I have no doubt that my past residents' blood continues to flow, as strong as my walls, and that provides me with a certain sense of wellbeing. You see, while I am happy to give my gift, I take as much from my guests as I give because they keep me young and alive after all these centuries.

Finally, I know from discussions among my guests as they await their golden moment, that my legend has truly spread to the corners of the world and, in the process, has created its own industry. As imitation is certainly the most genuine form of flattery, I don't object. In many respects it only adds to my appeal, however it does cause me to wonder about human behaviour.

As you must know by now, I am not some shrinking violet who shies from the limelight of public acclaim, however on occasion attempts to benefit or profit from my fame have seemed a bit over the top. I have heard, for example, that there are Blarney Stones to be kissed everywhere from Texas and Missouri in the United States to a virtual Blarney Stone available on a computer monitor. I know that bits of the Blarney Stone seem to have made their way to the four corners of the world, not unlike splinters from the true cross. I can assure you that I have been in constant contact with the Blarney Stone since she came to my walls nearly seven hundred years ago and no one has taken a piece of her yet. Although one particularly inebriated Australian did attempt to bite a bit off her but he broke a tooth instead.

And then there are the pubs, restaurants and shops all over the world which have taken some form of the name Blarney whether it be stone or castle. I have heard visitors speak of such establishments in nearly every part of North America from Boston to San Diego and from Alberta, Canada, to Naples, Florida. I even understand there are eight or ten such establishments in New York City alone. On this side of the Atlantic they can be found in Germany, Spain and any number of other European countries and in Asia and Australia as well. Remarkable, even if I do say so myself. But that is the stuff of legends so you won't hear me object or complain.

Anyway, for all the Blarney Stones all over the world and all the establishments that have borrowed my name, there is only one Blarney Castle and in it is firmly planted only one Blarney Stone. And that, I am happy to report, is myself and a part of my walls. I am not beautifully restored like my sisters Kilkenny and Malahide or my brothers Bunratty or Carrickfergus. When you climb my ramparts you will have to imagine what it was like to live within my walls hundreds of years ago because, quite honestly, I am a ruin. What remains, however, stands tall and strong and I am confident that I shall remain as you see me today, to be enjoyed by generations of humans to come. I am proud to join my brother and sister castles as one of Ireland's strongholds, perhaps its most famous stronghold, because I bring to Ireland and the world a most unique gift – the gift of eloquent speech.

BUNRATTY CASTLE

~

I A Most Inhospitable Beginning (1250–1400)

Welcome, welcome, *fáilte* to Bunratty. It is indeed a privilege to welcome you to my walls and to tell you the story of my existence. I think you will find my story to be particularly interesting because, while I am now famous throughout Ireland and indeed the world for the gracious hospitality I provide to my guests, my early days were quite different to say the least. You see, when I was a young castle, I was the scene of some of the bloodiest battles and sieges in the history of Ireland. And no sooner had I recovered from one battering than some other human beings were launching rocks, stones and other missiles at my walls.

If that weren't enough, along the way the behaviour of some of my occupants was so bad that it made my name synonymous with the worst violations of hospitality imaginable. And then just when I was beginning to feel normal, I was abandoned to fall into ruin. It seems that I was always in the proverbial wrong place at the wrong time. Yet, here I am, centuries later, in remarkably good condition and I am thrilled to provide the most gracious hospitality to those who call on my walls. I still marvel at this remarkable change in my fortunes and I am delighted to be able to tell you how this all transpired and perhaps you will share in my surprise.

I suppose it could be said that my roots go much deeper than nearly any of Ireland's other strongholds because the foundation stones on which my many incarnations have been built supported buildings in Viking times, over a thousand years ago. And if those foundation stones are to be believed, the Vikings were not the first. You see before modern engineering changed the landscape around my walls, I was located on a virtual island, surrounded on all sides by water, bogs and marshland and accessible only by a narrow tract of land. This made my site valuable because it was easy to defend and so various people took advantage of this special topography.

In the late twelfth century the Normans, who originally came from France and had conquered England a century earlier, invaded Ireland. The Normans were well trained and equipped with the most modern weapons and soon they had conquered many parts of Ireland, particularly in the north and east of the country. Their king, Henry II, parcelled out Ireland by granting leases to those who promised the best returns to the royal coffers. Henry didn't seem particularly interested in the fact that native people had far superior claims but that is the way of conquerors. Being closer to England, the eastern part of the country was distributed first to people like Strongbow, Talbot, and De Courcy. These Norman knights built stronghold castles called Kilkenny, Malahide and Carrickfergus, all of which were to play an important part in my own history.

It wasn't until the middle of the thirteenth century that the Norman King Henry III got around to distributing what is now called County Clare but was then part of a region called Thomond. That term is an anglicisation for the northern part of Munster province. Like his predecessors, Henry III was not particularly concerned that native families, particularly the O'Briens and the MacNamaras, had claims that extended back for centuries and this was to cause a great deal of the bloodshed within and around my walls.

The recipient of Henry's lease grant to Thomond was one Robert De Muscegros who agreed to pay an annual rent of thirty pounds provided the first two years were free so he could build a castle. De Muscegros built a wooden motte and bailey fort on the site where I now stand. He first established a proper foundation by adding dirt, rocks and stone to the existing rock footings until a hill – or motte – rose above the countryside at the back end of my island. I learnt much about De Muscegros, and indeed the history of the site, before I was constructed from those same rocks and stones that later became part of my own foundation and which remain part of me to this day. On the top of the motte he built a keep, or wooden tower house, three storeys high. A pathway led down from the motte to the remainder of the island. The bailey – or enclosed yard – with the motte at its centre covered nearly the entire island. There was no need for a moat because the bailey was surrounded by water.

When De Muscegros died a short time after he built this motte and bailey castle, his son, John, succeeded him and continued the business of encouraging commerce around the castle. The town of Bunratty accommodated this growth and grew just beyond my walls. Unfortunately for John's heirs when he died the king, Edward I, had other plans for Thomond. King Edward had a friend named Thomas De Clare who had accompanied him on a crusade to the Holy Land so Edward owed him a favour. Edward revoked the Muscegros lease and granted the whole of Thomond, including Bunratty, to De Clare.

Thomas De Clare was the man who, in 1277, first built my walls and my own story begins with this construction. De Clare was a great-grandson of Strongbow and a cousin to Isabel Marshall, the mistress of Kilkenny Castle, so he was well connected in Norman-Irish society. My first existence was as a rectangular-shaped keep rising forty feet in the air. I was three storeys high although the ground floor was used only for storage and stables. My first floor contained a kitchen, dining room and quarters for staff and soldiers while the second floor was reserved for the lord of the castle and his family. Defensive walls surrounded the stone tower in much the same way as De Muscegros' bailey. At the top of my walls were wide ramparts with high crests from which defenders could shoot down onto attackers. Looking back, I suppose I was little more than a fortified house of dressed stone, but my first memories of those days are when I served as the residence of Thomas De Clare. I thought of myself as a strong and comfortable castle and looked forward to my service to humankind.

Soon after the completion of my walls, any illusions I might have had about the nature of my service were abruptly changed. One evening in 1277, De Clare invited Brian Ruadh O'Brien as a guest of honour to dine in my hall. O'Brien had recently been deposed as the Irish King of Thomond by his nephew, Turlough Mór O'Brien, and he sought De Clare's assistance in regaining his throne.

The meal progressed through many courses interspersed with entertainment and I am sure that my pleasure at this, my first real opportunity to provide hospitality, caused me to emit a warmth that could be felt by all the participants. When the meal ended, the principals toasted each other.

Thomas De Clare first raised a cup into which a drop of each man's blood had been mingled with the wine and announced, 'To the eternal friendship between this house and Brian Ruadh O'Brien. I pledge that we shall always stand at your side and lend whatever support we can to the recovery of your property.'

Not to be outdone, O'Brien raised his cup, 'To Lord Thomas De Clare, by the blood of Christ and my blood mixed with yours and by all the holy relics, bells and crosiers of Munster, I pledge my undying loyalty and friendship to this house, and may I be struck dead if I violate this pledge.'

The pledges of mutual friendship and loyalty were greeted with many shouts of support and the parties returned to their libations. Some time later, De Clare leaned over to his guest and said, 'While I support your cause, I trust that you recognise that I am the lord of these lands holding from Henry III, by papal order the King of Ireland.'

O'Brien laughed causing his host's face to turn a shade of red. 'Whatever you say, M'lord,' O'Brien responded with a mock bow. 'You may have heard, however, that the O'Brien claim to these lands is a thousand years old.'

'Nevertheless,' came the terse reply, 'I am the lord of these lands and you are subservient to me.'

O'Brien laughed again, 'Whatever you say . . . whatever you say.'

'I'll tell you what I say,' De Clare shouted, rising from his seat. 'Guards, seize this man and take him from my house.'

Immediately five burly knights grabbed O'Brien while others subdued the remainder of O'Brien's party and they were all dragged

Here I am in the mid-fifteenth century soon after the
MacNamaras finished my construction. At the time I was
protected by water.

outside into my castle yard. Brian Ruadh was clearly shocked by this behaviour and he continued to protest, 'What is the problem? What of your pledge to eternal friendship?'

Once outside, De Clare's anger erupted into violence as he struck O'Brien with a type of heavy baton, knocking him to the ground. 'I will tell you what I say to you, you uncivilised Irish bastard. I tell you what I say to anyone who would dare to challenge my authority . . . Kill him! Kill him!'

The knights proceeded to beat the poor man to death stomping and kicking him until he lay still, after which they chopped off his head. His body was then tied to a pole, which was planted outside my front gate and his head was skewered to the top. 'Let this be a warning to anyone who questions my rule,' De Clare announced to the people who had gathered at the commotion.

Such behaviour was totally unknown to the native Irish who might have dispensed such retribution but certainly not while the victim was a guest of honour at a banquet. As for me, I felt as though a fog had descended on my walls. This was not what I imagined my role to be. This was certainly not hospitality.

As you might expect, the O'Briens did not forget this incident and much more blood was to flow in and around my walls as a result of it. You see, while the O'Briens may have had no scruples about fighting among themselves, an attack from the outside, especially by a hated Norman invader, required swift revenge.

A few months later Turlough Mór O'Brien, who had seized the kingship of Thomond from his now dead uncle, together with his brother Donal, gathered their clan to prepare for battle. In time, they attacked my walls in the night killing many soldiers and inhabitants living in the vicinity. While my walls held, the siege lasted for some months and many more people died as they lacked proper food and medical treatment. The siege was eventually lifted but the O'Brien memories lived on and so did their hatred of De Clare.

I remember several occasions during which Thomas De Clare tried to sort out his relationship with the native Irish but he had little success. I suspect that, because he had violated the basic Celtic principles of hospitality and honour, he could hardly expect better treatment. The O'Briens continued to besiege my walls and, for some time, I hosted Turlough's son, Donogh, as a hostage against further retribution by the O'Briens. Despite their common animosity towards De Clare, the various branches of the family continued to war between themselves. This made De Clare's position even more difficult because, even if he made peace with one side of the family, a different faction would attack.

Unfortunately, the O'Brien family was not the only problem facing my occupant, because the MacNamara family, who also demonstrated a pedigree of many hundred years, protested their loss of lands at the hands of De Clare. The MacNamaras were traditional allies of the O'Briens and they too were aggrieved that Brian Ruadh O'Brien had been so foully murdered. To demonstrate their displeasure they burned the town of Bunratty on two occasions before the fourteenth century had ended. My existence in those early years was very depressing because all I ever seemed to experience was assaults, fire and blood, and with all his problems, there was nothing my occupant could do about it.

In 1287 Thomas De Clare died peacefully in his bedchambers within my walls but the enmity of the O'Briens and the MacNamaras did not die with him. Thomas was succeed by his son, Gilbert, who himself died soon after, so my next real occupant was Thomas' second son, Richard. Any thought that the acrimony might end with this resident was quickly ended and, if anything, matters got worse.

In an attempt to find peace with at least one faction of the O'Brien family, Richard decided to support the claim of the descendants of Brian Ruadh O'Brien, the man his father had murdered and, for a time, it seemed that peace might result. As it happened, however, the descendants of Turlough Mór O'Brien found their own champion, another Norman knight called Richard De Burgh also known as the 'Red Earl', whose stronghold was a castle in Antrim called Carrickfergus.

'What is he like?' raged my occupant whose temper was not unlike his father's. 'He rules all of Connacht and Ulster and here he is poking his nose into my business.'

'Your orders, sir?' a subordinate asked after De Clare's complexion returned to normal.

'Orders? We will fight the bastard. Those are my orders,' was the reply.

Shortly thereafter, De Clare and his ally, Dermod O'Brien, met De Burgh on a hill within sight of my walls. The battle, if one could call it that, lasted only a matter of an hour or so before De Burgh's men fled for their lives with Dermod in hot pursuit. The Red Earl and his nobles valiantly surrendered and were put into custody within my walls. Although De Burgh was a captive, he was treated more as a guest and a feast was prepared. In the course of the conversation that followed, I heard all about my brother castle Carrickfergus that was, apparently, totally impregnable but a cold and miserable place to live.

'So why would you bother coming down here?' De Clare asked after he had listened to a litany of the Red Earl's conquests. 'Surely it isn't the weather.'

'Well at least it isn't as wet and cold as Antrim,' De Burgh laughed in reply. 'Actually, it's nothing personal. I just thought I'd check the state of this part of the country and, when young Murtagh O'Brien came along, I said why not. You did notice that I didn't put up much of a fight, didn't you?'

The two combatants had a good laugh over the whole thing and when the meal ended De Burgh was not stomped to death. They went on to discuss the activities of other Norman lords and I heard about castles like Malahide and Kilkenny. The two marvelled that the native clans around Dublin had been so quickly subdued which meant that the Talbots of Malahide could concentrate their efforts on making money and not defending their walls. Kilkenny, on the other hand, shared the same problem as De Clare, as the O'Briens had overrun and burned its motte and bailey castle to the ground. Shortly thereafter the Red Earl returned home and my own occupant returned to his problems with the O'Briens and the MacNamaras.

Richard De Clare's response to the MacNamaras was another of the vicious incidents that seemed to plague my walls in those days. When the MacNamaras refused De Clare's demands that they submit and end all violence against the town of Blarney, he hanged three young men whom he held hostage. Two of the boys were sons of Lochlain MacNamara and the third was the eldest son of MacCon MacNamara.

A fourth boy was spared when the clergy intervened and paid De Clare about one hundred pounds. Rather than causing them to submit, this action incensed the MacNamaras and earned De Clare yet another mortal enemy. Not long after, the MacNamaras again burned the town of Bunratty killing any soldier who might venture from the safety of my walls.

In the centuries that have followed, a scene that frequently haunts my memories is that of those young men hanging dead within my walls. I remember thinking, *What kind of existence could I look forward to if I had to accommodate humans who would do such a thing to mere boys?* At the time, I also remember wishing that I had never been built. I certainly had no interest in a future that would require me to accommodate this type of human behaviour but, of course, there was little I could do.

After sorting out the MacNamaras, to use the terms of my occupant, De Clare turned his attention to Murtagh O'Brien. A meeting had been arranged to discuss a peaceful resolution and Richard De Clare rode out to Limerick to negotiate. He was never to return to my walls but messengers to his wife, Johanna, reported the outcome.

When Murtagh refused to submit, De Clare decided to fight. His final stand was near the town of Corofin and it was there that the forces of Murtagh O'Brien and MacCon MacNamara overwhelmed Richard De Clare and his small force and De Clare was killed in the course of the battle. The atrocities committed against the O'Briens and the MacNamaras by De Clare were avenged. Unfortunately, they were not quite finished with me.

On hearing this news and a report that the O'Briens were on their way to ravage my walls, Johanna spent no time in mourning or agonising. She simply ordered that a boat be loaded with her most valuable possessions. When this was accomplished, she ordered that my wooden roofs and interior furnishings be put to the torch. Johanna sailed off to Limerick, never to return. Although my walls had never failed, I was ablaze at the hands of my own occupants. *What an ignoble end*, I thought, *to be destroyed not by attackers after a long defence, but by my own occupant, fleeing in terror.* When the O'Briens arrived at my open gates they found me deserted, empty and wrapped in flame, and departed in search of a more worthy foe.

I do remember the pain and agony of that experience, however there was also a cleansing element to my immolation as I again thought about the murder of Brian Ruadh O'Brien and the hanging of the three MacNamara boys. Perhaps this was what was required to rid me of the stain I acquired from the De Clares.

Although my wooden roof and floors were burned, my stone walls did not suffer greatly from the heat and, although I was damaged, I was not destroyed. A short time later, in 1322, a man by the name of Robert De Welle arrived on assignment from King Edward II to hold my walls until a decision was made about Norman control of Thomond. De Welle repaired my roof and floors so that I was habitable, but he apparently did not have the budget or the inclination to fully restore me to my former state.

A few years later another Norman called Maurice Fitz Thomas, who was to become the first Earl of Desmond decided that my status presented him with an opportunity to establish himself in Thomond. Fitz Thomas ignored the protests of De Welle, that he was awaiting orders from Edward II, and he took over my walls. Fitz Thomas assigned a constable called John Fitz Maurice to hold my walls and, for a few more years, I was nothing more than a pawn in a struggle between Normans.

Meanwhile, the O'Briens and the MacNamaras continued to grow in strength and, without a strong Norman force to contend with, they controlled the land around my walls. I recall Constable Fitz Maurice being particularly concerned about this and he frequently called on Fitz Thomas to provide him with additional forces to defend my walls. Apparently Fitz Thomas had more important matters that required his attention so no relief arrived. Finally, the word came that Brian O'Brien had defeated the forces of the Sheriff of Limerick and was laying waste to the entire countryside.

It soon became apparent to me that Constable Fitz Maurice's concerns for my safety were well founded as the word reached my walls that the O'Briens and the MacNamaras were marching on me, intent on driving the Normans out of Thomond. In 1332 the combined families had their final revenge for the atrocities they had endured within my walls. After a brief siege the constable surrendered and fled leaving me to the mercy of the Irish. Not surprisingly, they laid waste to my walls burning everything that could be torched. The resulting fire and the intense heat was enough to crack my walls in many places.

When the O'Briens and the MacNamaras left, I was effectively a ruin. In the quiet of the Clare countryside, with no occupants to secure and little to do except gaze out on the forests and hills, I thought about my existence. Here I was, only fifty years old and already I had been besieged on any number of occasions, captured three times, burned twice and was now in ruins. Unlike my brother, Carrickfergus, it could hardly be said that I was impregnable. Unlike my sister castles, Malahide and Kilkenny, the last thing that could be said was that I was hospitable. I know it might be said that I was only feeling sorry for myself, but you would have to admit that I was a sorry excuse for a castle, never mind one of Ireland's strongholds.

For over two decades I lay in ruins, a home for nothing more than animals seeking shelter from the rain. In truth I had become rather resigned to my plight because I had no expectations for myself or anyone else. Eventually I became comfortable with the fact that I would spend my days in a rather premature retirement, as it were, an old ruin like so many that dot the Irish countryside.

As it transpired, however, the Normans believed that the land on which I was located was too valuable to remain undeveloped so the king's justiciar, Sir Thomas De Rokeby, arrived at my walls intent on building a new castle. *A new beginning,* I thought, *just what I need. And maybe this time my occupants will do a proper job.*

Rokeby began his work by adding another thickness of rock and stone to the outside of my foundations so that there was no chance an attacker might undermine or destroy my base. I soon realised that he expected that I would be a permanent fixture for many generations to come. Unfortunately, in his position as justiciar, Rokeby was often out campaigning against families like the O'Byrnes in Leinster, the O'Nolans in Carlow and the McCarthys in Blarney. As a result his initial efforts became a hurried attempt to provide a serviceable castle rather than the extensive stronghold I thought I might become.

Rokeby had hardly finished the job when Roger Craddock, the

Bishop of Waterford, sent to my walls two prisoners who were members of the MacNamara family. The bishop's envoy told the custodian Rokeby had appointed in his absence, that the two had been found guilty of some offence against Our Lady and, as they resided within the Diocese of Killaloe, which included my island, they were to be burned at the stake within my walls.

Thinking it best not to challenge the bishop, the two were duly executed, much to my own horror and that of everyone who heard about it. That Craddock's superior, the Archbishop of Cashel, destroyed the Waterford bishop meant little to the MacNamaras who again combined with the O'Briens and overran my walls reducing me to ruins.

You can well imagine my feelings at that time about humans in general, and Normans in particular. At least during my first go I lasted fifty years before inhospitality reduced me to ruins. This time I had lasted less than five years but the result was no less painful or permanent. I was again a ruin and I fervently hoped that the whole human race would leave me to become part of the land from which I came and not bother reconstructing my walls.

My wish was not to be granted because the O'Briens themselves, attempting to ensure that they were well and truly rid of the Norman conquerors, decided that if a stronghold was to occupy my little island, the stronghold would be in the hands of the Irish. The English, as it transpired, were involved with their own domestic problems, known as the War of the Roses, and had little time for further conquest in the west of Ireland. The O'Briens and the MacNamaras, with no foreign power to harass them, became so strongly entrenched in the region around my walls, that it would be centuries before it was wrested from them.

It was these families, particularly the MacNamaras who decided that, if the Normans thought I was ideally placed to be one of Ireland's strongholds, a stronghold I would be. Not a Norman castle like Carrickfergus, Malahide or Kilkenny, but an Irish stronghold like Blarney.

II Days of Power and Beauty (1400–1650)

I know from those who have walked and talked within my walls that there are some beautiful castles across Ireland, many of which were built by the Normans. I suspect that the Irish recognised the power and strength of a castle and they too built strongholds of their own. I was proud to take my place among the Irish castles and, although I have no way of knowing, I believe that few castles of either origin can now match the splendour and stateliness of my walls.

With no wars to fight and no Normans to resist, MacCon MacNamara took nearly ten years to build me so that I would stand for centuries. He used De Rokeby's foundation and continued the pattern of expanding the parts of my old walls that would be used for corner turrets. This provided a more substantial base for these corner towers that were much higher than any of my previous walls.

MacCon first built four square towers, each of which would occupy a corner of my finished walls. Each tower had six floors connected by stairs and each floor contained a small room. After the towers were constructed, walls connected each of the towers and the main block was constructed in the middle. This block contained three floors, although the ground floor was used for storage and to house animals. Access to the upper floors was through a narrow, circular staircase through which only one person could pass at a time making it easy to defend. In addition, the staircase circled to the left so that a right-handed swordsman would have difficulty leading with his sword hand. Apparently MacCon decided that the vast majority of soldiers were right handed.

The first floor contained a vaulted hall, which was the main living room for the common soldiers and the servants of the house. Just off the main guard hall, stairs led down to a dungeon, which could only be accessed through the soldiers' quarters. One half of the second floor housed my great hall where the business of the castle was conducted while the remainder included a large kitchen and private apartments for the chieftain and his family. This floor also housed a small private chapel. The upper tower rooms contained guest apartments as well as a special room for the resident priest and a larger chapel used by the remainder of the soldiers and staff. Each of the tower rooms had particular uses from storage to soldier and staff quarters to toilets. To enter my walls it was necessary to cross a drawbridge and pass through a four-storey arch at the top of which was a murder hole. This opening in the parapet was directly over my main gate and it allowed my defenders to shoot down on anyone who would try to gain entry through the main entrance. Alternatively, the defenders would dump massive caldrons of boiling water, oil or pitch down on the attackers.

Unfortunately, MacCon MacNamara did not live to see the completion of my walls and his son, Sean Finn, finished the job. When my walls were completed in the latter half of the fifteenth century, I was much the same in appearance as you would see me today. That does not mean, however, that the next several hundred years would be any more peaceful for my occupants and I than had been my first two centuries. Of course I had already reconciled myself to such a fate and I could only dream of what it must be like to be in a position like Malahide where attack and destruction were not a concern.

I was only to remain in the MacNamara family for a few decades but it was not blood that finally delivered me to the O'Briens, it was a wedding. The two most powerful families of Thomond united when Turlough O'Brien, Prince of Thomond, married Raghnailt MacNamara, the daughter of the MacNamara clan chief in 1475. I well remember the sunny day in May when the two were united at the Friary Church at Quin and then returned to my great hall to celebrate the occasion.

The bride was particularly beautiful in a long off-white gown that was cinched around her bosom and waist with tiny white beads. Her long, curly brown hair hung loose, strewn with wild flowers. Turlough, tall and strong, stood by her side beaming with the pride of a young man deeply in love with a beautiful woman. The weather was sunny when they arrived but, shortly thereafter, it poured out of the heavens. Not that the weather had any affect on the party because by then they had gathered within the comfort of my great hall.

The bride and groom were seated at table on a raised platform at the top of the hall and the remaining guests took bench seats in front of them. A team of cooks had been working all day, not only in my kitchens, but also over specially constructed pits just outside my walls where many different types of meat and game were slowly roasted on spits. The early courses of the feast included eggs treated with wild flowers, a pie with currants and dates and several different types of fish and fowl. The second course included a wide variety of meats and game, including venison, pork, deer, rabbit, beef and lamb. The third included even more meats as well as chicken, pigeon, quail and pheasant. Finally a massive platter of fruits, vegetables, cheeses and pastries of all types was laid before the couple. The meal was washed down with large quantities of wine and mead, although many of the guests preferred a type of beer.

Between courses the entertainment included much singing and presentations by bards who recited their stories and poems, some of which had been written especially for the occasion. When the meal finished, a musical group appeared and tables were pushed aside enabling my hall to echo with the sounds of laughter and dancing.

The marriage of Turlough and Raghnailt, and the presence of the children born to them, was the first time that I embraced the idea that I might enjoy being a castle. I was finally a strong fortress and a comfortable residence. As a stronghold of the O'Briens, the lands throughout much of Thomond were ruled from my walls. I had been built for defence and, even though the O'Briens faced no serious threat from either their Irish neighbours or the Normans, I was confident that I would stand strong if an attack ever did come. Secondly, I delighted in the squeals of laughter as my residents' young children ran up and down my many staircases with what appeared to be a limitless pool of energy. And at night they slept in the spacious and well-appointed chieftain's quarters. And, finally, I rose majestically over the skyline of Clare commanding all before me, which did my ego a world of good after my years as a ruin.

While I enjoyed the respite from my days of blood and gore, the continuing dispute among the various O'Brien factions, not to mention the English interests, ensured that my existence would not remain peaceful indefinitely. In an attempt to obtain the recognition and support of the English crown, in 1542, Turlough's son and successor, Murrough, decided to make his submission to Henry VIII. This venture was debated within my walls and not everyone agreed with Murrough's decision.

'Why should you submit?' one man asked. 'We dominate Thomond and even though the English would like to think they own Ireland, we haven't even seen them in nearly a hundred years.'

'Nevertheless,' Murrough countered, 'they know how important this castle is to the control of the west and I have heard too much from other parts of the country to think that we will be able to stand against them forever. The northeast and east of Ireland are in Norman hands and the Irish. The English not only have unlimited forces but the most modern weapons and sooner or later they will come and we will have to face the possibility of defeat.'

'So we just give up everything our fathers and grandfathers have built?' another queried.

Murrough responded, 'No. That is what I am trying to say. The English king has announced that any chieftain that submits to his authority and turns over his lands and possessions to the crown will, after a suitable time during which his good faith is established, be returned to his lands with legal title from the crown. Then if our cousins decide to contest our rights, they will have to fight the English as well.'

'But we are Catholics,' another said. 'He is hardly going to make you an earl when you don't recognise his authority over the Church.'

'Don't you worry about that,' Murrough said with a smile. 'What I am here and what the king thinks I am are two entirely separate matters.'

Despite the protests from other members of the family, Murrough O'Brien travelled to London and made his submission to the crown. Henry VIII was apparently impressed as was the English court because word came back to my walls that the Lord Deputy found Murrough to be a man of 'much sobriety and towardness' and shortly thereafter Murrough returned, his lands and castles intact, as the first Earl of Thomond.

For reasons I don't understand, Murrough's son and the second earl, named Donogh, chose to live in another of the O'Brien castles in Ennis so I was occupied by a second son, called Turlough, who then disputed Donogh's right to my walls. The English sorted the dispute my naming a third party, Conor O'Brien, as the third earl and he took possession of my walls as well as those of several other castles including the one at Ennis.

I remember Conor as a big man with a quick temper who knew little about the niceties of dealing with the English representatives of the crown. In April of 1570 an English tax collector named Sir Edward Fitton became a particular subject of Conor's abuse and a decision was apparently taken to deal with Conor. The word soon reached my walls that the crown had declared that Thomond was in rebellion. When the English army began its march, Conor immediately realised the error of his ways and travelled to London to submit once again. In the meantime, James Butler, the Earl of Ormond and Conor's cousin, came over from Kilkenny Castle on orders from the crown and occupied my walls in the name of Queen Elizabeth I.

Like the first Earl of Thomond, Conor was obviously able to impress the queen with his remorse because, after he had surrendered his lands and castles to the crown, she regranted him the O'Brien lands including my walls. As a sign of his good faith, and perhaps as a hostage to his future good behaviour, Conor also left his son, Donogh, in London to be educated in the gentle ways of the English. Conor, meanwhile, spent most of his time at the O'Brien castle at Clonroad. On Conor's death, Donogh returned to Ireland as the fourth Earl of Thomond and immediately reinstated me as the chief seat of the O'Briens.

Since my construction by the MacNamaras over one hundred years earlier, little had been done to alter or improve my walls. I was, however, a strong fortress which had never been taken by force or, for that matter, been challenged. When Donogh came to live in my walls he brought with him an appreciation of the comfortable life in London. In considering my walls he was less interested in the security I provided and more interested in making me more comfortable and accommodating for entertaining his friends and associates.

To that end, Donogh replaced many of my archer's slits with wood-frame windows complete with leaded glass. He also covered my wooden roof with lead providing a far better protection against the elements. Donogh also crowned my corner towers with brick vaulting and rebuilt parts of my upper floors so that they would be a more

comfortable home for his family. He took special care with my great
hall, installing a cut-stone chimney piece and many floral and scroll
decorations made of plaster. I felt that the fourth earl's improvements
may have made me more comfortable for his family, but what I gained
in luxury, I lost in security.

The matter was the subject of discussion between Donogh O'Brien's
military commander, Tomás O'Brien, and himself.

'How are we to shoot out of glass windows?' Tomás inquired.

'And why would you be shooting anything out of my windows?'
Donogh asked in reply.

Trying hard to control his sarcasm Tomás replied, 'Well you see, this
is a fortress and in the event of attack it often becomes necessary to shoot
at the attackers and while it is easy and safe to shoot out of archer's
windows, it is difficult and unsafe to shoot out of a glass window.'

The sarcasm was completely lost on Donogh who had apparently,
forgotten the realities of Ireland during his pleasant days in London.
'Oh don't worry about that,' he replied. 'No one would dare attack us
as we have the sponsorship of the crown. If they do attack, the English
will send an army to sort out the blighters.'

Donogh spent most of his day in my great hall administering to the
matter of his estate from a throne-like chair at one end of the room. His
family lived on the floor above and servants and retainers slept in many
of the small rooms in the corner towers. When that seemed to intrude
on his family's privacy, Donogh built a vault between the north-facing
towers to house excess staff and thus increase his own living space. When
the work was completed, I had been transformed into more of a mansion
house than a castle fortress but everyone who called on my walls
marvelled at the beautiful workmanship. Donogh even began to develop
gardens beyond my walls in the style he had seen in London.

Although I was now an Elizabethan mansion, the earl had certainly
sacrificed much of the security that had made me a stronghold,
deeming it redundant. Unfortunately, he was premature in his
judgement because my days as a subject of bloodshed and death were
not entirely behind me.

War returned to the west of Ireland a few years later in the early
1640s while Barnabas O'Brien, the sixth Earl of Thomond, occupied

my walls. I recall Barnabas as a tall man with long, thinning hair and a furtive look about the eyes that gave the impression that trouble was just around the corner, as indeed it was. I must admit that I had as much difficulty following the contestants and allies as did my occupant and I suspect that any choice he made might have been the wrong one.

At the risk of confusing you, just as I was confused listening to the discussions within my walls, it appeared to me that a confederation of Old English and native Irish Catholic landowners had been established at my sister castle in Kilkenny to govern Ireland on behalf of the crown. This confederation was at war with the Royalists, including the crown they purported to act for as trustee, because the crown didn't care for this independent government acting without its control. The confederation was also at war with a group called the Parliamentarians who did not care for the way the crown was handling matters relating to Catholics. The Royalists and the Parliamentarians were also at war and ultimately the confederation supported the Royalists.

This battle was the continuation of a similar war in England where the English Protestants were concerned about the Catholic leanings of King Charles I, among other things. The parliament they controlled began a civil war against Charles with a man called Oliver Cromwell at the head of their army. After six years of fighting, Charles was defeated and dethroned, losing his head along the way, and Cromwell became the Protector of England.

Whatever about the politics of the day, Barnabas, being primarily concerned with maintaining his own property, sat in my great hall and met with any number of representatives from the various factions. During one such meeting, Donogh McCarthy from Blarney Castle, who happened also to be a step-nephew of my occupant, came over to seek support for the Confederation of Kilkenny.

'But the O'Briens are loyal to the crown,' Barnabas stated.

'As are we, my dear uncle,' McCarthy replied. 'All we are doing is joining together as Catholics to administer our estates in trust for the crown. With the dispute between the king and parliament in England, there is no support or direction coming from London so we are acting in the best interest of the king and the Catholics in Ireland. Why, we even have the support of the Pope.'

After some further conversation Barnabas said, 'Well, I believe you can count on my support but I will, of course, have to discuss the matter further with the family. And I certainly don't want to anger the crown.'

Barnabas then announced his decision to the family gathered in my great hall. He added that everyone would be required to take an oath of loyalty to King Charles reasoning, it appeared, that, since the confederation was in trust for the king, he could support the king without angering the confederates.

Some time later, however, Barnabas met with a distant cousin, Murrough O'Brien, the Baron Inchiquin, who supported Cromwell and the English parliament.

'You see,' Murrough concluded. 'When Charles is gone from the throne, you will want to be seen to have supported parliament, so while I can understand your interest in the confederation, remember that it claims to be interested in acting for the crown, which will ultimately rest with parliament.'

That too, made sense to Barnabas, so Murrough left my walls believing that his cousin was a neutral but had strong sympathies for the parliamentarians. As the matter escalated into a war between the various factions, Murrough sent a fleet of ships controlled by the parliament under the command of William Penn to my walls and Barnabas had little choice but to welcome the admiral. I remember that the whole affair caused my occupant to become physically ill so he sent a representative to meet with the parliamentary representatives. Faced with the immediate possibility that the forces at his door would remove him from my walls, Barnabas consented to join the parliamentary forces and Penn and his forces occupied my walls. By coincidence, I was to discover some years later that Penn had a son, also William, who became famous by founding the American state of Pennsylvania.

Shortly after, Donogh McCarthy returned with an army of his own and I found myself under siege by the confederates. In fairness, this particular siege was not really that dangerous to me because it soon became apparent that, despite his army of some three thousand foot and three hundred horse, Donogh had no interest in bombarding my walls or causing any real discomfort for his uncle. The reason for this,

I was to discover, was that McCarthy thought so highly of my walls that he thought it a pity to cause me damage. Then, too, Donogh was not able to completely blockade the river so William Penn had access to the sea and could occasionally resupply provisions for my occupants. Defence of my walls was assigned to Lieutenant Colonel MacAdam who was a strong leader and very organised so there was little chance I would be retaken by stealth.

Just because I did not sustain any significant damage does not mean that the siege was not long and bloody because it was and lasted for many months. During that time, Penn's forces of some seven hundred men frequently engaged McCarthy's army, often in an attempt to secure provisions, which resulted in casualties. In addition, the town of Bunratty was a target for many attacks and several buildings were burned and residents were killed. In response, Penn finally transported many of the old men, women and children out of the proximity of my walls delivering them to Limerick for safety.

My great hall was the scene of many discussions between Penn and Barnabas. Barnabas was a nervous wreck over the whole affair with a cousin on one side, a nephew on the other, his castle under siege and an army, which required maintenance and provisions, under his roof. In time, my resident's hair began to fall out in bunches. Meanwhile Penn was optimistic.

'I can assure you,' Penn said on one occasion, 'as long as your nephew does not see fit to bombard or fire the house we can hold out indefinitely. My information is that Cromwell will soon be in control in England so it is just a matter of time before he sorts out McCarthy and his people.'

Barnabas shook his head, 'Look at me. My health is shot, my children wake up screaming in the night. This is no way to live. If Donogh wants this place so badly, let him have it and then you can take it back after Cromwell comes. He's hardly likely to burn it once he has control. Meanwhile, I have had enough.'

Penn was surprised as much by his host's decision as by the fact that he was unable to convince Barnabas to change his mind. Barnabas, after all, had previously been quite malleable.

And so it was that in May 1646 Barnabas O'Brien, the sixth Earl of

Thomond and his family left my walls and walked onto a ship to sail
to the safety of Cork. Barnabas was to be the last Earl of Thomond to
occupy my walls. Penn, however remained and the siege continued for
several additional months. In the late spring, the fighting intensified
and it was clear to me that McCarthy intended to overrun Penn's
troops who were entrenched in my shadows.

Still Penn held on and from the discussions he conducted with
Lieutenant-Colonel MacAdam it was apparent that he believed that
relief would come in a matter of days, but the days and weeks stretched
on with no relief in sight. Finally, MacAdam was shot and killed by a
sniper as he looked out of one of my windows and the parliamentary
forces had lost their strong leader. That loss, combined with their
diminishing supplies, left Penn little choice but to withdraw. The
remnants of the defence forces took what few supplies remained and
sailed away from my walls. The Siege of Bunratty was over and
Donogh McCarthy, Earl of Muskerry, walked through my door and
took possession.

In the company of Donogh was the man Pope Innocent X had
designated Papal Nuncio to the Confederation of Kilkenny. Although
he was obviously accustomed to the finer things in life, it transpired
that Cardinal John Baptist Rinuccini had lived in an earthen hut
during the last few months of the siege and he was delighted with the
comfort of my walls.

In fact, I recall him dictating a letter to his secretary Massari in
which he proclaimed, 'I have no hesitancy in asserting that Bunratty is
the most beautiful spot I have ever seen. In Italy there is nothing like
the palace and grounds of Lord Thomond, nothing like its ponds and
parks, its three thousand head of deer.'

Massari added his own comment saying that 'nothing could be more
beautiful as Bunratty's walls are fit for an emperor'.

Of course I was delighted that the Pope's representative should heap
such high praise on me, but then I did consider that, after living in an
earthen shack, I must have been quite an improvement. The
confederation's victory at my walls was, perhaps, its greatest success
and, although Donogh returned to Blarney, for a time I was a centre
for their activities. From meetings held in my great room, it was clear

to me that the confederation was doomed as soon as Cromwell defeated Charles enabling the parliament to govern England. I heard that the confederation eventually joined with Royalists, who supported Charles I, in a treaty brokered by Ormond from Kilkenny Castle but, after he had taken control of England and beheaded the king, Cromwell landed in Ireland in August 1649.

III Days of Fire and Gloom (1650–1953)

It didn't take Cromwell's forces long to march through Ireland leaving behind a trail of death and destruction. Reports continued to reach my walls about his massacring of thousands of men, women and children at Drogheda and Wexford. I supposed that the confederation and Royalist forces were worn out from their fighting each other, as well as the Parliamentarians, but it was soon clear that there was no army that would stop Cromwell, or his inevitable march through Ireland. When my sister Kilkenny Castle fell in March of 1650, the confederation was well and truly destroyed and the mood among my occupants was nothing short of fear and panic.

Soon after the Parliamentary forces took Limerick City after a five-month siege and Clare Castle also fell; the end was in sight for the confederation and Royalist troops. My occupying Irish forces knew better than to stand and fight the English army, so they loaded onto wagons whatever valuables they could take and abandoned me to the wrath of Cromwell. Before they departed, however, my resident troops attempted to set me on fire so that I would not fall, intact, into the arms of the English.

I was shocked to feel flame for the first time in centuries, but it was certainly a reminder of my mortality, not to mention my previous burnings. In one sense, I was disappointed that no attempt was made to defend me against the attackers but then I was hardly a fortress any more and it was only wishful thinking to believe that I could have withstood an assault. For that reason, the shock was not nearly so great as it had been when I was abandoned and burned by Lady Johanna De Clare three hundred and twenty-five years earlier. I was fortunate on this occasion in that the lead roof prevented a major conflagration and damage was minor.

A short time later, the English army arrived and doused the few smouldering remnants of the attempted destruction. After a thorough inspection, they decided that I was a fit stronghold so a Captain Preston garrisoned my walls and I was again in English hands.

Preston had hardly settled into my walls when the Lieutenant-General of Cromwell's forces appeared at my gate in a desperate state altogether. Edmund Ludlow had contracted an illness when he was caught out in the rain and sleet after surviving the Siege of Limerick. His commander, General Henry Ireton, had ordered him to rest and he was near death before he found warmth and hospitality within my walls. While Ludlow regained his strength, it transpired that General Ireton had died of a similar malady so I now housed the commander-in-chief of Cromwell's army.

When he had sufficiently recovered, Ludlow returned to his wars but I was to hear about his subsequent successes when he later returned to me. Among his campaigns, Ludlow personally commanded his army against Donogh McCarthy from Blarney, who had successfully led the siege against my walls on behalf of the confederation. Like my own recent defenders, McCarthy had abandoned Blarney and he made his final stand at a castle called Ross in Killarney. McCarthy was defeated there by General Ludlow and he fled from there to exile in France with Charles II.

Some time after, Edmund Ludlow, who had been succeeded as commander-in-chief by a General Fleetwood, returned to my walls for some well-earned rest and relaxation. Obviously, he remembered his recovery from the fever, and he thought that the hospitality of my walls would provide a relaxing and restorative atmosphere. Since he was in residence for some time, I became well acquainted with the man.

For many years, Edmund Ludlow had been one of Cromwell's strongest supporters and that was the reason he attained such a high rank when Cromwell invaded Ireland. Along the way he made the unfortunate mistake of signing the death warrant of Charles I, making him a regicide. On several occasions guests would call on him to discuss the news of the day and, in the course of one such conversation, I realised that Cromwell's days might also be numbered.

'He what?' Ludlow raged.

His guest replied with a satisfied smirk, 'Cromwell has dissolved the House of Commons. It seems that he doesn't care for people telling him what to do.'

Ludlow sputtered, 'But . . . but that is why we got rid of Charles and put Cromwell in charge. Parliament is supposed to be answerable to the people. He can't do that.'

'Yet . . . nevertheless . . .' was the response.

Ludlow fumed about the matter for several days after which he began to write pamphlets protesting against Cromwell. Before too long he departed my walls having lost his position in Ireland for his troubles. Years later I was to learn that when Charles II was restored to the English throne, most of those who signed his father's death warrant were executed as regicides. That was the fate that befell Miles Corbett who had been rewarded with the occupancy of Malahide Castle after helping Cromwell. Even Cromwell himself, long dead at this stage, was dug up so that his head could be chopped off. My own Cromwellian occupant was apparently able to flee to Switzerland where he ultimately died of natural causes.

As for my own walls, I continued to garrison English soldiers and became the place to which local people would come when they had a grievance. I suppose I was a courthouse of sorts because I housed the baron's courts, where disputes between local residents were judged.

Like many of my brother and sister castles, after Cromwell died and Charles II was restored to the English throne, I was also restored to those who owned me before all the trouble began. In my case, I became the property of Henry O'Brien, the son of Barnabas and, in consequence, the seventh Earl of Thomond. Henry had business interests in Limerick and Cork and, although I caught sight of him one day looking curiously at my walls, he never bothered to take up residence. When Henry died his son, also called Henry, (the eighth earl) – who took a similar disinterest in me – succeeded him. When he died in 1741 the Thomond line of earls died with him and he was the last of the O'Brien earls to claim title to my walls.

Before departing this earth, Henry apparently sold my walls, subject to a mortgage, to a fellow named Thomas Armory who did take up residence for a short time. Armory was a strange chap who spent his time wandering around my walls talking to himself. His formal government position was Secretary for Forfeited Estates, but he also did a great deal of writing during his short residence and I later heard that he had some success in that career after returning to London. I suppose the wilds of Clare were too remote for Armory because he sold my walls on to Thomas Studdert in whose family I remained for the next two centuries. (In passing, and to avoid confusion, it seemed to me that most of the Studderts were called Thomas.)

I suppose I was not unlike my brother castle Blarney in that, when the powerful Irish families were driven away by the English, or by the disintegration of the great clans, we found ourselves in the hands of Anglo-Irish gentry who were allowed to pick the carrion left by the conquerors. When it suited, we were well treated but when it did not, we were allowed to fall into ruin, and that was, apparently to be my fate.

Thomas Studdert toured my walls after his acquisition and decided that I did not merit substantial time or resources. Studdert used my walls for storage and livestock and, for some fifty years, I was merely a curiosity – weathering, growing old, but serving little purpose.

In 1804 another Thomas Studdert built a substantial mansion adjacent to my walls and he made that house his residence. I believe my brother Blarney had a similar experience, but in fairness my new neighbour was not only an attractive building but also quite interesting and I got on well with her. In the years that followed when I was completely abandoned for human use, Blarney House not only kept me up do date on the news and information she got from her residents, but she also kept me entertained so that I never lost heart. This would prove to be important when I was rejuvenated many years later. I suspect that without her spirit and wit, I would have deteriorated much more quickly and would have been in no condition to embrace the opportunity that was eventually to be mine. So to Blarney House, my many thanks.

Anyway, the construction of Blarney House as the Studdert's residence had another benefit to me in that, being so close to his home, Thomas Studdert actively sought ways in which I might be of benefit to him and his finances. One of his first projects was to improve the quay so that ships might more easily discharge their cargoes as well increasing commerce in the area. He also built a bridge enabling better access to the main Limerick road, again with a view to increasing business in the area of my walls. For a time, Studdert used my walls for warehousing, which I must say, is not much more exciting than standing vacant. At least, however, there was more activity in the vicinity to keep me entertained.

Here I am in the early nineteenth century. As land was reclaimed from the water a flourishing community grew within my shadows.

Eventually Studdert undertook some basic repairs and was able to convince the local constabulary that I was an ideal location for a police station and jail. I suppose that it was an improvement on warehousing and several constables moved in with their wives and families. My front gate and entry were festooned with posters offering rewards for the capture of local brigands who, when captured, were held in what had once been the dungeon. I can't think of anyone of note who passed through my walls in those early days but justice was swift and sure and many young men spent their last night on earth confined in my dungeon. There were times, particularly when I was empty and abandoned, that I could still hear their mournful wails.

I was pleased to once again have human occupants. Although providing hospitality for people accused of various acts of violence and villainy, not to mention their jailers who were not the most pleasant people, is hardly the existence I envisioned for myself.

During the early 1840s, an English gentleman visited me on his tour of Ireland. While on the road to Limerick, William Makepeace Thackeray happened upon my walls and immediately entered into a discussion of my history with the head constable. A Sergeant Moloney accommodated Thackeray as he insisted on seeing nearly every room within my walls from the small tower rooms to the great hall. He stopped short of viewing the roof as he decided it was too treacherous but he was apparently greatly impressed with what he saw.

I was to discover that Thackeray was a famous English writer who published some well-known novels like *Vanity Fair* and *Barry Lyndon*, but he also wrote a travel book called *The Irish Sketch Book* in which he apparently romanticised my history and appeal. I decided that an ageing and decaying castle like myself can't get enough of this type of publicity and, perhaps, it contributed to my renovation some years later.

Subsequent generations of Studderts made some small efforts to preserve parts of my structure but, for the most part, the nineteenth century was particularly hard on my walls. With no heat generated from within, either by cooking fires or human bodies, I could feel the dampness loosening my mortar. Soon rocks were crumbling and I became a shadow of what I once was. The constables, known in the latter part of the nineteenth century and early part of the twentieth century as the Royal Irish Constabulary continued to use my walls as a police station. Because I had deteriorated to such a degree, no officers stayed within my walls and the families were long gone. The actual barracks was in the annexe vault that Donogh O'Brien had added to my northern walls some three hundred years earlier when he needed additional housing for his staff.

I recall a conversation in what had once been my main guard room on my first floor some time during the second decade of the twentieth century. The participants – the current incarnation of Thomas Studdert, my titleholder, a surveyor named Jones and a Constable Byrne – were considering my state of repair and what my future would be.

'I'm telling you, mate,' Byrne said, 'I cannot continue to agree to pay rent on this place unless you are prepared to make significant repairs. Last week one of my constables broke his leg falling down those crumbling stairs. A prisoner could nearly walk out of here, the doors are in such poor nick.'

Studdert replied, 'Do you have any idea what the most basic repairs would cost. You pay me twenty pounds per year, which would be hardly enough to repair the roof. Perhaps if the rent were increased . . .'

'Not a chance, mate,' came the quick response. 'Here is a list of what we require if you want us to continue to rent this mess.'

Studdert gingerly took the list as if it might burn him and handed it to the surveyor. 'What do you think?' he asked.

The surveyor glanced at the paper and responded, 'At a glance, I make it a couple of hundred pounds.'

'Which I certainly don't have. Do you have any suggestions, Mr Jones?'

Jones considered the matter for a moment and replied, 'I suppose you could donate it to the Board of Public Works and they could take it over for its historical value. You might even try to get some compensation for the money you put in to keep it standing but I wouldn't count on that because funds are tight.'

I understand that Studdert did take the surveyor's advice because some weeks letter other surveyors from the commissioner's office appeared in order to make an initial assessment. Soon I was beset by inspectors and surveyors who probed every part of my walls, floors and ceilings. Some time later, the entire board of the Royal Society of Antiquaries made an inspection and some archaeologists did some digging around my walls to determine if I had any historic value.

I followed these proceedings with interest because I believed that they would greatly influence my future. If I was found lacking I would doubtless continue to deteriorate and, like many castles in Ireland, I would serve little purpose except to provide another picturesque ruin to the Irish countryside. On the other hand, if I were to be found strong enough, remedial works might be undertaken and, at some future time, I might be restored. I knew that I would never again be a fortress or even a residence, but the words 'cultural centre' and 'museum' were particularly intriguing as possibilities for my future service to humankind.

I specifically recall the Chief Inspector from the Board of Public Works, who marched around, hands behind his back dictating notes to a secretary who trailed after him like a puppy trying to keep up.

Among Mr Salmond's most positive comments were, 'The castle walls are plumb and there are no serious cracks' and 'there is practically no vegetation or ivy which might weaken the mortar'. On the other hand, he also reported that, 'The turret roofs cannot be seen for the grass growing on them' and 'there is no roof over the main portion of the castle' and 'significant pointing and cleaning would be necessary'.

I subsequently discovered that I had passed the inspector's test and that he recommended that I be acquired as a national monument. Unfortunately negotiations with Thomas Studdert slowed the whole process because he did not particularly want to completely part with his ownership interest, especially when there was a chance he might be further compensated down the line. Little did I know that Studdert's conflicting interests would haunt me for many more years to come.

When there was little chance that I would be anything but a continuing drain on his resources, Studdert was happy to part company with me. If my walls were to become an historic sight to be visited by tourists and other interested parties, however, then he wanted a share of the admissions. On the other hand, Studdert lived in nearby Bunratty House and he did not want to be bothered by visitors who might call at inopportune times and disturb him in his enjoyment of his house. His definition of those times seemed to coincide with Saturdays, Sundays and holidays when visitors would be most interested in seeing my walls.

As I followed these discussions and negotiations, thanks in no small measure to my friend Bunratty House, I decided that Thomas Studdert vaguely reminded me of my former resident Barnabas O'Brien. Both were interested in being very sure that any decision they made would be the right decision and in consequence, made no decision at all. Perhaps, I thought, there is something about me that engenders such indicision.

Anyway, between the toing and the froing no decisions were made and the next thing I heard was that Ireland was involved in a War of Independence so the English government was no longer interested in acquiring castles in Clare or anywhere else for that matter. I sat abandoned for the next several years, still deteriorating and most concerned that, at a subsequent inspection, I might not be so fortunate.

I was not without some human company because Studdert, having been enlightened to the possibilities presented by visitors who might want to tour a structure of my character opened my doors for a small charge. His venture was neither professional nor safe but he was happy to take the odd shilling when it was available, which I will admit was not frequent during those troubled times.

Studdert was able to provide a general history of my walls but he seemed to concentrate on exaggerating the contributions of his own family, which were minimal in comparison with those of my previous occupants. Then, too, he was not inclined to climb my narrow staircases so he allowed the visitors the run of my castle. Because of my age and lack of maintenance, I was unable to provide a safe visit and many of my guests departed with one injury or another. These injuries caused me great regret because they reminded me of my continued deterioration and, of course, my failure to provide comfort and hospitality to those who visited.

Perhaps, I should not have worried about my condition, as it had been nearly three hundred years since I had been completely occupied and I still stood strong. The problem was that I noticed every little change in my condition. Each time a crack appeared it would accumulate water and in no time it seemed to become a gaping hole. In time I had another worry which was that some human visitors had little interest in my preservation and were vandalising my finishings or, indeed, my very structure. I was well aware from my earliest days that it is one thing to withstand the assaults of nature and quite another to withstand the assaults of humans intent on your demise.

I well remember these 'guests' who would establish themselves in one of my rooms or towers and pull down any loose wood they might find to light a fire for their picnic. In addition it seemed that carved brickwork was a souvenir worth taking, so bits of my mantels and cornices were pulled down causing further damage.

While it might have only been a few years, it seemed an eternity before Ireland had established its independence, survived a civil war and put together a government administration that was capable of addressing its antiquities, including myself. In 1935 negotiations with Mr Studdert were begun again but, unfortunately, he was no easier to deal with than he had been twenty years earlier. He was also ageing and there was little he could do to prevent the vandalism causing great concern among those who worried about my welfare.

In telling you about my history and those who made me what I am, I would be remiss if I did not mention one man who was my guardian in those days when entry was available to anyone who called on a neighbouring pub owned by a Mrs Ryan. Sergeant Longaigh of the local Garda station frequently called on my walls to inspect my condition and personally chased off several people who would cause me harm. He also posted notices on my walls warning of the dire consequences that would befall any vandal and he campaigned for my rescue from Mr Studdert.

The Irish government's Board of Works and National Monuments Advisory Council began negotiations with Mr Studdert and commissioned more surveys and studies. It seemed to me at the time that not a week passed without some team of surveyors probing my innards but I certainly recognised the importance of the exercise if I was to be rescued. Once again, however, Studdert who spoke generally about donating my walls to the State was reluctant to part with his full interest when completing the transaction was discussed. In time, the negotiations intensified but, once again, circumstances put my future development on hold.

On this occasion it was World War II and the Emergency that caused the Irish government to consider its monetary priorities and, although I am sure they thought that I was important, the security and survival of the nation was vital. Looking back on those days, I can laugh at the way my hopes and expectations rose to dizzying heights only to be dumped to the depths of doubt by matters totally beyond my control. One day plans would be laid for my role as a living museum welcoming guests from all over, and the next day old Mr Studdert would be insisting that he was not going to just give away his family heritage that he had so carefully protected. While I laugh now, you can imagine my frustration at the time.

Eventually the Emergency ended and post-war prosperity brought with it new hopes that I might be restored, or at least preserved. For once I was fortunate in that the government's plans for developing the tourist business began at Shannon just down the road from me. Shannon was to be Ireland's international airport and tourists, particularly from the United States would greet Ireland from its gates. Perhaps the first sight these tourists would see would be my imposing walls. Suddenly, it seemed, my rescue was an important part of the nation's plans to develop its tourism industry. And so, once again, I was beset by surveyors and planners.

I was well prepared for another long and protracted session of negotiations between various government agencies and my owner Mr Studdert and I hoped that this time my future would be secured. Studdert was very old but, perhaps, he was even less inclined to part with my walls. After all he had nieces and nephews, some of whom had assisted him in his attempts at maintaining my walls. Studdert made it clear that, if the government expected to make money from tourists who came to my walls, they should be willing to pay his family for their years of sacrifice. Having heard that song before, I did not allow my expectations to rise above mild curiosity.

What occurred in 1953 took me so totally by surprise that I have never quite gotten over the shock. Quite simply, an English lord with Irish roots appeared at my walls, as had many other visitors before him. Again, like others he marvelled at my imposing presence and asked many questions about my history after which he departed. I discovered some short time later that the gentleman marched over to my reluctant owner, Thomas Studdert, and offered him one thousand pounds for my walls and a bit of land around me. Perhaps it was the size of the offer that in those days was substantial, or perhaps he caught Studdert in the proper frame of mind but whatever the reason, Studdert accepted the offer and I was born again.

IV Days of Resurrection and Redemption (1953–Present)

While I was delighted to part company with Thomas Studdert, I was not immediately euphoric about my future. On too many occasions during the previous seven hundred years moving from one occupier to the other was not unlike jumping out of the frying pan and into the fire. However, I was delighted to discover that, on this occasion, not only was I in safe hands but my future was secure.

I quickly discovered that Robert Vereker, Lord Gort in the Irish peerage, was the new owner of my walls. Gort's family ties to Ireland dated to the seventeenth century when he took over lands confiscated from the O'Shaughnessys so I suppose that made his family Cromwellian Planters. In the twentieth century, however, Gort was an enthusiastic supporter of Ireland and its antiquities, which, I reluctantly admit, included myself. Anyway, Lord Gort had a great interest in the history of Ireland from the days his family first came to this country and a more general interest in medieval history. More importantly for me, however, was that he had the enthusiasm, resources and connections to restore me to a grandeur I hadn't known for over three hundred years.

Soon scores of architects, historians, archaeologists and builders swarmed over my walls, but this time the discussion was not about what might be done if I was available for development, rather what would be done. As I had long hoped, the plan was to restore my walls to the way I appeared before Barnabas O'Brien departed. I would then become a living museum so that people could learn about the times when I was the dominant stronghold in the west of Ireland. For the first time in years, I felt young again and when I looked at my wrinkles and cracks, I knew that they would soon be repaired.

I recall many discussions among developers and professionals in those early days and, in every case, the enthusiasm of my benefactors was clear. Lord Gort was a self-effacing man, with a good sense of humour and none of the pretence I might have expected of a titled gentleman.

'I am not a professional architect,' he declared, 'or any type of a professional come to think of it. A little law, perhaps, but that hardly counts now does it.'

'So you will be leaving all of the decisions to us, is that it?' an architect enquired.

'Quite,' Lord Gort replied. 'But I will be looking over your shoulder at every turn and I should like to be kept well informed on everything that is going on. You know I do have a bit of knowledge in these matters and I might have some ideas for you to consider.'

In time I realised that his 'bit of knowledge' was quite extensive and he had made medieval antiquities his life work. Lord Gort's ideas were always well reasoned and were accepted as often as not. Despite his status, my new owner was well liked by the men who actually worked on my walls and they were always happy to stop for a brief chat and show him what they were doing.

Although Lord Gort may not have formally qualified, I was to become quite accustomed to the presence of actual professionals who, in some respects, were my surgeons, cutting and sewing, bringing me back to health and life. That is not to say that they were always in agreement as to the manner in which the patient was to be treated. On occasion the opinions were rather strongly held and the debates quite volatile, but I put those down to the great interest and enthusiasm of my benefactors for my future.

One important professional was called Percy LeClerc from the Office of National Monuments. This man, who had been involved in the turbulent negotiations with Mr Studdert, was particularly pleased that my restoration had begun. The problem that he presented was that I had been taken into the guardianship of his office, which, as a rule, endorsed only preservation and not restoration. My understanding of the difference was that, according to the letter of the law, Mr LeClerc's office was empowered to acquire historic sights and ensure that they did not deteriorate further. Visitors could then view these sights in whatever state of rack or ruin they happened to be in.

When I heard LeClerc proclaim this restriction on any number of occasions, I thought it particularly unfortunate. Of course, I had become aware of castles, like Blarney for example, that had deteriorated to such a degree, that restoration would require rebuilding substantial parts of the original castle. That, however, was not my situation as I had survived my years of neglect in relatively sound shape. My restoration required repairing or replacing what had survived, rather than rebuilding what had fallen down.

Besides, I have been around humans long enough to know that it would take a rather vivid and knowledgeable imagination to appreciate life in a complete ruin. Although I was hardly a complete ruin, I thought I could be of far greater service if, properly restored, people could actually see and understand life in my walls many hundreds of years ago.

While Mr LeClerc was adamant about his responsibilities, he was flexible enough to see that I could be something special. As a result, he was able to bend the rules to allow the restoration effort but in deference to his office he was insistent that the job be done as precisely as possible presenting a true picture of what I once was. I became very familiar with Mr LeClerc because he was in nearly constant attendance to ensure that my restoration met this strict criterion.

Another professional who contributed greatly to the effort was an antiquarian and historian named John Hunt. Mr Hunt had participated in other castle restorations and was very familiar with the process. Although he certainly knew the detail that would be found in any particular historic period, Hunt believed that restored castles could be valuable tools for teaching history. This did not necessarily mean that my walls needed to be a precise duplicate of the way they assumed I had once appeared but rather I should present a concept from which visitors could learn.

This made some sense to me because, after all, I had been a castle for over seven hundred years and to attempt to recapture a moment, say August 1633, would not only be impossible (even if they consulted me as my memory is not what it once was) but not particularly instructive. History, after all, is not a snapshot, but a moving picture.

As you can imagine, Hunt did not always agree with LeClerc's insistence on precision. 'Precise to what?' he would often query. 'This fine castle has seen centuries and we would have to actually tear things down to make it a precise duplicate of anything in the sixteenth or seventeenth century.'

Another matter of contention also related to Hunt's historic interest. Knowing that my grounds must certainly contain valuable relics of my

Here I am today, welcoming guests from all over the world to my famous banquets.

existence, Hunt performed various archaeological digs, at one point excavating my basement. This activity also ran afoul of LeClerc's insistence that my basic structure be untouched so I witnessed a few 'discussions' relating to those diggings. On the other hand, one thing there was little dispute about was Hunt's expertise in identifying proper fixtures and furnishings and in consequence I was adorned with many very familiar pieces.

The Irish government was understandably interested in my restoration because I would certainly be important in promoting tourism. I understand that they assisted in the funding of my repairs and were represented among the professionals by Brendan O'Regan, the then Chairman of Bord Fáilte, as the Irish Tourist Board was called. Mr O'Regan co-ordinated this funding and he worked closely with the architects and historians as well as with the builders.

I soon came to understand that, with a castle of my age, it was very difficult to budget the cost that might be involved in restoration. I was aware from the many discussions over drawings in what had once been my main guard room, that funding was a constant concern and, over the next few years, work stopped on several occasions while the matter was sorted out. Fortunately, Mr O'Regan was strongly committed to my future so eventually work began again. In addition, I suspect by virtue of his training as a master of hospitality, O'Regan was well able to mediate disputes, and that was a skill that was certainly required during the course of my development.

There were many other professionals, including carpenters, brick masons and other tradesmen who contributed greatly to my new life, far to many for me to mention, yet without them I would still be a ruin. The government's Board of Works who had their own agenda, which was also preservation and not restoration, undertook the physical construction. While LeClerc might have been inclined to allow some latitude between the two, the Board of Works didn't. Fortunately Brendan O'Regan was the liaison person who was able to find enough common ground to ensure my completion.

Perhaps the most obvious example of all these conflicting interests was in my modernisation. You see, in my earlier days, I was not equipped with electricity, modern plumbing and heating or many of the amenities that people would expect in the twentieth and twenty-first centuries. In truth, although I was comfortable for the times, times change – and I would hardly be comfortable for modern guests. Not only that, but I would not be particularly safe, because a circular staircase that was constructed to guard against easy access by a right-handed medieval swordsman would be even more daunting for a sixty-year-old tourist. If I were to be a commercially viable attraction, as was certainly the hope of Mr O'Regan and Bord Fáilte, it was not possible that I exactly replicate my prior self either for any particular time or specific year. In fairness to all my professionals, this delicate issue was often discussed and argued over but it did not stop my restoration.

The actual work on my walls continued, with some interruptions, for over six years. I suppose by modern standards that is a considerable period of time but I remember that some earlier work on me took nearly as long. In any event, I was thrilled with the efforts and each day felt more and more revitalised. My walls were all pointed and cleaned and crumbling stones were replaced. My floors were completely refinished with stone tiles nearly identical to those trod by the O'Briens. My roofs and ceilings were also replaced and wall panels and fireplaces restored. I was amazed at the detail of the work, each step of which was supervised by an expert in castles of my vintage. Of course, that was one of the reasons it took so long to return me to my former glory. While a modern process might have taken less time, my workers were interested in restoration not mere building.

Finally, furnishings began to arrive that would truly replicate my past glory. Again, it was Lord Gort and John Hunt who provided many antiques from their personal collections. Not only were my walls much like they had been nearly four hundred years ago, but my furnishings were either original or remarkable replicas of the furniture and fixtures that I housed those many years ago. Of course, I knew that the twentieth century was over half gone, but I certainly felt centuries younger as if I was magically transformed into my previous existence with Donogh O'Brien, my Great Earl.

Once more, I towered over the Clare countryside, a proud monument to the greatness of the Irish people who built my walls. Once more I was one of Ireland's strongholds, albeit serving an entirely different purpose to that for which I was originally constructed. I need no longer worry about protecting my guests from the inhospitality of man, although safety from the elements was certainly part of my remit. Most of all, I was reborn to provide the most gracious hospitality for all who might enter my walls. After seven hundred years, I was thrilled to be able to provide that gift.

I well remember the day in May 1960 when my gates were thrown open and my new life as a centre of Irish hospitality was launched. The government minister responsible for formally launching my new existence was Erskine Childers who was the Minister for Transport and Power. I must admit to a little confusion about the connection between Childers' ministry and myself but as I was basking in the glow of the occasion I gave it only a passing thought. As he subsequently became the President of Ireland, I now feel honoured that he attended. The Bishop of Killaloe celebrated a Mass in the chapel off my great hall with a choir of priests providing Gregorian chant.

Those in attendance included, of course, Lord and Lady Gort, John Hunt and Brendan O'Regan although unfortunately Percy LeClerc was not in Ireland at the time. There were also celebrities including the famous film director John Huston and his daughter Angelica, who would subsequently become a famous movie star. I was also delighted to have an O'Brien, although I don't know the connection between the famous Limerick novelist Kate O'Brien and my previous occupants. Throughout the afternoon, John Hunt gave tours of my walls describing the detail of my restoration and furnishing.

For some reason that is entirely unclear to me, the luncheon celebrating my rebirth was held at some other venue but I did welcome a drinks reception at which a great deal of mead flowed freely, not unlike the feasts of my distant past.

When I had been officially opened for public viewing, I thought that, perhaps, visitors from all over Ireland and the world would soon flock to my gates. But I soon realised that it takes time and effort to promote any attraction. Promotion also costs money and in the early 1960s that was a commodity in short supply, at least in the west of Ireland. Fortunately the effort was in the capable hands of Shannon Development, which saw me as the foundation stone upon which tourism in the region would be built. In my first year of operation four thousand six hundred people toured my walls many of them from America.

Just as in the days when Robert De Muscegros first built me, commerce was attracted to the area around my walls and I became a hub for other tourist amenities. Ryan's pub, where keys to tour my walls could be collected in the Studdert days, experienced its own rebirth as Durty Nellie's pub, which has since become synonymous with a visit to my walls and has also acquired an international reputation.

I am particularly fond of the Bunratty Folk Park, also in the shadow of my walls. You see there were any number of critics who complained that, whatever about my renovated walls and the entertainment I provided, I was not a reasonable depiction of how the vast majority of people lived centuries ago. The Folk Park answers those critics by providing a wide range of displays showing the conditions under which Irish people lived in the last seven hundred years. The displays include a fine Georgian mansion in the form of my good friend Bunratty House at one end of the social spectrum to one-roomed thatched cottages where the poor lived. Nearly everything in between is also included and costumed guides are happy to assist visitors in understanding the trials and joys of ordinary people who lived within the shadow of my walls. The displays also include shops, mills, forges, schools and nearly any amenity you would likely find from those days. I take particular pleasure, on a fine summer's afternoon, in watching the delight that the park and especially the animals bring to the eyes of little children. Bunratty Folk Park has continued to grow and develop in the years since it opened and like myself, it gets better with each passing year.

I believe that it was in the second year after my doors were reopened when I heard a comment that redefined my service to humankind. I heard someone say that I was not a museum where people view relics of times long dead, but rather a vital and living place where people could step into history and actually experience life in those ancient times. That, I decided, was very special indeed because it gave me the opportunity to provide an even more gracious and hospitable atmosphere to those who called. Happily, it was an atmosphere with which I was most certainly familiar.

It was during that second year that the great medieval banquets returned to my walls and to my immense pleasure they have not left. Guests are invited to a feast in my great hall where they are seated on benches not unlike those in the time of the O'Briens. An Earl and Lady of Bunratty and Lords of the Feast are designated to preside over the banquet, which is served by a staff dressed remarkably like those who served so many years ago. In truth, the food served, is not quite the same due primarily to modern hygiene requirements, which is probably a good thing for my guests. Although the food does not include the numerous courses that were once served, the courses my guests currently eat are well presented and certainly enjoyed. They eat as in the days of my earlier banquets before the fork had been invented with knives, spoons and fingers.

A knave is also designated and he or she is promptly removed to the dungeon and then required to sing for his or her supper. I recall one such knave, a smallish, gingery fellow, who had been 'volunteered' by his sisters and two giant friends. To claim his supper he stood at the back of the hall singing a song entitled 'Oh Lord, It's Hard to be Humble'. Although I don't recall ever seeing such a thing in any of my previous experiences, it was all great fun and that, after all, is the reason for my current service to humankind.

Just as in days gone by, the meals at my banquets are washed down with unlimited quantities of mead. On occasion, snuff is provided for anyone who chooses to partake. Since most people have not had that particular experience before there follows a great deal of sneezing and watering of eyes. After the feast, the entertainment begins with music, song, recitations and dance which, I can assure you, sends waves of nostalgia flowing through my walls. I suppose one of the things I appreciate most about the entertainment is that it is authentic to the times with traditional Irish airs. It is quite unlike the modern Irish and Irish-American songs that I often hear in the singsongs after the entertainment concludes. In many respects, these banquets within my walls might as easily be hosted in the early 1600s instead of modern times and believe me, I could not be happier.

In truth, the banquets are not exact duplicates of what was once an occasional experience three hundred years ago. Rather, they present the visitor with a flavour of a history long past and no one knows that better than myself. I can assure you, however, that I have enjoyed every minute of my new existence and particularly these celebrations. After all, in addition to the tours of my walls, I am able to host two parties nearly every day.

And what wonderful parties they have been. I could not begin to tell you all about the thousands of people famous and not so famous who have celebrated within my walls or entertained my guests. I remember well some of those guests from years ago, including Princess Grace of Monaco. Being originally Grace Kelly of Irish heritage, she was particularly delighted with her experience and was the talk of my walls for some years after. More recently, I have hosted the Crown Prince and Princess of Japan, glamorous actresses like Demi Moore, famous actors like Peter Ustinov, modern singers like Harry Connick Jr, traditional Irish singers like Katie McMahon and Irish tenors like Anthony Kearns, to name but a few.

And then, of course, there are my entertainers. For many years, before equal status laws caught up with such things, they were all women but now men are also included. My entertainers are incredibly talented at singing, dancing and playing their musical instruments and are all beautiful in their own special way. As they are called Bunratty Performers, they have become world famous in their own right. I remember one young girl from the early 1990s called Noelle Fogerty. Not only could she sing like a bird but also, like many of my entertainers, she had a great way with the guests. I recall many older women who assured Noelle that their son back home in America, Australia or somewhere else was the perfect match for her.

I know that working within my walls is just a stop along these young people's journey through life, but I must say that I enjoy every minute they spend with me. I hope they remember me as much as I remember them. Each year I eagerly look forward to the new faces who will join me in providing hospitality and welcome to my guests for many years to come.

As for my future, I am confident that it is secure. In 1969 Lord and Lady Gort, recognising their own mortality, sold their ownership of my walls to a trust, which would be administered by an organisation called Shannon Development. The purchase price was ten thousand pounds, a fraction of my value and substantially less than they had invested in my rebirth.

The trust document requires that my walls are to be used as a contemporary national monument and made available to the public. I may also be used as a tourist amenity and entertainment venue provided that all profits are used for my maintenance and further development. When the documents were finally signed and sealed, I knew my future was secure because trusts, like buildings, tend to exist well beyond the life of any one person. In a remarkable display of generosity, my former owners Lord and Lady Gort then contributed the proceeds of the sale to acquire furniture and furnishings for my walls.

I would have had little contact with my various occupants who left my walls for different reasons over the course of the centuries and, when they died, it would have had little impact on me – if I were even aware of the death. However, when Lady Gort died in 1972 and Lord Gort died in 1976, I truly mourned their passing. This couple's kindness and generosity had rescued me from dereliction and ruin and provided me with an opportunity to continue to serve humankind. I trust that they know, wherever their souls may travel, that I will not disappoint them.

And so, here I am over seven hundred and fifty years old and in the prime of my life. I suppose I will always be scarred by the fire and destruction that accompanied my early years. I will certainly never forget the gross inhospitality of my early Norman residents, but I consider myself among the most fortunate castles in the world. You see, I have been given a chance to redeem my good name. For me, each day is another opportunity to welcome and provide hospitality to old and new friends from Ireland and all over the world. What existence could possibly be better than that? I am proud to be one of Ireland's strongholds, but my strength is now in my welcome, or *fáilte*, and I look forward to providing my unique service to humankind for many generations to come.

Important Dates for the Castles' Days of Power

1066   The Normans, under William the Conqueror, are victorious at the Battle of Hastings and take England

1118   Cormac McCarthy (**Blarney**) named King of South Munster

1154   Henry II becomes King of England

1155   Pope Adrian issues papal bull *Laudabiliter* authorising Henry II to invade Ireland and bring truth and the Christian religion to the 'rude and ignorant' Irish

1170   Richard De Clare (Strongbow) invades Ireland, captures Waterford and begins the Norman conquest of Ireland

1172   Strongbow first builds on site of **Kilkenny**

1174   Richard Talbot granted lease for **Malahide**

1176   John De Courcy (**Carrickfergus**) granted right to conquer Ulster

1177   Stone walls of **Carrickfergus** first constructed

1189   Richard I (Lionheart) succeeds his father Henry II as King of England

1190   Stone walls of **Malahide** first constructed

1191   Stone walls of **Kilkenny** first constructed

1199   John succeeds his brother Richard I as King of England

1204   Hugh De Lacy (Earl of Ulster) takes control of **Carrickfergus**

1210   King John captures **Carrickfergus**

1210   Stone walls of **Blarney** first constructed

1216   Henry III succeeds his father John as King of England

1242   **Carrickfergus** expanded to current configuration

1246   Robert De Muscegros granted lease to **Bunratty** and builds first castle

1262   De Burghs take control of **Carrickfergus**

1272   Edward I succeeds his father Henry III as King of England

1276   Thomas De Clare granted lease for **Bunratty**

1277   Stone walls of **Bunratty** first constructed

1280   On reaching majority, Richard De Burgh (the Red Earl) succeeds to **Carrickfergus**

1302   Robert Bruce marries Elizabeth De Burgh, daughter of the Red Earl (**Carrickfergus**)

1307   Edward II succeeds his father Edward I as King of England

1314	Robert Bruce defeats Edward II at Bannockburn and takes control of Scotland
1315	Edward Bruce (Robert's brother) invades Ireland
1315	Blarney Stone takes its place in **Blarney** Castle
1316	Edward Bruce crowns himself King of Ireland and takes **Carrickfergus**
1318	Edward Bruce is killed at Dundalk
1327	Edward III succeeds his father Edward II as King of England
1360	Norman knights meet in Kilkenny and petition Edward III for help in the control of Ireland
1361	Lionel, second son of Edward III, arrives with an army in response to the Norman petition
1366	Lionel forces passage of Statute of **Kilkenny**
1377	Richard II becomes King of England and later visits **Kilkenny**
1391	Butlers acquire **Kilkenny**
1446	**Blarney** Castle reconstructed to current configuration
1460	**Bunratty** Castle reconstructed to current configuration
1461	Edward IV becomes King of England as Henry VI is deposed
1509	Henry VIII succeeds his father Henry VII as King of England
1533	Henry VIII marries Anne Boleyn and breaks with the Church of Rome
1537	Church of Ireland is established
1546	Thomas (known as Black Tom) succeeds to the title of the tenth Earl of Ormond (**Kilkenny**)
1547	Edward VI succeeds his father Henry VIII as King of England
1549	Plantation of Laois and Offaly begins
1553	Mary I (Catholic daughter of Henry VIII and Catherine of Aragon) succeeds her half-brother Edward VI
1558	Elizabeth I (Protestant daughter of Henry VIII and Anne Boleyn) becomes Queen of England
1560	Clergy and secular officials required to swear an oath accepting Elizabeth's supremacy
1569	Desmond Rebellion in Munster

1580	Pope sends Spanish and Italian soldiers to support Desmond. They are defeated and massacred on orders of Elizabeth I
1583	Death of Cormac McTeige McCarthy (**Blarney**)
1593	O'Donnell and O'Neill revolt in Ulster
1601	O'Donnell and O'Neill defeated at Battle of Kinsale
1603	James VI of Scotland (son of Mary and grandson of Henry VIII) becomes James I of England, succeeding Elizabeth I, thus nominally uniting Scotland and England
1606	Potato is introduced into Ireland
1607	O'Donnell and O'Neill flee Ireland (Flight of the Earls)
1625	Charles I succeeds his father, James I, as King of England
1642	Civil war begins in England
1642	Confederation of Kilkenny established
1646	Barnabas O'Brien (the sixth Earl of Thomond) leaves **Bunratty**; he is the last of the O'Brien clan to control the castle
1647	Earl of Ormond (**Kilkenny**) surrenders Dublin to Roundhead forces
1648	Cromwell defeats Scots at Preston
1649	Cromwell becomes Lord Protector of England succeeding Charles I
1649	Charles I is executed
1649	Cromwell arrives in **Carrickfergus** with 20,000 men
1650	Cromwell returns to England
1650	**Kilkenny** bombarded into current configuration
1651	Charles II (son of Charles I) claims the throne, is defeated by Cromwell at Worcester and goes into exile in France
1653	Cromwellian settlement commences
1658	Cromwell dies and is succeeded by his son, Richard (September 3)
1660	Monarchy is restored and Charles II is proclaimed king
1672	Penal Laws against Catholics are suspended
1685	James II succeeds his brother, Charles II, as King of England
1687	Tyrconnell (Richard Talbot) establishes a Catholic army in Ireland
1688	William of Orange arrives in England with 15,000 troops at the invitation of the English parliament (November 5)
1688	James II is deposed and flees to France (December 23)

1689   William III (William of Orange) and Mary II (daughter of James II) are proclaimed joint King and Queen of England (13 February)

1689   James II lands at Kinsale (March 12)

1690   William of Orange lands at Carrickfergus (June 14)

1690   William defeats James at the Battle of the Boyne (July 1)

1694   Mary II dies

1702   Anne (daughter of James II) succeeds William III as Queen of England

1703   Sir James St John Jefferyes buys **Blarney**

1714   George I (great-grandson of James I) succeeds Anne as King of England